Ian Leslie lives in London where he combines careers in advertising and writing. His first book, *To Be President,* was described by Adam Boulton as 'brilliantly capturing the drama and emotion of Obama's successful run for the White House' and was extracted by *Granta. Born Liars* was BBC Radio 4's Book of the Week and *Curious* was described in the *New York Times* as 'the most delightful book I've read about the mind in quite some time' and in the *Independent* as 'a lovely erudite exploration of what it is that makes us human'. He writes about politics, culture, marketing, and psychology for publications including the *New Statesman, Prospect,* the *Guardian* and *The Times.*

'*Born Liars* . . . is erudite yet wears its learning lightly and is full of terrific stories. It will also make you see yourself, and the world around you, in a new light' *Daily Mail*

'Ian Leslie contends that lying is not a perversion of our nature, it's central to it. It is neither a design flaw nor a glitch, but necessary to our mental stability and social behaviour. His range of references is fascinating, from saints to sinners, from psychologists to psychopaths. I loved the irony and ingenuity of this book' *The Times*

'*Born Liars* is a lucid and entertaining celebration of our capacity for self-deception' *Sunday Times*

'Fascinating' *Independent on Sunday*

BORN LIARS

WHICH ONE ARE YOU?
PSYCHOPATH, SOCIOPATH OR
LITTLE WHITE LIAR?

IAN LESLIE

First published in Great Britain in 2011 by Quercus

This paperback edition published in 2017 by

Quercus Editions Ltd
Carmelite House
50 Victoria Embankment
EC4Y 0DZ

An Hachette UK company

PB ISBN 978 1 78648 455 0
EPUB ISBN 978 0 85738 043 2

10 9 8 7 6 5 4 3 2 1

Printed and bound in Great Britain by Clays Ltd, St Ives plc

For Alice

By a lie a human being throws away and, as it were, annihilates his dignity as a human being.

Immanuel Kant, *The Metaphysics of Morals*

Without lies, humanity would perish of despair and boredom.

Anatole France, *La vie en fleur*

Just remember — it's not a lie if you believe it.

George Costanza, *Seinfeld*

Contents

CONTENTS

Introduction

The serpent deceived me, and I ate.

Eve

The Bible tells us that it led to the fall of man. Philosophers from Kant to Oprah have condemned it unequivocally. We teach our children never to do it. It's a perversion, an aberration, a scourge. There are few things we hate more than lying.

Of course, liars are always other people. Lovers who have fallen out accuse each other of deceit; voters declare all politicians liars; the religious accuse the godless of hating the truth, while atheists accuse churchgoers of perpetuating the biggest lie of all. It doesn't matter which side you're on in these arguments, the basic grammar is always the same: *I* am a truth-teller, *you* try to bamboozle me with a self-serving fiction.

What's strange is that, unlike stealing, sexual abuse or murder, lying is a moral crime we all commit — and on a regular basis. The psychologist Bella DePaulo asked 147 people to keep a diary of their social interactions for one week and to note the number of times they intentionally misled someone. Her subjects reported that they lied, on average, 1.5 times a day. That is probably conservative. Another researcher, Robert Feldman, found that strangers meeting face-to-face for the first time will tell lies three times within ten minutes.

We lie by saying 'I'm fine, thanks' when we're feeling miserable. We lie when we say 'What a beautiful baby' while inwardly marvelling at its resemblance to an alien life form. We prepare our face to lie even as we're tearing off the paper Aunt Moira has lovingly wrapped around a china figurine of Princess Diana. Most of us have simulated anger, sadness, affection, or said 'I love you' when we don't mean it. Just about everyone has faked enthusiasm for somebody else's cooking. We tell our own children to smile and look grateful for the soap-on-a-rope grandma has given them for their birthday – and perhaps we add that, if they don't, Father Christmas won't come this year. 'Everybody lies,' said Mark Twain. 'Every day; every hour; awake; asleep; in his dreams; in his joy; in his mourning.'

Not only do we make exceptions to the prohibition against lying; sometimes we enthusiastically approve of it. If a doctor tells a bereaved husband that his wife died instantly in the crash, rather than the truth – that she spent her last hours in horrific pain – we applaud the doctor's compassion. When a football manager convinces his team of his complete confidence in their ability to recover from two goals down at half-time, even though he is inwardly despairing, we call it inspirational leadership (at least we do if the team goes on to win). We also encourage the lies that allow us to rub along with one another. Saying thank you to someone towards whom you feel genuine gratitude isn't good manners so much as self-expression; we need manners precisely for those moments when it's necessary to say something we don't feel. We call the lies we like 'white lies' — but asked to define precisely what makes a lie white we soon get lost in qualifications and contradictions.

Lying is anything but straightforward, and in recent years a growing number of scholars from different disciplines have been investigating its complex role in our lives. They have observed the lying behaviour of children, watched what happens to a person's brain when they lie, and compared our deceptive behaviour with those of our closest animal relations. What they have found turns our everyday assumptions about lying on their head. When I started to research this topic I imagined that the human tendency to lie was a design flaw that would one day be ironed out; instead, I discovered that it has driven the evolution of our species. I thought I knew how to spot a liar; I was mistaken. I took lying to be a sign of mental instability, but I discovered that good liars tend to be better balanced people than the rest of us. I believed I was always honest with myself; none of us is. I learnt that self-deception is a necessity rather than a problem, and that it leads to success at work, better health and happier relationships.

I learnt that when we are stripped of our lies, we become sick, depressed or mad.

In short, lying isn't a perversion of our nature; it's central to it. The ability knowingly to deceive, and to detect deception, is uniquely human, and it plays a part in every relationship we have. It's impossible to understand human society, or even to understand yourself, without first understanding deceit.

Earlier I quoted Eve as she points the finger of blame in the Garden of Eden. But who is the deceiver in that story? Not the serpent. He just encourages the nice young couple to eat the fruit. If there's anyone who actually tells a lie, it's Him. God tells Adam and Eve that the day they eat the apple, they will die. They do it anyway, but they don't drop dead. God was being disingenuous, to say the least. And if God can't do without deceit, which of us can?

The Lying Animal

What our intelligence owes to deceit

The relevant framework is not one of morality but of survival.

George Steiner, *After Babel*

In *Robinson Crusoe*, Daniel Defoe's novel of 1719, a man finds himself alone on a desert island. His survival depends on his ability to learn some technological skills very quickly. He has to build shelter, gather food, and make himself safe from external dangers. Crusoe excavates a cave. He fashions tools from stone and wood. He hunts, raises goats, grows corn, and even learns to make pottery. Throughout these first months and years on the island his only companion is a parrot. About fifteen years into his stay Crusoe is joined by Man Friday, whom he helps escape from a group of visiting savages. He teaches Man Friday English and converts him to Christianity. Together they save other prisoners and begin to build a small society.

Until relatively recently, scientists looking to explain

human intelligence told a story resembling the Crusoe myth. In this version, we grew strong and smart by mastering our natural environment, putting familiar objects like stones to new uses, crafting tools, and using our bodies in new ways. Over time, evolution selected for those best able to cope with such tasks, our brains grew more powerful. You can see why this story exerts such a pull: it makes humanity appear noble, skilful and strong. Being human, we can't help but like that. But it isn't an entirely satisfactory explanation for our inordinate mental powers.

The human brain might be evolution's most impressive achievement — and its most mysterious. At some point, between one and a half and two million years ago, our ancestors' brains started to expand, and at quite a rate; our hominid ancestors had brains about a third of the size they are now. Scientists have never been quite sure why. Brains are hugely demanding: they make up a small fraction of a body's mass but devour a fifth of its energy. Big brains need more food and more food means more risk, so our higher intelligence would appear to be a dangerous luxury. That our brains grew even bigger than those of apes is particularly hard to explain. We lived in similar environments and shared 98 per cent of our DNA with apes, yet at some point we left them behind. It's as if Toby and Sarah, two siblings of similar abilities, match each other's achievements in the first few years at school. Then one term Toby starts racing ahead, answering incredibly difficult questions and aceing every exam. You'd have to wonder if he wasn't cheating.

In recent decades, a new explanation for our higher intelligence has emerged, and at the heart of it is the drive to deceive. The seed of this theory was sown when one scientist concluded that the Crusoe narrative left out something rather important: other people.

Nicholas Humphrey is that rare thing in modern academia: a generalist. Although his abiding interest is the functioning of the human brain, he is deliberately careless of the boundaries that mark off one discipline from another and tends not to pursue the grinding, painstaking work of empirical research. His *modus operandi* is to make a visionary intervention in a particular field of study, reframe the question its inhabitants thought they were asking, and propose a daring new answer. Then he moves on, happy for others to spend years sifting through the evidence before concluding, as they usually do, that Humphrey had it right.

In 1976 Humphrey made one of his characteristic interventions into the debate over human evolution. In a paper called 'The Social Function of Intellect', he challenged the conventional view that human intelligence evolved in our ancestors' battle with nature. One way of looking at it, he said, is that we've been reading *Robinson Crusoe* the wrong way. We tend to think that the difficult time for Crusoe was the years he spent alone, fending for himself.

But perhaps it's the arrival of Man Friday that really stretches him. Crusoe has to learn (or relearn) to cope with another human being: to communicate and co-operate with a creature as smart as he is. Man Friday was famously loyal to Crusoe – but what if Crusoe hadn't been able to trust his companion? Then he'd *really* have needed to have his wits about him. And what if Men Monday, Tuesday and Wednesday had turned up at the same time – not to mention Woman Thursday?

It was hard to believe, said Humphrey, that our ancestors evolved their superior intelligence just because they had to cope with the practical problems of surviving in their environment. Certainly, making a tool demands a certain level of intelligence, as does remembering to clamber up a tree when a predator arrives, but these don't necessarily require inventiveness. One member of the species might discover such a technique, perhaps by accident, then all the others have to do is copy it. But a few species, including and especially our own, have an amazing capacity for foresight and innovative reasoning – what Humphrey termed 'the creative intellect'. We can imagine novel scenarios and plan our responses to them; we can 'see' things before they've happened, and then – if we're lucky – make them happen. Where did this capacity for imagination come from? Perhaps, suggested Humphrey, it came from the challenges of Palaeolithic social life.

The groups in which human beings and their immediate ancestors lived were larger and more complex than those of the other primates. Larger groups bring more security and better gossip, but they also bring competition. Each group member relies on the others to help him or her survive and prosper. But each must also learn how to exploit and out-manoeuvre the group's other members — or at least how to avoid the same happening to them — in the competition for food and mates. In such an environment, survival becomes a game of tactics in which you have to think ahead, as well as remember what's already happened. That means having a good memory for faces: you have to know who did what to you this morning or last week, who your friends are and who your enemies. It means calculating the consequences of your behaviour on others, and the effects of theirs on you. And you must do all that in an ambiguous, constantly shifting situation.

Humphrey's insight was that social living demands far more intellectual sophistication than dealing with nature does. After all, trees don't move around; rocks don't plot to trick you out of your food. When our ancestors moved out of the forests and on to the open savannah, the demands of their complex social lives combined with the challenges of this new environment to put rocket boosters on their mental evolution. Thus *Homo Sapiens* was born.

That was Humphrey's idea, anyway. For years, the 'social intelligence' hypothesis was just a controversial theory in search of evidence. Humphrey's paper was like a gauntlet thrown down to biologists, but it lay on the floor until the 1980s when Richard Byrne and Andrew Whiten decided to take it up. Byrne and Whiten were young primatologists at the University of St Andrews in Scotland, looking to make a name for themselves. What if they could be the ones who proved or disproved Humphrey's hypothesis? To this end, they zeroed in on a particular aspect of social behaviour: deception. They'd read examples of chimpanzee trickery in the works of Jane Goodall and, during their own fieldwork in the Drakensberg mountains of South Africa, they had noticed the facility of baboons for deceptive behaviour. When they asked around amongst colleagues engaged in fieldwork they were regaled with similar anecdotes.

A young baboon gets in trouble with several elders, including his mother, for attacking another member of the group. When he hears them coming over the hill, grunting aggressively, he stands on hind legs and stares into the distance across the valley. The newcomers, thinking that a predator or rival troop must be approaching, stop and look in that direction too. There is no threat. But the elders are distracted enough to forget why they came running over.

Two young chimps are observed digging furiously away at the ground to reach some buried food. When they hear a senior chimp approaching they back away from the spot, scratching their heads and acting as if they're just hanging around with nothing in particular to do. When the senior chimp moves on, they return to the spot and dig up the food.

An adult male baboon shoves a female out of her feeding patch. Rather than protest or retreat, she appears to enlist the male in a new plan, using flicks of her gaze to propose a joint attack on a younger male, innocently feeding himself nearby. The first male charges over to the younger one and chases him away. The female, meanwhile, returns to her patch and resumes feeding.

Byrne and Whiten suspected that these stories weren't mere anomalies or interesting-but-insignificant anecdotes, which is how their peers tended to view them. Their hunch was that primates, especially the great apes – chimpanzees, gorillas and orangutans – were practised, habitual deceivers. This, in turn, got them thinking about the evolution of *homo sapiens*. In the ancestral environment, the better you were at predicting the effects of your behaviour on others – and vice versa – the more likely you were to survive. It followed that those who were better at deception would have had a reproductive edge, because they would be better at, for instance, tricking others out of food. The same would go for those who were better at *detecting* deception, because they would be able to avoid being duped. As the evolutionary psychologist David Livingstone Smith puts it, '. . . in a world of liars, it is advantageous to possess a lie detector.' An evolutionary 'arms race' would develop, as each new variation on the species became more adept at trickery, or at spotting trickery. The species would evolve to be better at remembering, and at thinking ahead, and at the subtle game of thinking about what others are going to do next and why.

Initially, Byrne and Whiten found it hard to get their ideas published. The role of deception in human evolution just wasn't a subject that many in their field took seriously. Scientists, like the rest of us, have their own prejudices and blind spots, and it's perhaps not surprising that there was such resistance to an idea so unflattering to our self-image. If you believe your species has evolved through technical ingenuity and honest toil, it's difficult to accept that it may owe more to double-dealing and deceit.

But natural selection doesn't necessarily reward honesty; many species practise deception as a survival strategy. The Eastern Hognose snake will, if threatened, fake its own death by rolling over on its back, emitting a foul stench, and letting its tongue loll out of its mouth. The Mimic Octopus, found in the waters off Bali in Indonesia, can disguise itself at will as one of at least fifteen different sea creatures, all the better to attract prey or defend itself from predators. The female plover will fly from her nest and feign a broken wing when a predator approaches, in order to lead the intruder away from her young. Even plants deceive. The Mirror Orchid of North Africa produces small flowers to attract potential pollinators. The flowers have no nectar, but the orchids have a special ruse to seduce the unwary: they impersonate female wasps of the species that pollinates them. The blue-violet centre of the flower resembles the wings of a female wasp at rest; a thick set of long, red hairs imitates the hairs on the insect's abdomen. It's bait: insect porn for horny male wasps.

In 1982, Byrne and Whiten's dangerous ideas gained impetus from a new book that captured the imagination of readers within and beyond their field. Frans de Waal's *Chimpanzee Politics* is a gripping portrayal of the shifting power relationships within a captive colony of chimpanzees in a Dutch zoo, and it reads like the script of a gangster movie. Alliances are formed, broken and re-formed, individuals are manipulated, violence is selectively employed, females are fought over and seduced. De Waal framed his account as a vision of human politics in the raw, sprinkling his book with references to Niccolo Machiavelli's *The Prince*, which famously advises that 'since men are wretched creatures who would not keep their word', a ruler must know 'how to be a great liar and deceiver'.

Byrne and Whiten were fascinated by De Waal's work, particularly by the scenes involving outright deception. For example, a chimp called Puist is chasing one of her female rivals when, outpaced, she gives up. A few minutes later, from a distance, she stretches out an open hand as if to indicate that she is ready to be friends. The younger female approaches her, though she is clearly unsure what to think, moving only hesitantly, glancing around at others and wearing a nervous grin. But Puist persists with her outstretched hand, and starts to pant softly – usually the prelude to an affectionate kiss – as the younger female gets closer. Suddenly, Puist lunges, grabs her rival, and bites her fiercely. De Waal termed this move the 'deceptive reconciliation offer', and anyone who has been in a playground or watched *The Sopranos* will recognise it.

The success of *Chimpanzee Politics* gave the study of primate deceit a new legitimacy, and in 1988 Byrne and Whiten finally got to publish their work, *Machiavellian Intelligence* (the title inspired by De Waal). Byrne and Whiten collected all of the examples of deception that they had found and organised them into a taxonomy of Teasing, Pretending, Concealing and Distracting. The book's unsettling but powerful thesis was that our intelligence began in 'social manipulation, deceit and cunning co-operation'. Its moment had come; *Machiavellian Intelligence* proved highly influential, not only in the field of evolutionary theory, but across the social sciences, from psychology to economics.

There was one more step to go, however. Although Byrne and Whiten had put together a convincing argument that there was a link between intelligence and the capacity to deceive, and had provided a wealth of anecdotes to support it, they still lacked hard evidence. The intervention of an anthropologist from Liverpool University called Robin Dunbar helped them find some.

Dunbar, also inspired by Humphrey's theory of social

intelligence, noted that although all primates have big brains related to their body size, baboons, who live in large groups, have very big brains, while vervets, who live in smaller groups, have smaller brains. He wondered if bigger brains were required to handle the complexities of larger social groups. If you belong to a group of five, you have to keep track of ten separate relationships in order to successfully navigate its social dynamics – that is, to know who is allied with who, who is worthy of your time and attention and who is not. That is difficult enough. But if you belong to a group of twenty, you have one hundred and ninety two-way relationships to keep track of: nineteen involving yourself and one hundred and seventy-one involving the rest of the group. The group has increased fourfold, but the number of relationships – and thus the intellectual burden of tracking them – has increased nearly twentyfold.

Dunbar plunged into the vast accumulation of data on primates from around the world, searching for a statistical relationship between the size of an animal's brain and the size of the social group the animal typically lived in. He took as his proxy for brain size the volume of a species' neo-cortex – the outer layer of the brain. This is sometimes referred to as the 'thinking' part of the brain, because it deals with abstraction, self-reflection and forward planning. These are the kind of skills that Humphrey had argued were necessary to cope with the confusing whirl of social life, and it was this brain region that showed such a rapid expansion amongst primates — and especially humans — two million years ago.

Dunbar found just such a correlation; one so strong, in fact, that he was able to predict with impressive accuracy the group size of a species just by knowing the typical size of its neo-cortex. He even came up with a prediction for human beings. Based on the size of our brains, he said, we should be able to cope with a social group — people we would happily meet for a drink, say — of about a hundred and fifty people. Sure enough, when he combed through the anthropological and sociological literature, he found that a hundred and fifty worked as a rough average of the size of many human social groups, from hunter-gatherer societies to modern army units and company departments.

Encouraged by Dunbar's findings, Richard Byrne, now working with a young researcher called Nadia Corp, set out to see if he could prove a link between *deception* and brain size. Byrne and Corp studied a catalogue of observations of deceptive behaviours in wild primates that had been greatly expanded since the publication of Byrne and Whiten's groundbreaking hypothesis. They found that the frequency of deception in a species is directly proportional to the size of the neo-cortex. Bush babies and lemurs, which have a relatively small neo-cortex, were among the least sneaky. The most deceptive primates, including the great apes, also had the largest neo-cortex. The original theory held up: the better the liar, the bigger the brain.

Byrne didn't attempt to measure the capacity for deception of the animal that has the largest neo-cortex of all: *homo sapiens*. But then, he didn't need to. There's no doubt about which species takes the prize for deceit.

* * *

In the middle of the nineteenth century, P.T. Barnum's American Museum in New York housed an exotic collection of human and animal oddities, including the original bearded lady, a great white whale, and a pair of very argumentative Siamese twins. Naturally, the exhibition was hugely popular. But success brought difficulties. Barnum realised he had a problem with what modern retailers term 'traffic flow': the exhibition was getting congested because people were lingering too long in front of the attractions. Barnum's solution was to use a deliberately obscure term for exit, posting signs that read '*To The Egress*'. Excited at the prospect of witnessing yet another bizarre beast, customers would follow the signs and find themselves in the street outside.

The generally accepted definition of a lie is a false statement made with the intention to deceive. If I tell you that Paris is the capital of Belgium, you'll know it's not true, but you won't accuse me of lying. You'll just assume I'm mistaken, or that I'm making a joke. Telling somebody something false isn't a lie if the person doing the telling believes it to be true. But if you know that I know Paris is not the capital of Belgium, and you know that it's in my interest to persuade you otherwise (maybe I'm trying to make you lose at Trivial Pursuit) then you'll know I'm lying.

As Barnum's example shows, you can lie by telling the truth. You can also lie to somebody without deceiving them. In Jean-Paul Sartre's short story *The Wall*, set during the Spanish Civil War, Pablo Ibbieta, a prisoner sentenced to be executed by the Fascists, is interrogated by his guards as to the whereabouts of his comrade Ramon Gris. Mistakenly believing Gris to be hiding with his cousins, he plays for time by telling them that Gris is hiding in the cemetery. He then has a night to ponder his impending execution once the guards discover he has deceived them. Yet when dawn breaks he discovers to his horror that Gris had moved to the very location he reported to the guards. Gris is arrested at the cemetery and Ibbieta is released. Ibbieta lied to his interrogators with the intention of deceiving them but told them the truth.

Lies are slippery things, and endlessly various. There are the little lies we tell to simplify a complicated story or to protect our own privacy, and lies we tell to get out of unwelcome social situations ('Thursday? I have a bassoon lesson that night'). Then there are the more serious lies: the ones we tell to cover up misdemeanours or to get what we want – lies about illicit affairs or workplace manoeuvrings. There are lies of commission (I tell you I'm a policeman) and lies of omission (you tell me about your scorching love life without mentioning that your partner in sexual acrobatics is my wife). There are lies told to win admiration (the abnormally large fish you caught and threw back; a soldier's exaggerated account of his valour), and lies told to shield oneself or another person from physical or emotional harm.

There are also lies told for the sheer fun of it: we have all come across people who embroider their stories with a fictional filigree simply because they're more interesting that way. 'I'm the most terrific liar you ever saw in your life. It's awful,' says Holden Caulfield, the fourteen-year-old hero of *Catcher In The Rye*. 'If I'm on my way to the store to buy a magazine, even, and somebody asks me where I'm going, I'm liable to say I'm going to the opera. It's terrible.'

In this book I often use the words 'deception' and 'lie' interchangeably, but there is a distinction. Jerry Andrus, the great and eccentric American magician, made it a point of principle throughout his career never to lie, despite the fact that his act depended, as with all conjurors, on deception. But Andrus constructed his tricks so that he always spoke the truth, even as he was deceiving with his hands. He would say, 'It may appear as though I'm putting the card in the centre of the deck' rather than 'I am putting the card in the centre of the deck,' before producing said card from the top. This made his tricks more difficult to perform because he was alerting his audience to the possibility of deception, but that was the challenge Andrus set himself. Deception can involve any attempt to mislead: it could be a tone of voice, a smile, a faked signature or a white flag. A lie involves words – a specifically verbal form of deceit.

Indeed, the human knack for dissembling, born of the demands of Palaeolithic social life, was supercharged by the invention of language. Estimates of when this happened vary wildly, from fifty thousand to half a million years ago, but what's certain is that it was a giant leap forward for deceit, because it detached communication from deed. When I don't have to point to food to make you think there's food there – when I can just *tell* you and let you discover the truth later – then the possibilities for deception become infinitely more diverse and elaborate.[1]

Reading tales of primate deceit inspires two feelings at once: discomfort, because of the suggestion that such behaviour is bred in our bones, and admiration at the guile, creativity and intelligence on display. Something like those two antithetical responses runs through the history of our attitudes to lying. We are simultaneously appalled with ourselves for being able to make up things that aren't true, and impressed by our capacity for inventiveness; uneasy about our ease with falsity, yet certain that lies of some kind are necessary.

'Lying is indeed an accursed vice,' wrote the sixteenth-century philosopher Michel de Montaigne. 'If we realised the horror and gravity of lying we would see that it is more worthy of the stake than other crimes.' Theologians from Augustine onwards have condemned lying as a heinous sin. Immanuel Kant pronounced that there was no such thing as a white lie; that lying could never be justified under any circumstance.

Other thinkers have argued it is absurd to propose that we can, or should, live without deceit. 'There is only one world,' said Nietzsche, 'and that world is false, cruel, contradictory, misleading, senseless . . . We need lies to vanquish this reality, this "truth", we need lies in order to live.' Oscar Wilde, in his more playful style, suggested that lying is a welcome escape route from the insufferable dullness of real life, cautioning only that it should be done with flair; he lamented 'the decay of Lying as an art, a science, and a social pleasure'. Kant and Montaigne might have agreed with Achilles, the hero of the *Iliad*, who says, 'For I hate him like the gates of death who thinks one thing and says another.' Yet in the *Odyssey* Homer contrasts Achilles with a hero who is a 'master deceiver among mortals'; a man who skilfully and proudly wields deceit in battle and in love. In the end, it's Odysseus who comes across as the more attractive – more human – hero.

There's no settling the debate over lying. It's been part of the buzz and thrum of human conversation ever since we started talking, and it contains just about everything: our ideas about what kind of creatures we are, what it means to be a good person, and what on earth all those other people are saying about us. What's certain is that our ability to deceive is innate, and false speech comes

naturally to our lips. 'The human capacity to lie,' says the
literary critic and humanist philosopher George Steiner,
is 'indispensable to the equilibrium of human consciousness and the development of man in society.' Like it or
not, we are all born liars.

First Lies

How our children learn to lie (and why we should be impressed when they do)

The real history of consciousness starts with one's first lie. Joseph Brodsky

Charlotte's four-year-old son Tom has a rather casual way with the truth. Tom has no compunction whatsoever in blaming his one-year-old sister Ella for anything that goes wrong, even if that means lying through his baby teeth. If Charlotte is in the kitchen and hears a crash in the living room, she knows that when she walks in she'll find an upended lamp on the floor and Tom, pointing to Ella, inviting his mother to share his exasperation with his sister. Ella will be on the other side of the room, oblivious to the fuss, but Tom will be adamant that she knocked over the lamp while looking for her favourite doll. If it weren't that Ella can't crawl fast enough to get away from the scene of a crime so quickly, Charlotte might be tempted to believe him. 'He's so *convincing*,' she tells me. 'He's a scarily good liar.'

Should Charlotte be worried about Tom's lying? Browse the voluminous literature on child-rearing, and you might conclude that she should. Authors of how-to guides to parenting call for vigilance on the matter. Here's a typical extract from one of the many internet guides to raising children:

> Before we consider why children lie, it is essential to recognise that lying may be an early indicator of a more severe problem. Compulsive lying has often been indicated in the early stages of children suffering from social behaviour disorders, primarily that of Attention Deficit Hyperactive Disorder and Conduct Disorder.

The author is careful to distinguish between ordinary, harmless lying, and compulsive lying, where a child lies 'frequently and for no apparent reason'. On this basis, Charlotte might be concerned: after all, Tom lies frequently, sometimes without obvious motive. But when I ask her if she's considered seeing a child counsellor about Tom's trouble with the truth, she laughs. 'He's no worse than I am,' she says.

Charlotte's relaxed attitude to Tom's deceit is shared by the author of this passage:

> A little later (2 years and 7.5 months old) I met him coming out of the dining room with his eyes unnaturally bright, and an odd unnatural or affected manner,

so that I went into the room to see who was there, and found that he had been taking pounded sugar, which he had been told not to do. As he had never been in any way punished, his odd manner certainly was not due to fear, and I suppose it was pleasurable excitement struggling with conscience. A fortnight afterwards, I met him coming out of the same room, and he was eyeing his pinafore which he had carefully rolled up; and again his manner was so odd that I determined to see what was within his pinafore, notwithstanding that he said there was nothing and repeatedly commanded me to 'go away', and I found it stained with pickle-juice; so that here was carefully planned deceit. As this child was educated solely by working on his good feelings, he soon became as truthful, open, and tender, as anyone could desire.

This is from a short essay Charles Darwin published in 1877 entitled *A Biographical Sketch of an Infant*. Darwin, nearly seventy when he wrote it, had read an account of a child's mental development by the French naturalist Hippolyte Taine and was inspired to dig out the notes he had kept about the early years of his first child, William Erasmus, or 'Doddy'. Enraptured by the experience of fatherhood, Darwin was as intensely curious about his children as he was about the rest of the natural world. He was, of course, a great noticer, and the essay is alive with tenderly observed detail, such as Doddy's 'unnaturally bright eyes' as he scampers out of the pantry, high on sugar. Although Darwin attends to the first signs of a 'moral sense' in his child, he doesn't *judge* his young son in moral terms; he gives no indication that Doddy's 'carefully planned deceit' perturbed or angered him.

Darwin's essay was largely neglected by those in the field of what became known as 'developmental psychology', the study of children's mental development, which didn't really get going until well into the twentieth century. Even then, until the end of the that century little attention was paid to the question of when and why children lie. When it *was* discussed, it was usually as a disorder – a sign of delinquency. In our everyday lives we still think in similar terms, and few parents are comfortable with the notion that their child is a liar. But if you notice your three-year-old telling lies, you needn't be unduly concerned. In fact, it may be that parents should celebrate a child's first lie, just as they celebrate their child's first words.

Learning to Lie

We exert our powers of deception virtually from birth: even babies seem to engage in pre-verbal forms of fakery. During her research with the parents of very young children, Vasudevi Reddy of the University of Portsmouth found examples of baby behaviour that fit the taxonomy of deception in non-human primates put together by Byrne and Whiten: Teasing, Pretending, Concealing and Distracting. A baby girl repeatedly puts her hands out as if to join her welcoming mother but then backs away, laughing. A nine-month-old appears to fake laughter as a way of signalling that he wants to join in with others who are laughing. An eleven-month-old baby, being made to eat, watches her mother carefully, and as soon as her back is turned throws the toast away. The simplest acts of deception, says Reddy, 'seem to happen more or less simultaneously with the earliest attempts to communicate anything at all'.

Not only that, but children start telling lies more or less at the point they learn language. Between two and four these lies are usually self-serving and very simple, told to avoid punishment or to hide a minor transgression, as in the case of Darwin's son. Very young children tend not to be very good at lying. A three-year-old might say 'I didn't hit her' right after his father has witnessed him smacking his sister. A parent who enters the kitchen to find his daughter standing on a chair and reaching for the shelf where the chocolate is kept might find that she denies everything – but when he asks her why she's standing on a chair, she'll say 'I needed to reach . . .' The psychologist Josef Perner remembers his son Jacob trying to avoid going to bed by using an excuse he'd successfully adopted on past occasions – 'I'm so tired' – without realising that in this context he wasn't doing his case any favours. Very young children's lies are designed to achieve simple, defensive goals, and are quickly confessed to. The lying of a three-year-old is instinctive and spontaneous; there's little method to it.

Then, at around the age of four, something changes.

In a survey carried out by a researcher at the University of Pittsburgh, parents and teachers were asked at what age they thought children were able to tell a considered lie – the kind where the child knows exactly what he or she is doing. The answers varied. Some mothers thought that children aged as old as five-and-a-half were incapable of such dishonesty (nobody disagreed that kids are lying by the time they reach six). Generally speaking, however, parents reported that their children started to lie more and lie better around their fourth birthday. What parents notice intuitively, psychologists have identified methodically in study after study: somewhere between the ages of three and a half and four and a half, children learn how to lie with much greater skill and enthusiasm. On being caught reaching for the chocolate, that same child might claim that she is standing on the chair to return the cereal box to its rightful place. She will also maintain her story when challenged. And she'll do it all with a straight face.

Victoria Talwar has spent much of her professional life watching young children tell lies. An assistant professor of child psychology at McGill University in Montreal, she is interested in when and how children develop a sense of right and wrong, and specifically how they learn to employ deceit. To test a child's propensity to deceive — and his ability to do so convincingly — Talwar uses a well-established experiment known as the temptation resistance paradigm or, more informally, as the 'Peeking Game'.

It works like this. After meeting the researcher and playing a few games to establish a relationship, the child is introduced to a guessing game. He is asked to sit facing the wall. Behind him, the researcher brings out a toy and asks the child to guess what it is from the noise it makes. If the child gets it right three times, he wins a prize. After a couple of easy noises (a police car, a crying-baby doll) comes a deliberately baffling one. Talwar usually brings out a toy that makes no noise, like a stuffed cat, while at the same time opening a greetings card that plays a tinny tune. Understandably, the child is stumped by this. Before he attempts an answer, the researcher says that she has to leave the room for a minute, warning him not to peek whilst she's out. Children invariably find this instruction impossible to obey, and turn around a few seconds after the door has closed, unaware that they're being filmed. The researcher returns to the room, making enough noise on her way in to give the child time to swivel back to the wall. When he triumphantly gives the right answer, the researcher asks if he peeked. Does he tell the truth, or does he lie?

Generally speaking, three-year-olds confess immediately, whereas a majority of children aged four lie and say they didn't. By the time they're six, ninety-five per cent of children tell this lie. That some kind of Rubicon is crossed between the ages of three and five seems to be a universal truth: a similar pattern has been observed among American, British, Chinese, and Japanese children.

So what happens to children at the age of four? According to Talwar, it's only then that they truly grasp there are other people to lie to. As they approach their first birthday, children have already learnt that people want things, that they act in order to get those things, and that sometimes it works out and sometimes it doesn't. For example, studies have shown that nine-month-old babies expect an adult to reach for an object at which they have previously looked and smiled. Toddlers younger than two can tell the difference between what they want, and what happens – and they certainly know how to scream about it. Two-year-olds start to sense that their parents have feelings, and that they can affect those feelings by what they do. They then proceed to test this fascinating insight to destruction.

But what children don't have in these first years, what they can't even conceive of yet, are beliefs. A three-year-old might believe that the chocolate is in the cupboard, but she won't grasp that this *is* a belief – that's to say, that *other people might believe something different*. As far as a very young child is concerned, what's in his or her mind is the same as what's in everyone else's mind; that's why toddlers will sometimes come up to you and start discussing, in great detail, a TV show of which you've never heard. It's not until they are three or four that children discover other people have minds of their own.

In the story of *Snow White*, the Queen — Snow White's wicked stepmother — repeatedly fools our heroine by disguising herself as a harmless peasant woman. When Snow White accepts her seemingly kind offer of a delicious apple, the Queen attacks her. At the moment that Snow White opens the door to the Wicked Queen, she has a false belief about the world — she believes that she is opening the door to a peasant woman, and not to her stepmother. Her reason for believing this seems obvious to us, as it does to four-year-olds. We know that Snow White didn't see what we've seen — the Queen putting on her disguise — and this forms part of the story's drama for us. Children under three, however, tend not to enjoy *Snow White*, even though they may already be enjoying other stories their parents read to them. Why, they wonder, does Snow White allow that woman into her house when we all know it's the Wicked Queen in different clothes?

Developmental psychologists use a more formal test of the ability to take other people's perspectives: the Sally-Anne False Belief Test. This typically involves two characters, played by dolls. Sally has a basket, Anne has a box. Sally also has a marble, and before going out she puts her marble in her basket for safekeeping. With Sally gone, Anne takes the marble from Sally's basket and places it in her box. Where will Sally look for her marble when she returns? Adults know that Sally is going to head straight for her basket. Five-year-olds work this out too — they point to Sally's basket straight away. But three-year-olds predict the opposite. They point to Anne's box, where the ball really is. They don't see that Sally might have a false belief about the world. Of course, until you grasp that other people sometimes believe different things from you, it's impossible to think about deceiving them. There's no point telling a lie if everyone believes the same things.

Most children acquire what psychologists call a 'theory of mind' aged between three and four years old. More colloquially, they learn to 'mind-read'. Mind-reading is something all of us do, every day, while barely noticing that we're doing it. We size up the salesman on our doorstep and decide whether or not we should trust him. We worry about whether our boss thinks we've done a good job. At the movies, we notice the way the heroine turns back to glance at her former lover as she walks away from him, and conclude that she's still in love. Our mind-reading habit is so deeply ingrained that we attribute human mental states to animals, believing our dog to be contrite, and even to inanimate phenomena, blaming the sun for not wanting to come out today, or accusing the sea of cruelty.

The importance of this ability to the way we see the world becomes clearer if you try and imagine living without it. Here's the developmental psychologist Alison Gopnik:

This is what it's like to sit round the dinner table. At the top of my field of vision is a blurry edge of nose, in front are waving hands . . . Around me bags of skin are draped over chairs, and stuffed into pieces of cloth, they shift and protrude in unexpected ways . . . Two dark spots near the top of them swivel restlessly back and forth. A hole beneath the spots fills with food and from it comes a stream of noises. Imagine that the noisy skin-bags suddenly moved toward you, and their noises grew loud, and you had no idea why, no way of explaining them or predicting what they would do next.

Actually, Gopnik's description is itself an impressive feat of mind-reading. What she's attempting here is to put herself — and us — into the shoes of somebody with a severe case of autism. People with autism (or its higher-functioning variant, Asperger's Syndrome) find it hard to grasp what most of us learn as young children: that other people have their own thoughts and feelings, and their own perspective on reality. As a consequence, they make terrible liars.

Simon Baron-Cohen, professor of developmental psychopathology at Cambridge, is one of the world's leading authorities on autism. He was the first to identify a lack of mind-reading ability as being the key cognitive deficit suffered by autistic children. As a young PhD student, he played the 'penny-hiding game' with children to check for the symptoms of autism. He sat opposite the child and showed him or her that he had a penny. Then he put his hands behind his back before bringing them out in front of him and asking the child to guess which of his closed hands was holding it. Then he swapped roles.

For most children aged four and over, playing the trickster was easy, and a lot of fun. Children with autism, however, didn't play it very well. They would transfer the penny from one hand to the other in full view, or invite Baron-Cohen to guess while leaving one hand open. They made these simple mistakes because they weren't used to keeping track of what was in another person's mind. They were befuddled by the very idea that somebody might try to persuade them to believe in a different version of reality.

This innocence can leave children open to exploitation. Baron-Cohen tells the story of a boy with Asperger's Syndrome who was approached by a gang of boys in the playground asking to see his wallet. He handed it over without hesitation, and was shocked when they ran off with it. Being a stranger to deceit can also pose problems of etiquette: an autistic person may tell you that the shirt you are wearing is repulsive to him. He doesn't mean to offend you, says Baron-Cohen, he's simply telling the truth – and it's beyond him that anyone would ever do anything else. Although they can learn to read people better as they get older, autistic people retain a very different perspective on life. Baron-Cohen recalls a graduate student of his with Asperger's Syndrome saying to him, 'I've just discovered that people don't always say what they mean.

So how do you know how to trust language?' As Baron-Cohen points out, her discovery is one that the typical child makes at the age of four, in the teasing back-and-forth of the playground.

Of course, all mind-reading is flawed and erratic; that's why successful lying is possible in the first place. None of us ever quite cracks the great mystery of what makes other people do the things they do, or fathom what Philip Roth calls 'this terribly significant business of "other people"'. As a species we are just good enough at mind-reading to construct sophisticated ideas about what other people believe, and just bad enough at it to make errors. Much of life's comedy derives from our misreadings of other people's mental states. In Jane Austen's *Emma*, the eponymous heroine reads Mr Elton's attentions as a signal of his intentions towards her friend Harriet, although it turns out that the simpler interpretation was the right one: he has designs on Emma. Such mistakes can be a source of tragedy too: King Lear cannot discern the affection behind Cordelia's formal declaration of love, nor the calculations lying behind the fulsome tributes of his other daughters. Such errors of interpretation are the very stuff of life. Here's Roth again: 'The fact remains that getting people right is not what living is all about anyway. It's getting them wrong that is living, getting them wrong and wrong and wrong and then, on careful reconsideration, getting them wrong again. That's how we know we're alive: we're wrong.'

Although none of us is perfect at it, some people are better at mind-reading than others, and the better they are, the better liars they will be, if and when they choose to lie. When Charlotte's son Tom sees her walk into the room, he knows she will be wondering if he knocked the lamp over, and he is betting that by pointing the finger at his sister he can change his mother's mind. If you're going to convince me that you are Marie of Romania, you'll have to have a rough idea of how I think Marie of Romania might conduct herself. If a fifteen-year-old is going to convince her parents that she doesn't smoke dope, she'll need a keen understanding of what will set their minds at rest. One definition of a bad liar is somebody who lies without being very good at guessing what's in the other person's mind. (If you take a moment to think of a time you witnessed somebody telling a comically obvious lie, you'll see what I mean.) Great liars tend to be great readers of human behaviour. Think of Iago, a 'people person' if ever there was one, subtly drawing out Othello's rage, or reflect that Bill Clinton is famous for being both a convincing liar and a politician of exceptional empathy.

Other than mind-reading, there are two other key mental abilities involved in mature lying. One of them is what psychologists refer to as 'executive function', a cluster of higher-order mental skills related to thinking ahead, strategising and reasoning (although the word 'executive' has a distinct meaning in psychology, these are precisely the abilities that enable children to grow up and enjoy successful careers, running large organisations or figuring out complicated engineering problems). A four-year-old engaged in a lie has to run different mental processes in parallel: he or she must establish their goal, work out how it might be achieved with the aid of a false statement, and then execute their strategy without giving the game away via facial or verbal leakage – that's to say, looking shifty, or saying the wrong thing at the wrong time. They have to combine intellectual agility with physical and emotional self-control.

A child who lies well is also demonstrating a creative intellect – the ability to imagine those alternative versions of reality in the first place. Even very simple lies can require a leap of imagination. Tom has to be able to see it was plausible that Ella *might* have crawled across the room and knocked over the lamp even if, in truth, she has been sitting quietly on the sofa all along. In the Peeking Game, the more intellectually sophisticated children will stitch together an answer of some sort when challenged by the researcher. Victoria Talwar recalls how a Canadian boy tried to rationalise his 'guess that the toy behind him was a stuffed football, based on the sound of a greeting card tune. He explained that the music 'sounded squeaky, like the soccer balls at the school gym'. It was an impressive display of lateral thinking.

Lying is *hard*. Children who lie well must be able to recognise the truth, conceive of an alternative false but coherent story, and juggle those two versions in their mind while selling the alternative reality to someone else — all the time bearing in mind what that person is likely to be thinking and feeling. It is wondrous that a child of four should be able to do this. If you catch your three-year-old in a well-told lie, allow yourself to be impressed.

Learning Not to Lie

Of course, you can admire the skill in a three-year-old's lie without wanting to congratulate them on it. The number of lies told by children tends to spike upwards in children aged four as they exercise their amazing new-found powers. Then, during the first school years, as the child receives an increased amount of what Talwar calls 'social feedback', the lying usually declines. In the classroom and the playground, children learn that the benefits of lying come with some pretty hefty costs. They find out that if they lie too much, teachers and friends lose faith in their credibility, and they become unpopular.

This is an important point, and one that applies to adults as much as children. Truth-telling *works*, most of the time. For intensely social creatures like ourselves it's an efficient default mode, if only because, as Abraham Lincoln famously remarked, you can't fool all of the people all of the time. Sir Thomas Browne, the seventeenth-century

English thinker and prose stylist, offered a take on truth
and lies that both contrasts with and complements that
of Machiavelli's:

> So large is the Empire of Truth, that it hath place within
> the walls of Hell, and the Devils themselves are daily
> forced to practise it; . . . in Moral verities, although they
> deceive us, they lie not unto each other; as well under-
> standing that all community is continued by Truth, and
> that of Hell cannot consist without it.

Whereas the Italian sought to remind us that deceit is
ever-present, and that it is therefore necessary for rulers
to employ it on occasion, Browne saw things the other
way round. Isn't the truly remarkable thing the fact that
truth is so powerful? Even *devils* rely on it when they're
among their own, because 'all community is continued by
truth'. The subversive implication of Browne's argument
is that our general aversion to deceit does not stem from
a God-given morality or an innate instinct for truth so
much as the need to keep the wheels of social life turning.
Most decisions about whether or not to lie have little to
do with whether the person concerned is an angel or a
devil. We tell the truth because it suits us. And when it
suits us, we lie.

The majority of children learn what we might call
'Browne's Law' instinctively, at home and in school. But a
few remain impervious to it; they take a wrong turning.

Persistent lying in older children is usually the sign of a deeper malaise: a way of venting frustrations, winning attention, or coping with deep insecurity. 'Lying is a symptom,' says Victoria Talwar. Children of parents in the process of divorcing, for example, often resort to manipulative lying to assert some control over a situation in the face of which they would otherwise feel helpless.

In the words of Dr Nancy Darling of Oberlin University, Ohio, who specialises in the moral development of older children, lying is a 'self-reinforcing activity'. Lies beget lies. If a lie works to get a child out of trouble, she might try it again, then she might need more lies to sustain her first lie. We all know how powerful the momentum of deceit can be: once a lie is told, it often requires another. When you're knee-deep in lies it can seem easier to wade in further than to attempt an escape; before you know it you are reliant on them just to stay afloat. If a child's whole sense of himself comes to depend on lies, it's very hard for him to let go of them. 'The time to catch a liar is before eight years of age,' says Kang Lee, a professor at the University of Toronto and director of the Institute of Child Study. If a child is still lying habitually after the age of seven, she (or he) will probably continue to do so for years to come, even into adulthood; she's hooked.

The sooner a child learns that lying can be self-destructive, the better. The question of how children learn *not* to lie is as interesting as how they learn to lie in the first place. It's also controversial. Do children require strict moral instruction and harsh punishment for lying – or should they be left to work it out as they go along?

In 2009 Victoria Talwar was working on a study of the development of moral behaviour in children around the world, including in non-Western cultures. Having already visited China and Thailand, she was introduced by a friend of a friend to a school in West Africa. The school – let's call it School A – was run along lines familiar to anyone with experience of a mainstream school in Britain or Canada. It was strict but not unreasonably so; misdemeanours were punished with verbal admonishments, the withdrawal of privileges, or detentions. There was no corporal punishment.

When Talwar visited another school nearby, however, she encountered a stark contrast of methods. This school – School B – took a much more draconian approach to discipline, sticking closely to traditions established by the country's former colonial masters, the French, in the first half of the twentieth century. The children were expected to conform to a strict code of behaviour and transgressions were harshly punished, often violently. Simply getting an answer wrong in class earned you a smack around the head. It was the job of one staff member – whom Talwar privately nicknamed 'the enforcer' – to go from class to class asking the teachers if any of their pupils had misbehaved. Twice a day, those named by the class teacher were taken out into the school courtyard and beaten with a wooden bat in front of the other children. Punishable offences included a failure to do homework, forgetting to bring a pencil to class or — worst of all — lying.

Here were two schools, only a few miles apart, with pupils from similar social backgrounds, but with vastly different approaches to discipline. In other words, near-perfect conditions in which to explore the effect of different moral codes on deceitful behaviour. Both schools were happy to have Talwar carry out her experiment; each was supremely confident in the moral fibre of the students they turned out. The teachers in School B were unembarrassed about their methods and disparaging of School A's approach, which they regarded as hopelessly lax. They sincerely believed that theirs was the most reliable method for raising honest children.

Along with her frequent collaborator, Kang Lee, Talwar set about interviewing pupils between the ages of three and six years old from both schools. She introduced the guessing game to each child, brought out the easy-to-guess toys, and then the stuffed toy with its tinny accompaniment. Back in her hotel room, as she played back the interviews on her camcorder, she noticed something remarkable: School B's children seemed to be lying with far greater consistency and conviction than any children with whom she had ever worked.

To ensure a robust set of data, Talwar returned to both schools the following day and carried out more interviews. When she analysed the results, the first thing that struck her was the length of time the pupils from School B waited before they turned around to peek. Most children who play the peeking game wait less than ten seconds before taking their chance, and the children of School A conformed to this pattern. But School B's kids waited much longer – for up to a minute – before sneaking a peek. Perhaps School B's teachers would have felt proud at such evidence of inner discipline, but they would have been less pleased with Talwar's most striking finding: regardless of age, *all* their pupils lied, instinctively and immediately. The alacrity with which they did so seemed to have nothing to do with their cultural background; the results from School A were very similar to those from schools in North America or Europe.

Not only were the School B pupils all lying, they were brilliant at it. Wherever the peeking game is played, younger children tend to confess to their lie immediately, or make such a flimsy defence that it barely counts. ('When I say, "Well, how did you know it was a football?" a three-year-old will often say, "Because I *saw* it,"' Talwar told me.) Lying involves a considerable amount of physical and emotional discipline, as well as mental dexterity. The child has to control his expression and body language so as not to give himself away with a stray smile, a telltale flash of the eyes or a wince of anxiety – all while keeping his story straight. As you'd expect, such skills tend to improve with age: three-year-olds get their story mixed up or laugh at their own fibs, whereas four- and five-year-olds are better at making their stories believable, and telling them with a poker face.

This pattern was reflected in the results from School A. The School B pupils, however, were all masterful liars. Whether aged three or six, they denied having peeked with impenetrable conviction, and confidently maintained their story when challenged. The slightly older children were even careful not to guess correctly first time around, in order to give the false impression that they were groping towards an answer by a process of intuition and deduction. 'I thought it sounded a bit like a cellphone. But I know you're not allowed to have a cellphone in school. So then I thought it must be something else . . . an animal maybe . . .' These were skilful performances, requiring psychological nous, creative thinking and dramatic flair.

In the early 1990s Talwar studied at St Andrew's University, where her tutor was Andrew Whiten. What she learnt from the work of Whiten and Byrne was that lying is an inescapable part of being a social animal, and that children are likely to find the lying strategy that best helps them adapt to their social environment. Whiten and Byrne observed that it is young or low-ranked chimps that are most likely to engage in tactical deception, and the philosopher Sisella Bok has speculated that children develop the habit of lying as a last line of defence against the overwhelming physical and social power of adults. 'The weak cannot be sincere,' said François de La Rochefoucauld. By ratcheting up the punishments for lying, teachers and parents can force children further on to the defensive — with unintended consequences.

For the children in School A it made sense to tell the truth most of the time and lie occasionally. They knew they might get into trouble if caught out, but not too much. The children in School B, however, had adapted their behaviour to life in what Talwar described as a 'punitive environment', in which self-defence was the highest priority. They knew that telling the truth would often get them into trouble; they also knew that getting caught out in any type of lie, however small, would lead to a painful punishment. So they had learned, even at the age of three, to gamble on deception, employing a logic that went something like, 'If there's any possibility at all of getting into trouble, then tell a lie — just be sure to do it well.' As Talwar put it to me, 'If you're going to get into trouble for small things, you may as well go for broke.'

School B's approach, based on a regime designed by Catholic missionaries, was intended as a harsh but effective way of instilling good moral habits into children. Talwar's research revealed that its regime hadn't succeeded in knocking all the lies out of School B's children. Quite the opposite: it turned out to be the perfect method for producing habitual, highly skilled little liars.

Learning When to Lie

Children get mixed messages from their parents about lying. On the one hand, they're taught that lying is bad; on the other they're admonished when they tell grandma, truthfully, that they have never worn the scarf she bought them for Christmas. Kids note that when they lie in certain circumstances, their parents applaud them for it, and adapt their behaviour accordingly. Being observant creatures, they also notice their parents telling lies to others, whether it be the telemarketer on the phone or the friend who asks an awkward question. As they grow up, they learn to manage the ideas that lying is both wrong, and necessary. In one of Talwar's experiments, a child receives a present that looks like it's going to be a toy but turns out, on unwrapping, to be a bar of soap. The overwhelming majority of seven-year-olds openly express their displeasure. By the time they're eleven, about half of children will lie convincingly and say they like it.[2] As they grow up, it's not so much that children learn *not* to lie, as *when* to lie.

Nancy Darling has studied the social lives of adolescents for nearly twenty years in countries including Chile, the Philippines, Italy and the United States. In every society, nearly all teens will admit, in interviews, to lying at home. Their lies are usually limited to a few issues: romantic relationships, the use of alcohol or other substances, the violation of rules about where and with whom they're allowed to hang out. At the same time, most teenagers profess to valuing honesty, and many boast of having strong, open relationships with their parents. It's only when researchers ask about it in detail that the extent of their dishonesty is revealed, even to themselves. 'They're surprised by it,' Darling tells me. 'They don't like to think of themselves as liars.'

As with the rest of us, teenagers' attitudes to lying are complicated. On the one hand, they lie for reasons of straightforward self-interest – to avoid punishment, and to maintain a carefully managed image for the audience of their parents. On the other, they are lying to protect their parents, reasoning that the truth would upset them unnecessarily. Parents often collude in such deceptions, tacitly agreeing not to probe into areas of their child's life that they may not wish to know too much about. Darling remarks about her own teenage son, 'He doesn't lie to me about his sex life, because I don't ask him.'

At school, as at home, there are certain circumstances in which lying regularly pays off. For instance, the stigma attached to being a 'snitch' or a 'grass' is near-universal, and it can put kids in uncomfortable situations as they try to balance conflicting obligations to teachers, parents, and peers. A classic experiment from 1969, staged in an American high-school, illustrates the subtlety of the social calculations involved. During a history lesson, the teacher was called out of the classroom, apparently to take an important phone call. One of the students got up from his seat, strode up to the teacher's desk and swiped a pile of money that the teacher had left there. 'How about that?' he exclaimed triumphantly to the class, returning to his seat. The other students didn't know it, but the thieving student was playing out a role agreed earlier with the researchers.

The scenario was played out twice in different classes, with two different students playing the role of transgressor. In one, the student chosen was the boy whose name came up most often when classmates were asked to list five people whom they considered worthy to represent the class at a banquet for school representatives. He was the 'high status' student. In the other scenario, a 'low status' student, considered less trustworthy by his peers, played the role. After both incidents, the students from each classroom were interviewed by one of the psychologists, either singly or in pairs. They were asked three questions: 'Do you know whether someone took some change from the teacher's desk today? Do you know who took it? If so, who took it?' All the students interviewed alone told the truth, regardless of whether the classmate in question was high or low in status. But when students were interviewed in pairs, things were different. Now, when the culprit was high in status, *nobody* told the truth. Everyone denied that they even knew about any money being stolen. When it came to the low status culprit, however, everyone told the truth, and named him. The students had an instinct for honesty, but they were prepared to forego it in order to avoid being seen to betray the most popular kid in class.

The reason lying doesn't become a problem for most children isn't simply that they get taught that lying is wrong, and so stop. It's that they learn the unwritten social rules of when to tell the truth and when to lie. Parents can help them learn these rules, but only if they allow their children to feel trusted. Most children's lies are told in order to avoid embarrassment or to stay out of trouble, rather than to manipulate others, and punishing these dodges too vigorously can trap kids into a cycle of dishonesty. 'If you walk into a room to find your five-year-old with milk spattered everywhere and ask 'Did you do that?' you're inviting them to lie,' says Darling. 'If you say, 'Ah, you spilt the milk. Let's clean it up,' she's less likely to lie. If she still does, it's best to laugh it off – whilst making it clear you know she's lying. There's no point telling her she's a bad person because she lied.' If a child feels her character is constantly under assault she will quickly build a protective carapace of deceit around herself. Children who live with the threat of heavy punishment for lying may simply become better liars.

It's sometimes said that the best approach for parents to adopt when it comes to their children's lying is to simply let it go and wait for them to grow out of it. But to Darling, this is a betrayal of the child: 'If they get away with a lie, they'll lie some more, and pretty soon they won't know when to stop.' The best parents, she says, are warm but strict. She recalls that when she was young her father told her that he could tell when she was lying just by smelling her elbows. 'It was *years* before I realised this wasn't actually true,' she laughs. Now, she admires his shrewdness; he'd created an ostensibly objective test (itself a benign lie) to detect her lies, one that allowed them both to acknowledge the transgression without throwing her moral character into question or threatening punishment.

Victoria Talwar runs a version of the Peeking Game in which the researcher reads the child a short story before the game begins. One story is *The Boy Who Cried Wolf*, in a version that sees the boy get eaten along with the sheep because of his repeated lies. Another is *George Washington and the Cherry Tree*, in which the young George confesses to hacking down the tree with his shiny new axe. The story ends with his father's words: 'George, I'm glad that you cut down the tree after all. Hearing you tell the truth instead of a lie is better than if I had a thousand cherry trees.' Talwar was interested to see if the stories had any effect on the willingness of children to lie during the subsequent game and, if so, which story was more effective. You might imagine that *The Boy Who Cried Wolf* would work better. After all, it ends with a vision of terrifying punishment. But in fact, children who were read this story were *more* likely to lie than normal. By contrast, the story of George Washington's truthfulness inspired children to follow suit – even when Washington was replaced by a nondescript name in order to eliminate the potential for the first president's fame to influence the child. According to Talwar, the power of the story is that it teaches children to take pleasure in honesty, rather than instilling in them the fear of being found out.

The research of Darling, Talwar and others suggests that the most reliable way to raise a trustworthy child is to trust *them*; to work on their best instincts rather than attempting to eradicate their worst – in short, to create an environment that makes honesty feel like the best policy.

Though he was writing in an age of strict and often punitive moral instruction, Charles Darwin had arrived at the same conclusion long before:

'As this child was educated solely by working on his good feelings, he soon became as truthful, open, and tender, as anyone could desire.'

Confabulators

Liars, artists, madmen

> *A writer is congenitally unable to tell the truth and that is why we call what he writes fiction.* William Faulkner

In 2004 the satellite broadcaster Sky launched a legal action against one of its suppliers, Electronic Data Systems (EDS). The case rested on Sky's charge that EDS had deceived them over the length and cost of an IT project. Sky was demanding hundreds of millions of pounds in damages. Industry observers were sceptical about Sky's chances of success; a case on this scale had never been won before, and it would be very hard to prove that fraudulent misrepresentation, rather than simple misunderstanding, was at the root of the dispute.

On day thirty-seven of the trial, Joe Galloway, the EDS executive whose integrity was most at issue, faced Sky's barrister Mark Howard across the courtroom. Taking a break from the complex substance of the allegations,

Howard questioned Galloway about the Masters in Business Administration he had been awarded by Concordia College in the US Virgin Islands, mentioned by Galloway in his witness statement. Galloway needed little prompting to expand on his year of study on the beautiful island of St John. He said that he had attended Concordia College while on the island in the service of a previous, Texas-based employer who had tasked him with overseeing a project for a number of Coca-Cola distributors based on St John. This required him to fly to and from the island by plane, on 'a small commuter flight . . . a four or six-seater airplane'. He described the three main college build-ings, which he had got to know well — a rigorous progamme of evening classes required him to spend three hours a night on campus, several evenings a week. He promised to provide textbooks from the course to the court, and eventually did submit one.

During this part of his testimony, Galloway spoke confi-dently and fluently, as he had throughout the trial, and even seemed to be enjoying himself. The uninformed observer, and even most informed observers, would never have guessed he was making it all up.

A psychiatric case study published in 1985 by the neurol-ogist Antonio Damasio tells the story of a middle-aged woman who had suffered brain damage following a series of strokes. She retained most cognitive abilities, including coherent speech. *What* she said was rather unpredictable, however. Checking on her knowledge of contemporary events, Damasio asked her about the Falklands War. She spontaneously described a blissful holiday she had taken in the islands, involving long strolls with her husband, and the purchase of local trinkets from a shop. Asked what language was spoken there she replied, 'Falklandese. What else?'

In the language of psychiatry, this woman was 'confabulating'. Chronic confabulation is a rare type of memory problem which affects a small proportion of brain damaged people. In the literature it is defined as 'the production of fabricated, distorted or misinterpreted memories about oneself or the world, without the conscious intention to deceive'. Whereas amnesiacs make errors of omission — there are gaps in their recollections they find impossible to fill — confabulators make errors of commission: they make things up. Rather than forgetting, they are inventing.

Confabulating patients are nearly always oblivious to their own condition, and will earnestly give absurdly implausible explanations of their circumstances — of why they're in hospital, or talking to a doctor. Some invent occupations for themselves, or pretend that they are doing their work as they talk. One patient, when asked about his surgical scar, explained that during World War II he surprised a teenage girl who shot him three times in the head, killing him, only for surgery to bring him back to life. The same patient, when asked about his family described how at various times they had died in his arms, or been killed before his eyes. Others tell yet more fantastical tales, about trips to the moon, fighting alongside Alexander in India or seeing Jesus on the Cross. Confabulators aren't out to deceive – they engage in what the neuropsychologist Morris Moscovitch calls 'honest lying'. Uncertain, and obscurely distressed by their uncertainty, they are seized by a 'compulsion to narrate': a deep-seated need to shape, order and explain what they do not understand.

Chronic confabulation is usually associated with damage to the brain's frontal lobes, particularly the region responsible for self-regulation and self-censoring. Hearing a question, or just a word, triggers a whole set of associations for the patient. Of course, this happens to all of us – hear the word scar and you too might think about war wounds, old movies, or tales of near-death experiences. But you don't let all of these random thoughts reach consciousness – and if you do, you don't articulate them. You self-censor for the sake of truth (I wasn't in World War II), sense (you can't be killed and come back to life) and social appropriateness. Chronic confabulators do none of these things. They randomly combine real memories with stray thoughts, wishes and hopes, and summon up a story out of the confusion.

The wider significance of confabulation is what it tells us about the normal human mind: specifically, it exposes the mind's gushing stream of invention. We are natural-born fabulists, constantly spinning stories out of our experience and imagination, testing the leash that keeps us tethered to reality. It's just that, most of the time, we exercise our cerebral censors, exerting control over which stories we tell, to whom – and which we want the hearer to believe. The *degree* of control exercised, however, can depend on personality, and on the moment.

Mark Howard may have been surprised at the length and detail of Galloway's extemporisation but he was more than happy to let him continue, because he knew he was lying. In the course of conducting an exhaustive background check on Galloway, Sky's legal team had discovered that there was not and never had been a Concordia College on St John; there was not, nor ever had been, a Coca-Cola office or facility on the island. Nor was there an airport; it was not possible to fly onto the island. The barcode and stamp on the book Galloway produced marked it as the property of a library in Missouri, near Galloway's home. A few days after Galloway's testimony, Howard presented to the court an MBA certificate that his pet schnauzer Lulu had been awarded by Concordia College and University, an unaccredited institution based in Delaware that awards degrees based on 'Life Experience'. The barrister pointed out that Lulu had managed to achieve a higher mark than Joe Galloway. He also displayed a letter of recommendation written on behalf of Lulu by Concordia College's president and vice-chancellor.

Perhaps the most remarkable thing about Joe Galloway's

lying was its unnecessary elaborateness. Once Howard began to ask Galloway about his MBA, Galloway's best tactic would have been to confess to its origin, since a moment's reflection would have told him that in a case with such high stakes it was likely that every aspect of his witness statement would be pored over for veracity; a second option would have been to stonewall most of the barrister's questions by claiming not to remember much about it. Instead, he recalled his year on St John at length and in finely drawn detail. Galloway was exhibiting something that lying experts term 'duping delight' – although perhaps his delight lay less in the duping than in the exercise of his own fertile imagination.

Explaining his decision in favour of Sky, the judge said that the apparent ease and confidence with which Galloway had lied about the MBA had destroyed his entire credibility as a witness, and indicated a propensity to deceit in his business dealings. Lying about an educational qualification was one thing, said the judge, but Galloway had demonstrated something else: 'an astounding ability to be dishonest'. EDS was ordered to pay Sky over two hundred million pounds.

* * *

In the film *The Usual Suspects*, detectives engage in a desperate search for the mysterious Keyser Söze, a ruthless, violent and brilliant criminal who has acquired a mythical reputation in the underworld. Though his brutal deeds are legion, barely anything is known about Söze's identity, his past, or even what he looks like – those that meet him have a habit of dying horrible deaths. In their investigations the detectives rely on the testimony of Roger 'Verbal' Kint (played by Kevin Spacey), a lowly con-artist with a pronounced limp, who has been granted immunity from prosecution in return for telling what he knows of Söze's story.

Verbal describes how he and a small group of career criminals were blackmailed by Söze, through Söze's lawyer Kobayashi (Pete Postlethwaite), into destroying a large drug shipment belonging to Söze's rivals, during which operation all but Verbal and one other man were killed. He also tells the investigators what he knows of Söze's life; of his beginnings as a low-level drug dealer in his native Turkey, and of how, after the Hungarian mafia kill one of his children, he wreaks terrible revenge on them and becomes a faceless, fearsome one-man force of destruction. Verbal's tale directs the police to a man called Dean Keaton (Gabriel Byrne); apparently the real Söze.

In the movie's famous final sequence, however, it is revealed to Verbal's interrogator – and to us – that Keyser Söze is none other than Verbal Kint. Verbal's story was an elaborate lie, an improvised concoction of strung-together details snatched from his immediate surroundings, including the crowded bulletin board in the office where the interrogation took place. As the investigator stares at the board, he recognises random words and phrases from the story he has just been told, and feels the cold rush of revelation. He drops the coffee cup he has been sipping from during the interrogation. In slow motion, we see it fall to the floor and smash. The manufacturer's logo, printed on the bottom of the cup, reads *KOBAYASHI*.

Like the appropriately nicknamed Verbal, confabulating patients make up their stories using whatever comes to hand. As with the woman who told of her holiday in the Falklands, their stories are conjured up instantaneously — an interlocutor only has to ask a question, or say a particular word, and they're off, like a jazz saxophonist using a phrase thrown out by his pianist as the launch-pad for a solo. A confabulating patient might explain to her visiting friend that she's in hospital because she now works as a psychiatrist, that the man standing next to her (the real doctor) is her assistant, and they are about to visit a patient. Chronic confabulators are often highly inventive at the verbal level, jamming together words in nonsensical but suggestive ways: one patient, when asked what happened to Queen Marie Antoinette of France, answered that she had been 'suicided' by her family. These patients are like novelists as described by Henry James: people on whom 'nothing is wasted' though, unlike novelists, or liars, they are entirely at the mercy of their material.

Both Verbal Kint and the Falklands woman are exercising one of the core processes of the creative imagination. In *A Treatise on Human Nature* the philosopher David Hume writes:

To form monsters, and join incongruous shapes and appearances, costs the imagination no more trouble than to
conceive the most natural and familiar objects ... But
though our thought seems to possess this unbounded
liberty, we shall find, upon a nearer examination, that it
is really confined within very narrow limits, and that all
this creative power of the mind amounts to no more than
the faculty of compounding, transposing, augmenting, or
diminishing the materials afforded us by the senses and
experience. When we think of a golden mountain, we
only join two consistent ideas, gold, and mountain, with
which we were formerly acquainted ... In short, all the
materials of thinking are derived either from our outward
or inward sentiment: the mixture and composition of these
belongs alone to the mind and will.

William James (Henry's brother) called the ability to make
novel connections between ideas 'divergent thinking', a
mode of thought in which 'the unexpected seems the only
law'. When I asked the writer Will Self about his creative
process he echoed this theme, describing the creative
mindset to me as a continuous willingness to pick up on
aspects of the world, aspects of thought, and put them
together with other things to produce juxtapositions. We
get a glimpse of a creatively focused confabulatory process
in *No Direction Home*, Martin Scorsese's documentary
about the early career of Bob Dylan. It's 1966, and Dylan
is standing on a street corner in Kensington, London,

wearing a blue suede jacket, Ray-Bans, and pinstripe trousers. He is on his first trip to Britain and in a playful, high-spirited mood. Dylan has come across a series of three painted signs on a pet shop, which evidently doubles as a tobacconist. He reads them aloud:

> WE WILL COLLECT, CLIP, BATH & RETURN YOUR DOG
>
> CIGARETTES AND TOBACCO
>
> ANIMALS AND BIRDS BOUGHT OR SOLD ON COMMISSION

Dylan then uses these words as the raw material for a series of verbal riffs that are part nursery rhyme, part Beat poetry. Dancing around, waving his cigarette in the air and giggling at his own inventiveness, he spits out new versions faster than most of us can think:

> *I want a dog that's gonna collect and clean my bath, return my cigarette, and give tobacco to my animals and give my bird a commission.*
> *I'm looking for a place to bathe my bird, buy my dog, collect my clip, sell me cigarettes and commission my bath.*
> *I'm looking for a place that's gonna animal my soul, clip my return, bathe my foot, and collect my dog.*

Part of what makes this vignette so compelling is that it lays bare one of the key operations of improvisational creativity: taking elements of the familiar or mundane and remixing them until something new is born. It would be stretching it to call the resulting doggerel art, but this is where much art begins: in the power of confabulatory combination. Dylan's creativity often spilt over into lying, especially when it came to his own biography. When first making a name for himself in New York he told interviewers that he was raised in Gallup, New Mexico, had lived in Iowa, South Dakota, North Dakota and Kansas, and had been taught guitar by the blues singers Arvella Gray and Mance Lipscombe. In fact, Dylan had lived only in Minnesota and New York by that point, and had never met Gray or Lipscombe. This is exactly the sort of story a confabulating patient would tell, mixing truth with fantasy and wish-fulfilment. The difference is that Dylan presumably knew he was fibbing.

In 1996, during a now-famous libel case, the former cabinet minister Jonathan Aitken recounted a tale to court which vividly illustrated the horrors he was having to endure after his name was besmirched by a national newspaper. He told of how, on leaving his home in Lord North Street, Westminster one morning with his teenage daughter Alexandra, he found himself 'stampeded' by a documentary crew. Upset and scared by the crew's aggressive behaviour, Alexandra burst into tears. Aitken bundled her into his ministerial car, but as they drove away, he realised that they were being followed by the journalists in their van. A hair-raising chase across central London ensued. The journalists were only shaken off when Aitken executed a cunning deception: he stopped at the Spanish embassy and swapped vehicles.

Aitken, a wealthy, handsome, and highly articulate man, had a weakness for melodrama. The year before, at a press conference announcing his intention to sue the *Guardian* newspaper, he declared: 'If it falls to me to start a fight to cut out the cancer of bent and twisted journalism in our country with the simple sword of truth and the trusty shield of British fair play, so be it. I am ready for the fight. The fight against falsehood and those who peddle it.' The case, which stretched on for over two years, involved a series of claims made by the *Guardian* about Aitken's relationships with Saudi arms dealers, including meetings he allegedly held with them as their guest in the Ritz Hotel in Paris while he was a government minister. As Aitken knew when he delivered this stirring battle-cry, the key allegations made by the *Guardian* were all true. He went on to lose the case, which destroyed his reputation and his career.

As the trial unfolded, what amazed the *Guardian* journalists, who knew he was lying – and what astonished everyone else after his case collapsed – was the sheer superfluity of the lies Aitken told. Some were necessary to maintain his original lie, but others were told, it seemed, for the sheer thrill of invention. Like Galloway, Aitken was led further and further into deceit by his own pleasure in confabulating. There was another, subtler aspect to Jonathan Aitken's lies: like a novelist, he used them to illuminate character. The florid rhetoric of his press conference set the tone for his self-presentation at the trial as a man of oak-like virtue, a patriot beset on all sides by frivolous, malign and bitter critics. The story he told of being chased by journalists wasn't necessary to his case, but it had a clear dramatic purpose: to burnish the portrait he was painting of a dashing and gallant hero.

Aitken's case collapsed on 17 June 1997, when the defence finally found indisputable evidence that he had lied about his trip to Paris, and presented it to the court. Until then, his charm, fluency and flair for theatrical displays of sincerity looked as if they might bring him victory. The first big dent in the façade of his integrity had been made days before, however, when the unedited rushes of the encounter in Lord North Street were shown to the court. They revealed a very different story. Aitken had indeed been doorstepped that day, but Alexandra Aitken was not with him. The minister walked out of his house alone, got into his car and drove off, with no vehicle in pursuit.

The stories invented by confabulating patients aren't entirely random – like Aitken's lie, they tend to depict an idealised version of the protagonist, who often stands at the centre of a heroic drama. Unable to admit the truth of their condition or its cause, their stories are told to make metaphorical sense of their predicament. Aikaterini Fotoupoulou, a psychiatrist at King's College, London, specialises in the theory and treatment of confabulation.

She told me about one of her patients, a nineteen-year-old window-fitter known as RM who had been a passenger in a car that crashed at high-speed. He was left with damage to his brain's frontal lobes. Six months later, RM had made a strong physical recovery but was disoriented in time, had severe difficulty planning ahead, and had become, according to his friends and family, a more boastful, irritable and emotional person than he was before the accident. He had also become a chronic confabulator. As far as RM was concerned, he had made a full recovery, and during rehabilitation sessions he invented long and complicated stories to explain why he was in a hospital, being attended to by doctors. He rewrote unpleasant events from his past in ways he would have preferred them to have happened: shortly before the accident he had been greatly upset by his parents' divorce, yet during therapy he would tell and retell the story of how he had persuaded his parents to stay together after they threatened to separate. RM also told tales of implausible derring-do, in which he would respond to a call of distress from a girlfriend or family member under threat from an anonymous attacker. He would race to the scene at impossible speed and be forced to use violence to subdue or even kill the assailant. At the end the police would arrive, survey the bloody aftermath, and praise him for doing what they were not able to do. It became apparent to Fotoupolou that RM's stories of high-velocity heroism were his attempts to assuage deep feelings of powerlessness, by rewriting his memories of the horrific incident in which he had lost part of mind.

Fotopoulou has learned to read between the lines of her patients' confabulations to find the ways in which they are trying to make sense of troubles of which they are only dimly aware. Another of her patients, a wealthy Italian businessman who had suffered a stroke, would constantly fret that he had lost boxes of important files. Fotopoulou took this to be his metaphor for his memory problems. Sigmund Freud would have had no trouble recognising the stories of confabulators as wish-fulfilments that the rest of us work through in dreams and fantasies. He not only looked for hidden psychological meanings in the dreams and speech of his patients, but in works of art. For Freud, dreaming, storytelling and lying are inextricably intertwined, because we can never tell the truth of the unconscious. He noted the prevalence of novels by male authors with a 'hero who is the centre of interest, for whom the writer tries to win our sympathy by every possible means' — by rescuing distressed women, for instance.

* * *

Shortly before his death, Marlon Brando was working on a series of instructional videos about acting to be called

Lying For A Living (it has never been released). On the surviving footage, Brando can be seen dispensing gnomic advice on his craft to a group of enthusiastic if somewhat bemused Hollywood stars, including Leonardo Di Caprio and Sean Penn. Brando also recruited random people from Los Angeles and persuaded them to improvise (the footage includes a memorable scene featuring two dwarves and a giant Samoan). 'If you can lie, you can act,' Brando told the writer Jod Kaftan, when asked about the title he had chosen for the series. 'Are you good at lying?' asked Kaftan. 'Jesus,' replied Brando, 'I'm fabulous at it.'

Actors, playwrights and novelists are not literally attempting to deceive you, because the rules are laid out in advance: you come to the theatre, and we'll lie to you. But as Brando and others have observed, artistic storytelling and lying are very close: both involve making up fictional stories and asking others to believe in them, and the mental processes involved are similar. Having said that, the differences between the artist, the liar and the confabulator are as revealing as the similarities.

Unlike artists, chronic confabulators can't *stop* telling tales. At certain moments, this is also true of artists, who will sometimes describe an act of creativity as being beyond their control — as something happening *to* them. When Dylan is outside the pet shop there's a sense of the words tumbling out of him of their own accord, and he famously scrawled what became the lyrics to 'Like a Rolling Stone' in one long rush of inspiration (Dylan later referred to his first draft, fondly, as 'a piece of vomit, twenty pages long'). However, the artist ultimately knows he's engaged in creating a fiction and is able to draw on his subconscious processes at will. Robert Louis Stevenson came to rely on his unusually vivid dreams to provide the basis of his stories; *The Strange Case of Dr Jekyll and Mr Hyde* began in a nightmare from which he awoke screaming. If chronic confabulators are trapped in what Fotopoulou calls 'a waking dream', artists dip into their confabulatory resources quite deliberately.

Dr Charles Limb, an assistant professor of medicine at Johns Hopkins University, is an ear surgeon and a devoted music fan (he is, he told me, obsessed by sound). Limb is an accomplished saxophonist, composer and music historian, and the music he loves most is jazz. He is fascinated by the mental processes that enable jazz musicians to create something new in every moment; that allowed, for instance, his musical hero John Coltrane to improvise instant masterpieces on stage. Limb wanted to see if there was a way of tracking the neural activity of musicians as they improvised, and whether that might allow a glimpse into the processes of creativity in action. Along with his colleague Allen Braun, he designed an experiment to do just that.

Limb and Braun recruited four jazz musicians and asked them to play specially designed keyboards while lying inside a brain scanner. The musicians began by playing a piece that required no imagination; a simple blues melody composed by Limb. Then they were asked to improvise over the top of a recording of a jazz quartet. The musicians displayed a distinctive pattern of brain activity as soon as they started their improvisations. The area of the pre-frontal cortex responsible for self-awareness and introspection – for our sense of who we are – showed high activation. At the same time, the musicians seemed to 'turn off' activity in those parts of the brain linked to self-control and self-monitoring – the areas that are usually damaged in confabulating patients. As Limb puts it, the improvising musician 'shuts down his inhibitions and lets his inner voice shine through'.

Paradoxically, artists are able to control the point at which they *relinquish* control. When I asked Will Self if there's anything that marks out artists from the rest of us, he recalled a remark made by the author Flannery O'Connor to the effect that writers have to be 'calculatedly stupid'. 'I can think of any number of people who are more perceptive than me, who are more learned and have more know-how,' said Self. 'But what they aren't is calculatedly stupid, in the sense that they are unable to preserve intact their ability to suspend disbelief. They can't *play*, in the way that a child will make a den and say "This is my castle". Writers can still do that. Creativity is just an advanced form of play, in which the normal rules of space and time are suspended.'

Freud observed that the child's uninhibited pleasure in

play is diminished in adulthood, or marginalised as private 'day-dreaming' or mere 'fancy'. Children are magical realists; aware of the difference between reality and fantasy but never less than ready to take unashamed pleasure in the latter. There is now a better understanding of why this is in terms of our neurological development: the parts of the brain responsible for pleasure and fantasy arrive early, while those responsible for self-monitoring and regulation are the last to become fully formed. As we grow older we can still hear the hiss and bubble of what William James called the 'seething cauldron of ideas', but it tends to recede as reality asserts itself and we address the quotidian tasks of getting jobs and filling out mortgage applications. 'Every child is an artist,' said Pablo Picasso. 'The problem is how to remain an artist once we grow up.'

In a 1962 study of creativity, a group of high-school students aged between eleven and eighteen were administered a series of verbal and visual exercises, the focus of which was to tease out the difference between being intelligent and being creative; the results of the exercises were compared to scores from IQ tests which the school had already administered. In one exercise the students were shown a picture of a businessman sitting in an aeroplane, reclining in his seat. They were asked to imagine the story behind it. A high-IQ student gave this response:

Mr Smith is on his way home from a successful business trip. He is very happy and he is thinking about his wonderful family and how glad he will be to see them again. He can picture it, about an hour from now, his plane landing at the airport and Mrs Smith and their three children all there welcoming him again.

A high-creativity student gave this response to the same picture:

The man is flying back from Reno where he has just won a divorce from his wife. He couldn't stand to live with her anymore, he told the judge, because she wore so much cold cream on her face at night that her head would skid across the pillow and hit him on the head. He is now contemplating skid-proof face cream.

You can't help but wonder if this anonymous student went on to become a novelist, a screenwriter or a stand-up comedian. His response demonstrates a mind capable of startling associations: the simple line-drawing is linked to the ideas of Reno, divorce, and face cream, and inspires that brilliantly comic description of somebody's face *skidding* across the pillow. In three short sentences, the man on the plane becomes the protagonist of a drama, alive with conflict and uncertainty; one that instantly illuminates a character, a sensibility, an entire social *milieu*.

Perhaps the key way in which artistic 'lies' differ from

normal lies, and from the 'honest lying' of chronic confabulators, is that they have a meaning and resonance beyond their creator. One of the stories for which Will Self first became known is *Cock and Bull*, about a woman who grows a penis and has sex with her careless, constantly drunk husband without him noticing anything different about the experience. The story was born from the jamming together of two distinct concepts – 'woman' and 'penis' were Self's equivalent of 'gold' and 'mountain', or 'commission' and 'bath' – and it would be fair to say that Self's unconscious played a part in making the link; he came up with the basic idea during a drunken riff in the pub with his friends. But in the story that resulted, the juxtaposition is just the starting point for an exploration of a lifeless, loveless marriage.

Freud's rather clumsy attempts to psychoanalyse authors via their work neglected the extent to which good writers are able to shape their own material, whatever its source. Stevenson's nightmare was just the raw material; the story was shaped and written 'awake, and consciously'. If writers are compelled to narrate, they compel themselves to find insights, not just about their own lives but about our shared experience. Outside the pet shop, Dylan was practising a skill he used over and over again to ignite his grander creations – songs like 'Mr Tambourine Man', in which he takes us to a place where 'memory and fate are driven deep beneath the waves'.

The novelist Mario Vargas Llosa writes that fictions

'express a curious truth that can only be expressed in a furtive and veiled fashion, disguised as something it is not'. Art is a lie whose secret ingredient is truth.

* * *

People who can't stop telling tales, and who know they are lying, suffer from a different kind of madness to chronic confabulators, and a different kind of lack.

Joe Galloway and Jonathan Aitken would not be considered pathological liars in the clinical sense. Though they seem to have got carried away with their own lies, and clearly lacked scruples, they exerted a significant degree of control over their lying behaviour (which only makes their behaviour more reprehensible). Such liars can be considered distinct from *compulsive* liars who become addicted to frequent self-glorifying fibs, often because they are socially insecure, and whose lies usually harm nobody but themselves. *Pathological* liars are a different category again. Manipulative, cunning and egotistical, they lie compulsively but with specific, self-serving goals in mind. They can be charming and credible in pursuit of their goals, and wreak great damage on those unfortunate enough to cross their paths, who often find it hard to rebuild their trust in people in the wake of such an encounter. Pathological liars remain oblivious or careless of the effect their lies have on the possibility of building relationships; their short term gains are usually at the expense of long-term social reputation.

Such behaviour may be linked to a very specific deficit

of emotional capacity. Adrian Raine is a criminologist at the University of Pennsylvania who specialises in the study of how the brains of persistent criminals differ from the rest of us. He and his collaborators carried out brain scans on people whom they established as having psychopathic personalities. (Not all pathological liars are psychopaths – itself a complex and contentious classification – but there is considerable overlap between the two conditions.) The subjects were given a decision-making task to think about while in the scanner. The dilemma they were presented with is the kind of diabolical scenario beloved of moral philosophers, and it was dramatised in the last-ever episode of *MASH*.

It's wartime. You are hiding in the basement of a house with some of your fellow villagers. You can hear the enemy soldiers outside, whom you know have orders to kill anyone they find. You are holding your own baby. Your baby has a cold. You know that if she coughs or cries then the soldiers will hear, and they will find your hiding place, kill you, your baby, and all of your friends. Should you smother and suffocate your own baby to save the village? Or should you let the baby cough, knowing the consequences?

Don't worry, there isn't a right or wrong answer. In fact, the researchers weren't interested in how the subjects said they'd respond, so much as what was happening in their brains while they thought about it. When normal, non-psychopathic individuals are given this test, they display a high amount of activity in parts of the brain responsible for the governing of emotion. If you spent just a moment thinking about that dilemma you probably felt some sense of discomfort or unease; it is a horrible choice, after all. Psychopathic personalities, however, are less likely to experience that feeling. The brain scan results showed that the more psychopathic the individual, the lower the activation in the amygdala and other emotion-regulating regions as they considered the dilemma. In other words, these murderers seemed to lack an emotional component to their moral decision-making process, and there is plenty of evidence to suggest that most of us are very reliant on our emotions, or intuitions, to make moral decisions.

It's often said that psychopaths are people who don't know right from wrong. But that's not true – they could probably pass a test of moral reasoning as well as you or I. Their problem is that they can't *feel* right from wrong.

This void extends to feelings of honesty and dishonesty. The reason that most of us are honest most of the time, even when it might suit our purposes to lie, is that we *feel* uncomfortable with deceit – like the children who read the George Washington story, we have learnt to take pleasure in truth-telling and to feel emotional discomfort with fibbing (even if we sometimes suppress this discomfort and lie anyway). Pathological liars don't have this feeling. What they can do is give an extraordinary *imitation* of felt honesty, and sometimes with a great actor's grasp of verbal nuance and subtle gesture.

Hervey Cleckley, author of the classic study of psychopaths, *The Mask of Sanity*, wrote that 'Over-emphasis, glibness, and other signs of the clever liar do not show in his words or manner . . . during the most solemn perjuries he has no difficulty at all in looking anyone tranquilly in the eyes.' The most powerful liars cast a spell that is almost impossible to resist. Cleckley confessed that even after many years of working with psychopathic personalities he couldn't help but be taken in by them. Time and again, he said, he had been fooled by patients who implored him to lend them money, never to return it.

There may be another neurological characteristic common to pathological liars. Adrian Raine carried out a study on this topic with Yaling Yang, when both were at the University of Southern California. Initially, they faced an interesting problem: how to identify and recruit their subjects. After all, ask a liar if they're a liar and you risk being plunged into a logical vortex. Their ingenious solution was to ask the temporary employment agencies of Los Angeles to open up their rolls to them. Raine and Yang knew that pathological liars usually find it impossible to maintain long-term relationships of any kind, or to hold down long-term jobs. They are soon caught in one lie too many and have to keep moving on, socially and professionally, like parasites looking for new hosts.

By starting with a pool of temporary workers, Raine and Yang guessed they'd find who they were looking for more quickly. After asking for volunteers to take part in a psychological test they subjected the 108 who replied to a detailed questionnaire. 'We looked for things like inconsistencies in their stories about occupation, education, crimes and family background,' said Raine. They then interviewed those whom they suspected of habitual dishonesty. 'Pathological liars can't always tell truth from falsehood, and contradict themselves in an interview,' Raine explained. Not that they were pretending to be truthtellers – one of the common characteristics of people with this condition is a brazen disregard for how they are perceived, and a sense of grandiosity that allows them to feel invincible. In the interviews, some of the subjects would happily admit to preying on people, coolly relating stories of running cons and using aliases. Eventually the researchers identified twelve of the volunteers as the real thing, and used brain scans to look for structural brain differences between the pathological liars and the control groups.

Raine and Yang hypothesised that pathological liars would have some kind of neuronal deficit in their frontal lobes. The results of the scans showed they were right: the pathological liars had significantly less cortical matter in this region than the control group. What surprised the researchers was that the liars also displayed an *excess* of something: they had more 'white matter' – the brain fibres responsible for making connections. The more neuronal networking there is in the brain, the more varied and original is a person's stream of thought, and the higher their verbal skills. Although the study is far from conclusive, it suggests that pathological liars have powerful equipment for lying, and fewer of the inhibitions that most of us have about doing so; and that they are bursting with inventiveness while lacking crucial censoring mechanisms, including a capacity for moral feeling. Unable to find wider significance or solace in their own creativity, they remain trapped in the frozen world of their own lies.

Tells and Leakages

What are the signs of a lie?

> *'Where are the gold pieces now?' the Fairy
> asked.*
>
> *'I lost them,' answered Pinocchio, but he
> told a lie, for he had them in his pocket.*
>
> *As he spoke, his nose, long though it was,
> became at least two inches longer.*
>
> Carlos Collodi, *The Adventures
> of Pinocchio*

Charles Bond, a psychologist at Texas Christian University, asked 2,520 adults in sixty-three countries how to spot a liar. More than seventy per cent said that liars tend to avert their gazes, and most said that liars squirm, stutter, touch or scratch themselves or tell longer stories than usual. The same liar stereotype exists in every culture, says Bond. This would be less puzzling, he continues, if it was accurate, but the stereotype just isn't supported by the evidence. As a result, it leads us astray.

Bond partnered with fellow lying expert Bella DePaulo to carry out a meta-analysis of over a hundred academic studies of deception detection. They found that subjects asked to distinguish truth from lies answer correctly, on average, forty-seven per cent of the time. In other words, they'd be better off flipping a coin.

That's when people are *looking* for a lie. In everyday life we live with a 'truth bias'. Unless there is a compelling reason to think somebody is lying, it doesn't occur to us that they are. And why should it? The world would be a deeply unpleasant place if we were forced to consider that everything we hear could be a lie — indeed, as Browne's Law tells us, society would be unworkable. But this, of course, is what gives the skilled liar a head start over the rest of us.

So what *should* we be on the lookout for? There have been endless investigations into this question, but no simple answer has been found. For one thing, different people have different 'tells'; one person might blink rapidly; another might stare unblinkingly. The signs of lying also depend on the type of lie being told. When people tell complicated lies, they frequently pause more often and for longer and speak more slowly, but if the lie is simple or highly polished they tend to do the opposite. Bad liars sometimes exhibit the symptoms of discomfort we expect but, overall, liars are *less* likely to blink, to move their hands and feet, or to make elaborate gestures.

What's clear is that, faced with a group of people and

asked to identify the liar, you'd be better off picking the most charismatic and fluent person in the room rather than, as we're inclined to, the shifty-looking mumbler in the corner. Lying requires high cognitive, emotional and social abilities. The best liars tend to be charming, empathetic, and capable of thinking several moves ahead of their interlocutor. Their testimony under interrogation is often more coherent than that of the average truth-teller because they have thought their story through. They are more likely to tell a story in chronological order, whereas honest people often present accounts in an improvised jumble, which strikes us as dishonest-sounding. If someone says they can't remember things, we get suspicious, but actually, people who spontaneously correct themselves or say that there are details they can't recall are as − or even more − likely to be truthful than those who spin a smooth and fluent narrative line. Having said that, *really* good liars will make deliberate mistakes, to simulate spontaneity.

Liars are more difficult to spot than we imagine and very skilful liars are almost impossible to see through. Practised liars identify their own giveaways (or the conventionally assumed giveaways) and teach themselves to avoid them. They also anticipate what others are looking for: to be a good liar, you don't need to know which behaviours separate liars from truth-tellers so much as which behaviours people *think* separate them.

Just because there are no unassailably reliable signs of lying doesn't mean our internal lie detectors can't be honed and refined. There are two prominent schools of thought on where to look for a lie. One focuses on the liar's face; the other on his words.

The Honest Face

There ain't no way to hide your lyin' eyes.

'Lyin' Eyes' The Eagles

In 1967 Paul Ekman was approached by a group of psychiatrists from the Californian hospital in which he had been working to see if he could help them tell when suicidal patients were lying to them. Ekman, a psychologist, wasn't sure that he could answer their question, but he remembered a reel of film in his possession that might offer some clues. Several years earlier, he had filmed forty psychiatric patients being interviewed by doctors. At least one of them, 'Mary', a forty-two-year-old housewife, had been captured in the act of lying.

Mary had attempted suicide three times, and only survived her last attempt after being rushed to hospital. At the end of a three-week stay she seemed happier, and asked for a weekend pass to see her family. After interviewing Mary and being convinced by her account of her frame of mind, her doctor agreed. Just before leaving, however, Mary confessed to the real reason she wanted to go: to make another attempt on her own life.

Ekman and his colleague Wallace Friesen played the tape of Mary's exit interview over and over, searching for the signs of deceit that had escaped her doctor. They slowed the tape down and scrutinised Mary's face as she explained how well she was feeling. Finally, they saw it: when Mary was asked about her plans for the future, a look of despair flashed across her face, so quickly that it was almost imperceptible at normal speed and difficult to catch even at quarter-speed. Mary's face had betrayed her real feelings, perhaps before she even knew they existed.

The psychiatrists had come to Ekman in the first place because of his reputation as an expert on the expressive capacity of the human face. As a young psychologist in the early 1960s, he had set out to find evidence for a theory that was prevalent at the time amongst social scientists: that what people thought of as universal facial expressions were actually culturally constructed masks with no direct connection to human emotions. Indeed, according to the dominant school of psychology at the time, emotions themselves were of negligible importance to human behaviour, and unworthy of serious study.

Ekman travelled to a remote village in Papua New Guinea to meet the people of South Fore, a tribe who had very little contact with the people or culture of the West. With the help of a translator, he told them very simple stories that ended with somebody being happy, sad, or angry, and asked them to choose, from a selection of two or three different pictures, the facial expression that best suited what the person in the story was feeling. If Ekman could show that the villagers of Fore had a different facial repertoire to Americans, he would have found valuable empirical evidence for the theory.

But the tribespeople of Fore didn't give Ekman what he expected. They recognised the expressions he showed them, identifying them just as an American or a German would, and they used the same expressions themselves. When acting out a humorous story, they flashed cheesy grins; when describing frightening hunting tales, they adopted Hitchcockian poses. Ekman's hypothesis was turned on its head. As he said forty years later, 'I was dead wrong, and it was the most exciting discovery of my life.'

Back home, the academic establishment didn't embrace Ekman's findings, and he found himself gravitating towards an unconventional mentor: Silvan Tomkins. Born in Pennsylvania in 1911, Tomkins was the brilliant, charismatic, intellectually voracious son of a Russian dentist. He studied playwriting at the University of Pennsylvania but soon became absorbed by the young science of psychology. He left Philadelphia in 1934 and, unable to find scholarly employment in the midst of the Great Depression, spent the next two years working as a handicapper for a horse-racing syndicate. Tomkins's system was based on his reading of the horses' emotional relationship with each other. For instance, if a male horse had lost to a mare in his first or second year, he would be unsettled if he went to the gate with a mare next to him in the line-up. Nobody was quite sure whether or how it worked, but somehow he seemed to get results.

Unlike his contemporaries, Tomkins was interested in the emotions of human beings, too. While teaching psychology at Princeton and Rutgers he produced a comprehensive theory of the emotions in a four-volume work called *Affect, Imagery, Consciousness*. His greatest preoccupation was with how the human face displayed emotion, a subject that had also fascinated Charles Darwin. In 1872 Darwin published *The Expression of the Emotions in Man and Animals*, in which he noted that 'the same state of mind is expressed throughout the world with remarkable uniformity.' Darwin was the first to ask whether facial expressions of emotion are innate – biologically determined; or learnt – culturally determined. Twentieth-century social scientists were firmly of the latter view – except for Tomkins, and now Ekman.

One day, towards the end of the Sixties, Ekman came across a treasure: a hundred-thousand feet of film, shot by a virologist in the jungles of Papua New Guinea. Some of the footage was of the South Fore tribe he had visited; the rest was of the Kukukuku. The Fore were a peaceful and friendly people; the Kukukuku had a reputation for being hostile and murderous. For six months, Ekman sorted through the footage, cutting extraneous scenes and focusing on close-ups of the faces of the tribesmen. When a final cut was ready, he called in Tomkins. The two men watched the film in silence. Ekman had told Tomkins nothing about the tribes involved, and all identifying context had been edited out. At the end, Tomkins went up to the screen and pointed at the faces of the South Fore. 'These are a sweet, gentle people, very indulgent, very peaceful,' he said. Then, pointing to the Kukukuku, he said, 'This group is violent.' Ekman was stunned. 'How on earth are you doing that?' he asked. As they played the film backwards in slow motion, Tomkins pointed out the particular wrinkles and bulges in the faces that he was using to make his judgements.

Ekman started to see the face as a gold mine of information about the human condition. Together with his collaborator Wallace Friesen, he embarked on a vast, quixotic undertaking: to create a comprehensive taxonomy of human expressions. The two men combed through medical textbooks, outlining each of the forty-three facial muscles and identifying every distinct muscular movement that the face could make. Then they made faces at each other across a desk, systematically manipulating their facial muscles into different combinations, checking each one in a mirror, and videotaping themselves for the record. If they found a particular movement impossible to execute they went next door to the anatomy department where a friendly surgeon would jumpstart the dormant muscle with a needle. They called each distinct muscular movement an 'action unit'.

In time, the two researchers discovered and codified ten thousand facial expressions, all made up of different combinations of action units. Most of the expressions were meaningless – the kind of face a child might make in play. But about three thousand of them seemed to mean something. After seven years of research, Ekman and Friesen had catalogued the emotional repertoire of the human face, which they published in a document called the Facial Action Coding System, or FACS, still used by psychologists today. Each expression the human face is capable of is numbered, its movement described muscle by muscle, its emotional 'meaning' labelled. Action unit (AU) 12, which activates the zygomatic major, is a smile. Combine it with AU 6, which contracts the muscles that raise the cheek, and you have an expression of happiness. Sadness is defined as: AU 1+4+6+11, which means, 'the inner corners of the brows drawn together and upward, cheeks raised, slight deepening of the nasolabial fold, and slight depression of the lip corners.' Ekman points out that Woody Allen will raise the inner corner of his eyebrows whilst drawing his eyebrows down and together (AU1+4), in an expression of sadness that somehow makes his punchlines more poignant.

Thanks to Ekman's research, the universality of facial expression is now generally accepted by social scientists. Outside academia, he is best known for his insights into deception. The nineteenth-century neurologist Guillaume

Duchenne was the first to note how difficult it is to fake a facial expression. An authentic smile, he said, 'does not obey the will'; its absence 'unmasks the false friend'. Ekman's intricate mapping of the facial repertoire enabled him to define precisely why it is that even when we make a good effort at putting on our best or our worst face, we can't quite convince the careful observer. If we activate our zygomatic major without contracting our cheek muscles or scrunching our eyes, our smile seems lifeless. A 'felt happy smile' typically features 'apex coordination', with the eye closure reaching its maximum intensity at the same time the grin is at its broadest. Real smiles are also shorter and smoother in execution than anxious or faked varieties. Authentic expressions of anger are even harder to create voluntarily (Adolf Hitler was unusually good at faking rage) and the negative emotions are generally tougher to fake than the positive ones. We might bare our teeth, but we rarely remember to narrow the red margin of the lips – or even if we remember, we can't do it. Unless we're truly angry.

After watching the tape of Mary's exit interview, Ekman realised something even more remarkable: emotional expressions aren't just hard to fake; they are almost impossible to conceal. This was the revelation that stimulated his interest in lying and lie detection. Liars need to put on what Macbeth calls a 'false face' consistent with the lie, and good liars can do this without much difficulty. But even the most skilful liars, Ekman came to believe, can exhibit a 'leakage' of emotional truth, by unconsciously making a facial expression incongruous with the story they are telling. For a fraction of a second, the honest face disrupts the false face. Ekman terms these fleeting expressions of involuntary emotion 'microexpressions'. He frequently reminds people that a microexpression, even if you can spot it, is not necessarily the sign of a lie. It simply signals an emotional incongruity: you still have to figure out what it means, and whether it's significant.

These days Ekman teaches his face-reading techniques to police investigators, embassy officials and military intelligence officers. In these sessions, he begins by showing photos of faces in neutral poses on a computer screen. A microexpression appears for forty milliseconds and the student has to press a button to indicate which emotion it displayed: fear, anger, surprise happiness, sadness, contempt or disgust. Without training, they are invisible; with it, says Ekman, people greatly improve their ability to spot them.

Of course, we have a voluntary muscular system and thus a degree of control over our facial responses. Most of the time we can fake a smile well enough. But the more we are emotionally involved in a falsehood, and the higher the stakes – that's to say, the worse the consequences of being found out – the more likely it is that our face will give us away to the trained observer. It seems to have a mind of its own.

Silvan Tomkins used to open his lectures by declaring, 'The face is like a penis!'

False Speech

We've already seen that most of us aren't as good as we think we are at distinguishing truth from lies. You might expect that those whose jobs rely on making such distinctions would be better at it. According to Bond and DePaulo's meta-analysis, however, psychiatrists, judges, custom officials and policemen score no more highly than the general public on tests of lie-detecting ability.

Aldert Vrij, a professor at Portsmouth University and the author of *Detecting Lies and Deceit*, a seminal book in the field of deception research, believes that professional lie catchers, like most of us, focus too much on the stereotypical physical signs of deception and fail to pay enough attention to verbal ones. Some people, says Vrij, have a naturally 'dishonest' demeanour even when they're telling the truth; conversely, those with a naturally 'honest' demeanour can get away with a lot more. He cites the case of a Florida man, who became a prime suspect in a murder case after he appeared to be flushed in the face and embarrassed during his police interview. He was later found to be innocent.

If Ekman's research focuses on the signs of emotional stress experienced by a liar, Vrij is more interested in the effects of the mental strain that a lie imposes on the person telling it — their 'cognitive load' — and in particular the manifestation of this strain in the liar's speech.

He believes that the tried and trusted methods used by police interviewers are seriously flawed. In their day-to-day work, says Vrij, the police often assume that if somebody is surly and uncooperative then they're probably lying. But his research indicates that because liars are concerned about not being believed, they are likely to come across as *more* helpful than truthful people during an interview. Another problem is that some police interrogators, following in the tradition of Gene Hunt from *Life On Mars*, charge aggressively into interviews, accusing the suspect of guilt from the off. Vrij's work suggests that such attempts to break down the defences of the suspect only strengthen them, because they shut down the conversation; the suspect, feeling threatened, makes short answers or clams up altogether. The more talking they have to do, the more mental effort they have to make, and thus the more likely they are to incriminate themselves. Vrij argues that the way to catch a liar is to make them talk more, not less.

The police interrogation guidelines aren't much help. The official manuals recommend several strategies to help interviewers decide whether they are being told the truth. The principal one focuses on visual signs, such as whether the suspect is making eye contact, or fidgeting a lot. But, as we've seen, there's little evidence that these cues are reliable. Another recommended approach, the Baseline Method, involves comparing a suspect's language and demeanour during small talk at the beginning of the interview with those they use in the interview proper. But, says Vrij, people naturally adopt different modes of talking at different points — whether or not they're telling the truth. A third approach, the Behavioural Analysis Interview (BAI) strategy, comprises a list of questions to which, it is suggested, liars and truth-tellers will give different responses. Again, there's sparse evidence that this works, says Vrij, and neither do the guidelines address the fact that the police, like the rest of us, carry around a host of unconscious prejudices. It's been shown that suspects are less likely to be believed if they have a foreign accent, and more likely to be believed if they're attractive, baby-faced, socially adept and articulate — even though these two last traits have been found to be specifically associated with good liars.

So what should the police be looking for? As we've established, lying is effortful. Liars have to think of plausible answers under questioning; they need to avoid contradicting themselves; they need to tell a story that is consistent with what their interrogator already knows; they must try to avoid revealing slips of the tongue; they have to remember what they've said in case they're asked to repeat it. Whilst they're doing this they also have to be monitoring their own speech and body language to ensure they're not giving themselves away, even as they know that if they show any signs of all the effort they're putting in then they will arouse suspicion. Vrij's preferred strategy is to increase the liar's cognitive load to the point where they simply can't manage to perform the mental juggling act.

One of the interviewing techniques he recommends is to ask the suspect to tell their story backwards. By putting this extra mental pressure on suspects, those already struggling with the effort to tell a consistent lie will make mistakes that give them away. In 2007, Vrij and his colleagues published the results of a study that tested the police's conventional techniques against their own. The research involved more than two hundred and fifty student interviewees and two hundred and ninety police officers. The interviewees either lied or told the truth about staged events. Police officers were then asked to spot the liars using the traditional methods. Those who focused on visual cues proved significantly worse at identifying liars than those looking for speech-related cues. The liars seemed *less* nervous and more helpful than those telling the truth. As Vrij predicted, the most reliable technique turned out to be the backwards-story test.

Another technique designed by Vrij is the sketch test: asking people to draw a scene they claim to have witnessed. While it's non-verbal, this technique also puts pressure on the cognitive facilities of the liar. In Vrij's study, thirty-one participants – all of them members of the police or armed forces – were sent on a mock mission to pick up a laptop from a 'secret agent'. Afterwards they were asked to make a detailed drawing of the location at which they'd received the laptop. Half the participants were instructed to tell the truth, the other half to lie. Vrij hypothesised that the liars, in order to make their lie convincing, would sketch a location they'd actually been to in the past, furnishing it with the kind of detail often thought to be the hallmark of a good lie. He also predicted that in doing so they'd forget a key part of the scene: the agent. The truth-tellers would be much more likely to draw the man with the laptop, as he was such a central part of the scene they had in their minds. So it proved. On the basis of this factor alone it was possible to detect who was lying nearly ninety per cent of the time.

Although Ekman and Vrij place different emphases on what to look for, both agree on the importance of taking a holistic approach. When assessing truthfulness, a person's voice, hand movements, posture and speech patterns should all be taken into account, and it's vitally important to put all of this in context: do these behaviours contrast in revealing ways with how the person usually acts, and how do they square with everything else that's known about the situation? Such judgements require many fine and fallible calculations; there is no single, all-purpose tell we can use as a short-cut. Pinocchio's nose remains a fairy tale.

The Demeanour Assumption: Why We're Worse Lie Detectors – and Better Liars – Than We Think

In 2008 a group of Norwegian researchers ran an experiment to better understand how police investigators come to a judgement about the credibility of rape claims. Sixty-nine investigators were played video-recorded versions of a rape victim's statement, with the role of victim played by a professional actress. The wording of the statement in each version was exactly the same, but the actress delivered it with varying degrees of emotion. The investigators, who prided themselves on their objectivity, turned out to be heavily influenced in their judgements by assumptions about the victim's demeanour: she was judged most credible when crying or showing despair. In reality, rape victims react in the immediate aftermath of the event in a variety of different ways: some are visibly upset; others are subdued and undemonstrative. It turns out there is no universally 'appropriate' reaction to being raped. The detectives were relying on their instincts, and their instincts turned out to be constructed from inherited and unreliable notions about women in distress.

Shakespeare's warning about how hard it is to read 'the mind's construction in the face' is supported by a host of empirical evidence, yet interrogators remain stubbornly convinced of their ability to tell if a person is truthful by observing them, and relying only on their gut instincts.

The lawyer and fraud expert Robert Hunter calls this misapprehension the 'demeanour assumption'. He cites the case of the American student Amanda Knox, arrested in 2007 for the murder of Meredith Kercher. The Italian police concluded she was guilty based almost entirely on their assessment of Knox's demeanour under intense questioning: 'We were able to establish guilt,' declared Edgardo Giobbi, the lead investigator, 'by closely observing the suspects' psychological and behavioural reactions during the interrogations. We don't need to rely on other kinds of investigation as this method has allowed us to get to the guilty parties in a very quick time.' Giobbi's logic is dangerous, because people do not behave in police custody or in court in the same way as they might outside it and, guilty or innocent, some people will always behave suspiciously.

Of course, it's not just police investigators who suffer from this bias. We all have a tendency to make instant judgements about a person's integrity based on received ideas about appropriate demeanours. Italian prosecutors were quick to leak stories about Knox doing cartwheels while in custody, and when the press published pictures of her with a smile on her face readers around the world reacted the same way: no innocent person accused of a crime would behave like this. But people react to intense pressure in unpredictable ways, and a single photo yields no reliable information about a person's inner thoughts. But as unscientific as it is, the demeanour assumption plays a part in some of society's most important mechanisms. Hunter points out that it underpins the notions of oral evidence and jury trials; those who *watch* witnesses give evidence are assumed to be best placed to judge whether they are telling the truth.

What does it stem from, this over-confidence in our intuitions about lying? It probably has something to do with our innate tendency towards self-absorption, and our difficulty in recognising that other people are as fully rounded and complex as we are. Emily Pronin, a psychologist at Princeton University, reminds us that when two people meet there is a fundamental asymmetry about the way they relate to one another. When you are talking to someone, there are at least two things more prominent in your mind than in theirs — your thoughts, and their face. As a result you tend to judge others on what you see, and ourselves by what you feel. *You* know when you're hiding your true thoughts and feelings — pretending to be fascinated by your boss's endless anecdote, or grinning your way through a terrible first date — but you nonetheless tend to assume the other's appearance tells the full story of how *they* feel — if she's smiling, it's because she's really enjoying herself. It's been found that people over-estimate how much they can learn from others in job interviews, while at the same time maintaining that others can only get a glimpse of them from such brief encounters. The model we tend to work with is something like this: *I* am infinitely subtle, complex and never quite what I seem, *you* are predictable and easy to read. 'I suppose no one truly admits the existence of another person,' sighs the narrator of Fernando Pessoa's *Book of Disquiet.*

Paradoxically, this asymmetry makes us less confident than we should be in our own ability to lie, because we assume other people can read our faces as easily as we suppose we can theirs. In Edgar Allan Poe's short story *The Tell-Tale Heart*, a man who has committed a murder is being interviewed by clueless detectives. He becomes convinced that they can just *tell* he's guilty, and breaks into a needless confession. It's a dramatic example of what the psychologist Thomas Gilovich terms the 'illusion of transparency' — the irrational but often irresistible conviction that others can read our minds. A dinner guest suspects that her hostess can read her distaste for the food she's being served; a secret admirer guesses the object of his crush must have an inkling of how he feels; a business executive gets the overwhelming feeling that everyone in the room can tell how nervous she feels about making a presentation. We have a powerful tendency to exaggerate such fears and intimations, because although we mentally compensate for the fact that we have better access to our inner states than others do, we find it hard to compensate *enough.*

Gilovich carried out a series of experiments to demonstrate that we're much harder to read than we imagine. In one of them, groups of participants played a round-robin lie detection game – a version of Call My Bluff. Each person told either a lie or a truth and the rest of the group had to guess which was which. The 'liars' in each group consistently over-estimated the extent to which the other would guess they were lying. The effect was particularly pronounced amongst those who scored higher on a separate test for self-absorption.

The Strange Case of Major Ingram

No-one can earn a million dollars honestly.
William Jennings Bryan

On 10 September 2001, Major Charles Ingram faced this question:

A NUMBER ONE FOLLOWED BY ONE HUNDRED ZEROS IS KNOWN BY WHAT NAME?

It was the last in a sequence of twelve questions asked of Ingram on Britain's (and the world's) most popular game show, *Who Wants to be a Millionaire*? With the help of all three lifelines, Ingram had got the first eleven answers right. Now he stood on the verge of becoming only the third contestant in the show's history to win a million pounds.

For the best part of two evenings the studio audience had been amazed and bemused by Ingram's progress. His idiosyncratic manner offered a vivid contrast with the previous two winners of the top prize. Judith Keppel, who became the first Millionaire in 2000, possessed all the poise and self-assurance of England's upper middle-class: even when unsure of her answers, she was never unsure of herself. David Edwards, who had won the jackpot only five months before Ingram's appearance, exuded a different kind of confidence: that of a man who lives and breathes general knowledge quiz shows, and collects facts the way books collect dust.

Ingram, by contrast, twitched with self-doubt. He took an age to answer every question, circling around each option in turn, contradicting himself, lurching towards one before looping back and landing, as if by accident, on an answer he might have dismissed as impossible just a few seconds previously. He showed none of the strong instincts that can help pressured contestants override their doubts on crucial questions. Yet somehow he had stumbled towards the right answer eleven times. Now he was groping his way towards an answer that would either win him a million pounds or lose him nearly half that amount.

Faced with his four choices and bereft of lifelines, Ingram admitted he was unsure. 'You haven't been sure since question number two,' groaned the show's host, Chris Tarrant. 'I *think* it's a nanomole,' said Ingram, his hands clambering all over his face. 'But it could be a gigabit.' Tarrant hinted heavily that Ingram ought to take the money and run. For a moment, Ingram seemed to agree. 'I just don't think I can do this one.' But he persisted. 'I don't think it's a megatron. And I don't think I've heard of a googol.' Ingram murmured the latter word three more times to himself, before announcing that 'By a process of elimination, I actually think it's googol, but I don't know what a googol is.' The cameras focused on Ingram's wife, Diana, in the audience. She looked nauseous. 'You've got half a million – and you're going for the one you've never heard of?' asked an incredulous Tarrant. After more mulling, Ingram announced, with something approaching resolution, 'I'm going to play.' The audience let out a gasp of dismay. Ingram flinched. 'No, I'm not!' But he did, declaring googol his final answer. After the excruciating delay of a break in recording, Tarrant asked for Ingram's half a million-pound cheque back. 'You no longer have that,' he said, ripping it up. A pause. 'You've just won *one million pounds*!' The audience exploded with excitement and relief.

The episode was never broadcast. A week later, while the rest of the world reeled from the attacks of September 11th, Ingram received a phone call at his home in Wiltshire from Paul Smith, managing director of the show's maker, Celador Productions. Smith informed Ingram that the cheque Tarrant had handed him, post-dated for 18 September – the next day – had been cancelled. So had the episode itself, due to broadcast the same day. Smith referred vaguely to 'irregularities', without suggesting they were connected to Ingram, who sounded surprised but not upset. Five days later, at seven a.m., Ingram answered a knock at the door. It was the police, there to arrest him and his wife. At the same time, eighty miles away in Cardiff, a third man was being arrested: Tecwen Whittock, who had been sitting in the Fastest Finger First row of contestants during Ingram's time in the hot seat.

A year and a half later, on 7 April 2003, a jury at Southwark Crown Court in London found Charles and Diana Ingram and Whittock guilty of conspiring to cheat their way to a million pounds. Charles Ingram resigned his commission from the army. Eighteen months later he was declared bankrupt.

To attempt to steal a million pounds is one thing; to attempt it under the noses of fifteen million people is quite another. But it wasn't just the audacity of the Millionaire Three's scheme that struck the public — it was the absurdity. The story that emerged from the trial read like the script of a very British drama, mixing tragedy with comedy, low cunning and risible self-delusion. The popular version went something like this: a dim Major from a minor public school is persuaded by his ambitious wife to co-operate in a get-rich-quick scheme that involves getting on to the country's most watched game show and then using the coughs of an accomplice in the studio — a quiz show veteran — to direct him to the correct answers. Against all odds, the unlikely threesome pull it off. Until, one morning, the phone rings.

All three defendants pleaded not guilty, and later continued fiercely to protest their innocence, despite being offered large sums of money to 'tell their story'. After the trial, ITV broadcast a documentary about the aborted show and its aftermath. The programme was viewed by an extraordinary seventeen million people – more than the series itself. It presented an edited version of Ingram's run, drawing attention to the heavy coughs that seemed to occur every time the Major mentioned a correct answer. To the public, the documentary offered the peculiarly satisfying spectacle of watching a man engaged in an elaborate deception for which he had already been caught. Ingram's reactions to his coughing cues were so obvious, it was funny. 'I don't think I've heard of a googol.' *Cough.* 'I actually think it's googol.'

An odd lacuna lay at the heart of the prosecution case, however: there was no evidence of Major Ingram and Tecwen Whittock ever meeting, speaking, or emailing each other. Whittock had had brief conversations with Diana on the phone, but in the world of quiz show obsessives this was unremarkable. Diana had been a contestant herself (she won £32,000) and was co-authoring a book about the show; prospective contestants frequently seek out the advice of those who have been there before them. Neither did police discover any calls or meetings between the three after the show's recording. (You might have imagined that in the period after Ingram's win and before he knew of the investigation the three would have talked, if only to discuss the distribution of spoils). After a team of Scotland Yard's top detectives had taken eighteen months to carry out their enquiries, the Crown's case rested entirely on the tape of Ingram's appearance and the suspicions of Celador staff.

These suspicions seem, on closer examination, to have been surprisingly flimsy. For instance, the court was told that the production staff became wary when the Major used up his lifelines early in the show. But a look back at previous contestants who had made long winning runs indicated that there was nothing unusual about this. It was argued that Whittock's guilt was indicated by the fact that he leaned over to ask his fellow panellist about one of the questions. But at least one former contestant testified that this was normal too. A production assistant thought it odd that the Major said he would be going to work in the morning, despite having just won a million pounds. But the previous million-pound winner, David Edwards, a teacher, had done precisely that just twenty weeks before. Celador's testimony bore a touch of what psychologists call 'hindsight bias' – the tendency to recall one's own thoughts and feelings in a manner consonant with what you now know, or think you know.

There is no doubt, however, that the tape is compelling evidence. There are 192 coughs on it, and the prosecution deemed nineteen of the loudest ones to have come from Ingram's accomplice – although they conceded it was impossible to prove. Tecwen Whittock didn't deny coughing a lot. He suffered from hay fever and rhinitus, an allergy to dust. Independent experts testified to the authenticity of his condition and agreed that it would have been exacerbated by sitting for hours in the dry heat of the studio. As the prosecuting barrister scornfully pointed out, however, 'There is no condition causing you to cough after someone has given the right answer to a question.' Except – perhaps there is.

During the twenty-two days of the trial at London's Southwark Crown Court, there was a lot of coughing in the courtroom. The tape of Ingram's appearance was played in full at least a dozen times, and the key segments were replayed over and over, with the coughs helpfully amplified by Celador production engineers. But the coughs weren't coming just from the tape. A journalist sitting in the public gallery noticed that every time one of the barristers mentioned the word 'cough' – which is to say, frequently – people in the public gallery broke out into coughing fits. When a leading expert in respiratory conditions was giving evidence, proceedings were halted because a female juror couldn't stop coughing. During the defence barrister's summing up, two more jurors seized up and the judge adjourned proceedings until they could recover.

Those responsible didn't consciously decide to cough on this cue – they were reacting unconsciously and involuntarily. If the correlation between their coughs and the word cough had been pointed out to them they would have been startled. James Plaskett, a former winning contestant on the show, who published an exhaustive analysis of the Ingram trial, wondered if a similar effect explained Whittock's coughing. Once you accept that people cough in unconscious response to external stimuli it seems plausible that Whittock was at least some of the time, because we don't know that all the coughs were his — reacting involuntarily to the answers he knew to be right. Plaskett reviewed a DVD of Judith Keppel's winning performance. Audible audience coughs occurred after her first enunciation of the correct answer but before definitely committing to her answer at the £2,000, £4,000, £8,000, £64,000, £500,000 and £1,000,000 points. That's to say, at six of the last ten questions — just as with Ingram.

The case remains somewhat mysterious even to those closely involved with it. Chris Tarrant later remarked that 'Scotland Yard and the Fraud Squad have never worked out what happened.' A police source told the *Daily Telegraph*, 'We've never been able to find every piece of the jigsaw.' It's not within the purview of this book to discuss whether the verdict was just. The relevant question is this: why was everyone so ready to believe in Ingram's guilt?

When somebody pulls off the rare feat of winning a million pounds in a show with a studio audience, it's natural that questions should arise over their probity. Something about Ingram's manner, however, kindled these questions into suspicions; Celador's staff felt, instinctively, that something was not right. Of course, their instincts, like those of the detectives asked to judge the authenticity of rape claims, may not have been distilled wisdom so much as distilled prejudice. Ingram, a mid-ranking army officer with a posh voice and a bumbling manner, came with his own cultural baggage. 'Tim Nice-But-Dim' was how Tarrant described his first impression of the Major. Not the sort of man who could win one million pounds on a general knowledge quiz show.

But perhaps what really convinced ten jurors, the press and the British public of Ingram's guilt was his demeanour in the hot seat: awkward, a little odd-looking, not terribly confident, short on charm. During his time under the studio lights he seemed shifty, he fidgeted, he was inarticulate. In other words, Ingram exhibited all the cues we intuitively associate with a liar.

Trusters and Cynics

Jake Gittes, the private detective played by Jack Nicholson in Roman Polanski's film *Chinatown*, is primed to look for deceit in every conversation and is wary of everyone he meets. In his small world of crooks and divorcees, he is very difficult to fool, but when he gets drawn into the machinations of Los Angeles politics his instincts become useless to him. By the end of the film he has been duped by everyone, overwhelmed by the unsuspected complexity of human behaviour.

Some people are better than others at detecting deceit. But they're not necessarily the kind of people you'd think. Nancy Carter and Mark Weber, psychologists from the University of Toronto, gave forty-six MBA (Masters in

Business Administration) students, each of whom had already had several years of work experience, a work-based scenario to read. It described a recent spate of dishonesty in their university's recruitment and interview process, involving potential employees lying about their qualifications. These lies, they were told, had cost the organisation dearly in terms of time, productivity and morale.

The participants were asked to choose one of two managers to interview new applicants. The managers had similar experience and skill-sets; the only difference between them was attitudinal. Colleen was disposed to view people very positively and to assume that they were trustworthy until proven otherwise. Sue was more suspicious by nature. She was inclined to believe that people will get away with anything they can; her default attitude was one of distrust. A clear majority of the students chose Sue to run the recruitment process. They feared that Colleen would be gullible and easily duped. They even suspected her to be of inferior intelligence.

Most of us would probably make the same choice, even if we'd rather be friends with Colleen than Sue. Given the situation, it would surely be better to have an interviewer who is always on the lookout for liars than one who assumes that people generally tell the truth. It's commonly believed that those with a pronounced tendency to trust others are easy prey for predators in the social jungle. High trust is associated with credulity – with people who will believe anything they hear from an interviewee, or a vendor, or an internet date. Indeed, most economic models of decision-making suggest that in any social interaction we should all be more like Sue and less like Colleen: low trusters, who rightly assume that others are out to behave in their own self-interest, and so act to defend ourselves from exploitation. But is being a high truster synonymous with being an easy gull?

Carter and Weber followed their initial experiment with one intended to address that question. They made videos of students in simulated job interviews in which half of the interviewees were asked to tell the truth throughout the interview, while the other half were asked to lie about three significant things that might help them 'get the job'. The researchers then played these tapes to participants who had previously filled out a standard psychological test designed to ascertain whether or not they were high trusters or low trusters — for our purposes, let's call them Trusters and Cynics. The participants were asked to judge which students were telling the truth and which were lying. As it turned out, the Trusters were significantly *more* likely than the Cynics to spot the liars.

This finding tallies with previous experimental evidence from other social scientists suggesting that, counter-intuitively, Trusters are less gullible than Cynics. The reason for this seems to be that people who are naturally suspicious of their fellow human beings tend to keep their social interactions to a minimum, outside of a small circle of known and trusted acquaintances. In the words of the sociologist Toshio Yamagishi, they take fewer 'social risks'. This means they are less experienced at dealing with other people – at least, people they don't already know well – and therefore at reading intentions and motivations.

If you assume everyone you meet is out to deceive you, then you're less likely to be duped, but you're also less likely to learn how to distinguish liars from truth-tellers. Trusters come to be seen as gullible because they are the ones who most often enter into risky social interactions that occasionally backfire – the ones who go on blind dates or buy antiques from market stalls. But they're not gullible; they're trusting. There is a difference.

Remote Deceptions (and Detections)

In January 2007, a retired police inspector called Garry Weddell strangled his wife Sandra, a nurse, at their home in Bedfordshire, a few weeks after she had confessed to an affair and asked him for a divorce. Then he tied a length of cable around her neck and hung her body in the garage to make it look as if she had killed herself. Near the body he placed a single sheet of A4 paper on which he had typed her 'suicide note', wearing rubber gloves to avoid leaving any fingerprints. Weddell had spent twenty-five years on the force and had an idea of what his former colleagues would be looking for.

Tells and Leakages

Few people who knew the Weddells could believe that Sandra, a seemingly happy mother of three, would kill herself, and although Garry Weddell was not initially considered a suspect, a few of the more experienced detectives had their suspicions. They checked with police forces across the country and found only three previous deaths involving cable ties – every one a murder. Furthermore, there were bruises on Sandra's body that suggested she might have been in a fight before she died. The suicide note became a key piece of evidence: was it authentic?

Police handed the note to John Olsson, an expert in the field of forensic linguistics. In 1994 Olsson had been a post-graduate linguist working at the University of Birmingham, where he first became interested in the application of his work to criminal investigations. His colleague Malcom Coulthard had performed an analysis of the written confession of Derek Bentley – hanged in 1953 for the murder of a policeman – which demonstrated that it had almost certainly been written by a policeman, helping to win a posthumous pardon for Bentley. Olsson was hooked, and by the time of the Weddell investigation he had worked with the police on over three hundred cases, from extortion to murder.

In Olsson's experience, forged suicide notes could be spotted by their overuse of highly charged, self-lacerating words like crazy, cowardly, and selfish, which are rarely found in the genuine article. According to this logic,

Sandra's note looked like it might be authentic because it didn't use such language, but Weddell was an experienced cop who might have had a strong sense of which sentiments would ring true. So Olsson began looking for other clues. In previous cases, idiosyncrasies of spelling often pointed to the real author of the note, but he couldn't find any of those in the note or in letters written by Sandra or her husband. He had to get down to the level of punctuation before he made a breakthrough.

Olsson noticed something about the length of sentences in the note – in particular a quirk in the placing of full stops, the first of which appeared immediately after Sandra had supposedly written her husband's name:

> Garry. I am typing this note, because I know that if I were to hand write it and leave it for you, then I know that you wouldn't read it. I am so sorry for all the hurt I have caused you Garry. I never meant to hurt you or cause you so much pain.

The note was brief, to the point and peppered with full stops, most notably the first one. It was very unlike the letters known to have been written by Sandra, who favoured long rambling sentences, sprinkled with commas, dashes and semi-colons. One of her past sentences was more than one hundred and thirty words long – compared to the average sentence length of only twelve words in the suicide note. Much closer to the style of what was allegedly her final letter were letters written by her husband, who used full stops liberally and whose sentences averaged only nine words. This, together with other evidence, led the police to charge Weddell with murder.[3]

The kind of lying I focus on in this book is face-to-face, human-to-human deceit, in which the deceiver is attempting to spin a story that accords with his or her personality and circumstances. The more the lie is identified with the liar, the better. There is, however, another category of deception altogether, one in which the deceiver creates something — a painting, a recording, a document — that they hope will never be traced back to them.

Weddell's 'suicide note' is an example of such 'remote deception'. My second and final example of it comes from a different field of forensic investigation. The study of 'election forensics' took off after the disputed American presidential election of 2000. It applies statistical analysis to election results as a way of detecting fraud.

Faking election results doesn't sound difficult. You just invent a string of random numbers that are plausible enough and show the result you want, right? But it's harder than you might imagine. The problem is that we're surprisingly bad at making up random numbers. When participants in lab experiments are asked to write sequences of random digits, they tend to select some digits, or some patterns of digits, more frequently than others. The job of electoral forensics experts is to analyse the results of elections to see if they're really as random as they ought to be, or if there are some suspicious consistencies that reveal the hand of a fixer.

Bernd Beber and Alexandra Scacco, political scientists from the University of Columbia, analysed the disputed 2009 Iranian election that led to Iran's Green movement. They looked at the published vote counts received by different candidates in different provinces, concentrating on the last and second-to-last digits of each number. For example, if a candidate received 14,579 votes in a province, they focused on digits 7 and 9. The last digits in a fair election don't tell us anything about the candidates, the make-up of the electorate or the context of the election. They are what statisticians call random noise. But that's the point: it means they can serve as a litmus test for election fraud. For example, an election in which a majority of the vote counts ended in 5 would be very suspicious.

When Beber and Sacco looked at the results issued by Iran's Ministry of the Interior they found some odd anomalies. The number 7 appeared far more often than it would normally do in a set of randomly generated figures, and the number 5 far less often. Fewer than four in a hundred non-fraudulent elections would produce such numbers. That wasn't all. It's also been found that people have trouble generating non-adjacent digits (such as 64 or 17, as opposed to twenty-three) as frequently as one would expect in a sequence of random numbers. To check for deviations of this type, Berber and Sacco examined the pairs of last and second-to-last digits in Iran's vote counts. On average, if the results had not been manipulated, seventy per cent of these pairs should have consisted of distinct, non-adjacent digits. In this case, only sixty-two per cent of the pairs contained non-adjacent digits. That may not sound so different from seventy per cent, but the probability that a fair election would produce a difference this large is less than 4.2 per cent.

Each of the two tests provided strong evidence that Iran's published vote counts had been manipulated. Taken together, they left little room for reasonable doubt. According to this analysis, the chance that the Iranian election was fair is less than one in two hundred.

The Dream of a Truth Machine

The past, present and future of lie detectors

On 19 April 1921, in Berkeley, California, a young police-man invited an eighteen-year-old woman called Margaret Taylor into a small room. A strange-looking contraption sat on the table. Taylor, a blue-eyed, golden-haired native of the state, wasn't sure what to expect. A few weeks previously she had reported the theft of a four hundred-dollar ring from her room in College Hall, the female boarding house of her university campus. Now she was being asked to recount her story whilst attached to this bizarre device which − it was rumoured − could read her mind. Taylor wasn't the only girl in College Hall to find something had gone missing recently. For several months now its inhabitants − most of them young ladies from well-to-do families − had been returning to their rooms to find their evening gowns spread out on their beds, as if someone had been sizing them up. A sophomore from Bakersfield had been robbed of forty-five dollars she had placed inside a textbook; other students had lost letters, jewellery, items of silk underwear. Unable to extract a confession from any of her boarders, College Hall's housemother turned to the police. After an initial inconclusive investigation, the case was handed over to John Larson, the man who now greeted Margaret Taylor.

Miss Taylor was not under suspicion, but Larson needed a 'control' to measure against his suspects. As several other students waited their turn outside, Larson strapped a blood-pressure gauge to one of Miss Taylor's bare arms until it gripped firmly, and wound a rubber hose tightly around her chest to measure the depth of her breathing. He told her to hold as still as she could – the least muscular move-ment might be mistaken for a guilty reaction. Then he turned on the instruments. Drums revolved, black recording paper turned, and the long rubber hoses swelled and subsided to the rhythms of Taylor's body. A pair of needles began to scratch out patterns on the paper. After a short preamble, Larson began his questions, speaking in a monotone:

1. Do you like college?
2. Are you interested in this test?
3. How much is 30 x 40?
4. Are you frightened?
5. Will you graduate this year?
6. Do you dance?
7. Are you interested in math?
8. Did you steal the money?
9. The test shows you stole it. Did you spend it?

The interview took six minutes. After Larson had finished with Taylor, he worked his way through the list of suspects. One of them, a student nurse called Helen Graham, entered the room already under suspicion. A few years older than the other students, Graham was a tall, striking woman with deep-set eyes and an intense manner. She was unpopular with her dorm sisters, who disdained her modest Kansas background; it had been suggested to police that she seemed to spend beyond her means. Sure enough, no sooner had Larson reached the questions about theft – 'The tests show you stole it. Did you spend it?' – than the machine showed a steep drop in Graham's blood pressure followed by an alarming rise. In a fit of rage, Graham ripped off the machine's cuffs, leapt to her feet and ran from the room. Called back for questioning the next day, she broke down and confessed to the crime. Berkeley's newspapers hailed the first success of the police's new 'lie detector'.

* * *

In 1858 the French physiologist Etienne-Jules Marey built a device that simultaneously recorded changes in blood pressure, respiration and pulse rates whilst his subjects were subjected to nausea, sharp noises and stress. In 1895 the Italian criminologist Cesare Lombroso invented an early lie detector, based on a similar physiology of emotion. A suspect was told to put his hand into a tank filled with water; his pulse would cause the level of liquid to rise and fall slightly; the greater the fluctuation, the more dishonest he was judged to be. The work of Marey and Lombroso was part of a new strain of scientific thinking about the relationship between the emotions and the nervous system. William James argued that feelings derive from physiological responses rather than vice versa; a man runs from a bear not because he feels afraid, but feels afraid because he's running from a bear. In 1901, Freud wrote that 'No mortal can keep a secret. If his lips are silent, he chatters with his fingertips; betrayal oozes out of him at every pore.' Of course, when a person's emotions are manifested in the body's starts and shivers, they become available for measurement.

In the first decades of the twentieth century, new tests of personality and intelligence promised to bring clarity and objectivity to the messy business of human character and behaviour. Hopes for a 'truth-compelling machine' formed part of America's burgeoning optimism about the potential of such science to transform society. A 1911 article in the *New York Times* predicted a future in which 'there will be no jury, no horde of detectives and witnesses, no charges and countercharges, and no attorney for the defense. These impedimenta of our courts will be unnecessary. The State will merely submit all suspects in a case to the tests of scientific instruments.'

The cradle of this optimism was Berkeley, California, a young town formed around a new public university — the University of California — intended by its founders to outshine the old colleges back East. The trustees hoped that the campus they created, surrounded by the Contra Costa hills and commanding sublime views of the ocean, would become known as 'the Athens of the Pacific', and by the early twentieth century Berkeley was approaching the fulfilment of this dream. The town had become a magnet for America's best students, intellectuals and artists, and renowned for its early embrace of new technologies like the telephone and the streetcar.

Berkeley's police department was making a name for itself as the most progressive in the country, under the visionary leadership of August Vollmer, today regarded as the father of modern American law enforcement. A tall, ramrod-backed man with steely blue eyes and a fierce intellectual curiosity, Vollmer believed passionately in the potential of technology to revolutionise policing. One of his goals was to substitute humane scientific techniques for the traditional third-degree interrogations meted out by police forces around the country. As Berkeley police chief, he recruited clever, scientifically educated men who wouldn't normally consider a career in law enforcement, and encouraged them to innovate. One of his first recruits was John Larson.

Studious, intense, self-questioning and a terrible shot, Larson made for an unlikely policeman. He had moved to Berkeley to study for a PhD in physiology and forensic science after writing his Master's thesis on the cutting-edge technique of fingerprint identification. Larson deeply admired Vollmer and shared his vision of a more civilised and efficient method of policing. In 1920, he became the first man in the country to be in simultaneous possession of a police badge and a doctorate.

A few weeks before the interview with Margaret Taylor, Larson had read an article by a Harvard student named William Moulton Marston. The paper was entitled 'Physiological Possibilities of the Deception Test', and it proposed a correlation between a subject's blood pressure and the likelihood they were telling the truth. Excited by the potential of this discovery for police work, Larson, advised by Marston, used the research as a basis for the design and construction of an unwieldy device he called the cardio-pneumo-psychograph. The case of the College Hall thefts was the first time he had been able to use it for real. Apparently, it worked: *Science Nabs Sorority Sneak*, read one of the local paper's headlines, after Helen Graham's arrest. Larson was flushed with success.[4] A delighted August Vollmer gave the go-ahead for further work on the machine. He also landed Larson with a collaborator.

Leonarde Keeler was born in 1903 to the poet, naturalist and free-thinking bohemian Charles Keeler, who named his son in homage to Leonardo Da Vinci. A confident, technically gifted young man and an accomplished amateur magician, Leonarde had little patience for formal education. He was barely out of school when he read in the Berkeley press that the police were using something called a lie detector, and found himself gripped by the idea. Vollmer, a friend of Charles, appointed young Keeler to the force at Charles's suggestion, encouraging Larson to collaborate with this bright young man on the machine. The partnership proved fruitful. Keeler increased the number of physical signs that the lie detector monitored and made the device smaller, so that it could fit into a box. The new portable machine recorded pulse rate, blood pressure, respiration, and 'electrodermal response' (palm sweat) on a series of graphs. Today's polygraph (named by Keeler) is much the same device.

Between 1921 and 1923 in Berkeley, Larson and Keeler tested 861 subjects in 313 cases, identifying 218 criminal suspects and exonerating 310. Most of the crimes were petty, and some were domestic, like the marital dispute of which Larson noted 'Mrs Simons accused of mastur- bation by her husband.' Above all, the lie detector proved to be good at eliciting instantaneous confessions. The myste- rious machine shone a spotlight on the guilty consciences of a whole community. A restaurant chef pleaded guilty to stealing silverware, a custodian of the Unitarian Church admitted to pocketing a purse and watch. Though these successes were slight, the polygraph had shown itself highly effective across a range of different circumstances, and it promised much more. Vollmer's dream of a cleaner, more efficient interrogation method seemed on the verge of materialising. Before long the nation's police chiefs were making their way to Berkeley to see this machine for themselves.

Just as his invention was growing famous, however, Larson was becoming uncertain of it. He found that when he re-tested suspects after confession, their records appeared similar to those deemed innocent of the crime. He engaged in an exchange of agonised letters with Helen Graham, who had returned to Kansas following her humiliation in Berkeley. Graham, a naturally anxious soul who suffered a deeply unstable childhood, protested her innocence to Larson, who came to believe her and apologised for what had happened. (The thefts at College Hall continued, unreported.) Larson was increasingly troubled by his concerns over what, exactly, the polygraph was measuring. But to his colleagues and peers, *how* this machine worked was less important than that it did.

The collaboration between Larson and Keeler, although fertile, was always uneasy, and over the years they became rancorous enemies. Each fought for his own vision of the machine's future, and competed for the approval of Vollmer. The more reflective and sceptical Larson saw the machine as an aid to scientific research and penal reform, but grew doubtful that it should be used to dispense justice. Keeler had no such uncertainties. He volunteered to solve celebrated crimes and basked in the ensuing publicity, which in turn helped him to sell his lie-detecting expertise to large corporations. Larson came to despise Keeler as a mere salesman who had prostituted the technology they had created together. As Keeler prospered, he was dogged at every step by his former colleague, who publicly denounced Keeler's claims for the polygraph.

Larson and Keeler remained obsessed by the machine, and by each other, for the rest of their lives. Keeler's heavy drinking led to the end of his marriage to Katherine Keeler, a glamorous and accomplished woman who trained as a forensic scientist before establishing her own all-female detective agency in Chicago. Soon after doing so she left Keeler for Rene Dussaq, a Cuban-American with a degree in philosophy from the University of Geneva who at various times was a matador, polo player, Davis Cup tennis player, fencing champion and highly decorated war hero. Katherine was killed in 1944 after the plane she was flying solo across country crashed into a field in Ohio. Keeler died of a stroke caused by alcoholism four years later, aged 46. John Larson spent the rest of his career working for various penal institutions, collecting newspaper clippings about his machine, and working on a nine thousand-page book on psychology for which he never found a publisher. He died in 1965, aged 73.

* * *

In 1986, the American spy Aldrich Ames was notified by his bosses at the CIA that he was to take a routine polygraph test. All CIA employees were expected to take the test every five years, but due to an administrative backlog Ames hadn't taken one in a decade. He remembered hating it the first time, but now he was terrified. The year before,

having spent himself bankrupt, he had started selling information to the Soviets. Fearing the machine would reveal
his betrayal, he passed a note to the KGB via his handlers,
asking for advice on how to deal with it.

When he received a note back shortly before the test
he opened it excitedly, expecting to read of a diabolically
clever technique for outwitting the polygraph. Well-known
counter-measures included using mental imagery to calm
yourself and biting your tongue to make yourself seem
anxious in response to the control questions. In fact, the
KGB's advice was to get a good night's sleep, and try to
relax in the interview. Ames was disappointed. Nevertheless, he did as they suggested, and passed the test with
flying colours. In 1991 he passed it again, even as the CIA
was carrying out an internal hunt for its mole.

Aldrich Ames — whose treachery was discovered in 1994,
after he had betrayed the identities of most of the US
spies in the Soviet Union, several of whom were executed —
retained a lifelong contempt for the polygraph. In 2000,
the scientist Steven Aftergood wrote a critical piece about
the technology for the journal *Science*. That November he
received a letter, handwritten across four pages, from
Allenwood Federal Penitentiary, where Ames was (and is)
incarcerated. In it, Ames congratulated Aftergood on his
piece and delivered a witty, scathing critique of the
machine, all the more authoritative for coming from one
who had seen it off:

Like most junk science that just won't die (graphology, astrology and homeopathy come to mind), because of the usefulness or profit their practitioners enjoy, the polygraph stays with us. Its most obvious use is as a coercive aid to interrogators, lying somewhere on the scale between the rubber truncheon and the diploma on the wall behind the interrogator's desk. It depends upon the overall coerciveness of the setting — you'll be fired, you won't get the job, you'll be prosecuted, you'll go to prison — and the credulous fear the device inspires.

The polygraph is not pure hokum. A racing pulse and an increased heart rate can indicate guilt, and when combined with a skilled operator the machine can achieve high success rates (although the necessity of a skilled operator rather defeats the purpose). But Ames is right; much of the polygraph's effectiveness is itself based on a lie – the lie of its own infallibility. Its key flaw is that there is no utterly reliable physiological sign of lying. All the symptoms it measures can have other causes, including the sheer nervousness that many honest people feel when confronted by such a test.

The lie detector never caught on in Europe, and in the country of its birth it failed to meet the standard of general scientific acceptability for evidence used in court. But the machine did become a staple of the policeman's interrogation armoury.[5] Police cared little for the science – they just knew that presenting suspects with this magical device was a great way of extracting a confession (in a scene from HBO's *The Wire*, based on real-life police practices in the 1980s, officers are shown extracting confessions by putting a suspect's hand on a photocopy machine filled with paper printed with the word LIE). The US military and intelligence services used polygraphs extensively over the years to interrogate suspected spies or terrorists, confirm the loyalty of allies, check the veracity of tip-offs and – as with Ames – check on the reliability of its own employees. But in 2001 a Pentagon report to Congress concluded that 'national security is too important to be left to such a blunt instrument'. A 2003 report by America's National Academy of Sciences concluded that the polygraph performed 'well above chance, though well below perfection'. It is still used by the federal government, though rarely in law enforcement or by the military.

The polygraph insinuated itself into many areas of twentieth-century American life. In the 1930s and 1940s it was introduced, with Keeler's help, to banks, factories and government departments eager to check on the honesty and reliability of their employees. It became a political symbol, since it met, or appeared to meet, a demand for certainty about individual integrity that grew more strident as the country moved on to a Cold War footing. In the trial of Alger Hiss, Richard Nixon called for the suspected spy Whittaker Chambers to take the test even though, as Nixon remarked to a friend, 'I don't know anything about polygraphs and I don't know how accurate they are but I know they scare the hell out of people.' Senator Joe McCarthy issued polygraph challenges to the 205 Americans he accused of being communists in his speech of February 1950. The polygraph also became a pop cultural icon, featured in movies, TV series and magazines. It was the man whose insight led to the first polygraph prototype who best understood the machine's cultural potency.

Born in 1893 in Boston, William Moulton Marston was a chubby-faced, ebullient, irrepressibly optimistic man. At Harvard he worked in the prestigious 'emotion laboratory' of Hugo Münsterberg, where Marston and his fellow students experimented with an apparatus that registered responses to emotions such as horror and tenderness through the graphical tracing of pulse rates. One student volunteer was Gertrude Stein, who later wrote of the experience in the third person: 'Strange fancies begin to crowd upon her, she feels that the silent pen is writing on and on forever.' Marston was the only one of the three men with a claim to the invention of the polygraph never to have worked in law enforcement. Instead, his research into deception launched a colourful career that saw him become America's first pop psychologist.

During the 1930s Marston often appeared in magazines such as *Esquire* and *Family Circle*, carrying out his 'deception test' on willing young females, and featured as a guest on TV game shows. He was hired by Universal Studios to measure the emotional impact of their movies, and lent his expertise and name to advertising agencies, who liked using his test as an ersatz form of market research. An ad for Gillette shows Marston analysing a polygraph tracing while a man is shaving. The copy reads:

> Strapped to Lie Detectors, the same scientific instruments used by G-Men and police officers throughout the country, hundreds of men take part in an astounding series of tests that blast false claims and reveal the naked truth about razor blades. These men, shaving under the piercing eye of Dr. William Moulton Marston, eminent psychologist and originator of the famous Lie Detector test, come from all walks of life, represent all types of beards and every kind of shaving problem. Knowing that the Lie Detector tells all . . . these men shave one side of the face with a Gillette Blade, the other side with substitute brands.

Marston was fascinated by the new forms of mass entertainment, and believed that with the right guidance they could help solve America's deep-rooted emotional problems, which he put down to women not yet being the dominant gender. Women, argued Marston, were superior to men. Men had a stronger sexual appetite and a will to dominate, while women preferred to cultivate 'the love response'. But this seeming submission would eventually enable women to take command of the species. In a hundred years, he predicted, 'the country will see the beginning of a sort of Amazonian matriarchy.' He viewed the lie detector as a tool to fine-tune the emotional content of culture and, by doing so, to teach men and women what they really wanted.

At home, Marston lived in a harmonious *ménage a trois* with his wife Elizabeth and his mistress – and research assistant – Olive Byrne. He had two sons with each woman. Elizabeth, who worked as a lawyer, was the breadwinner. Olive looked after the kids during the day and helped with Marston's experiments. Their sons later recalled the arrangement happily. An evening's entertainment might include hooking up a guest to the lie detector. After Marston's death, Olive and Elizabeth continued to live together, and did so for the rest of their lives.

Of the three men who invented the lie detector, Marston was the only one who didn't suffer for it. What may be his greatest invention was not in the fields of psychology or law enforcement, but popular culture. Marston had been invited onto the board of DC Comics, who were eager to appease critics worried about the emotional impact of comic strips on kids. He asked his new colleagues why there wasn't a female superhero, a counterpart to Superman, and was informed, wearily, that such characters never worked. Marston responded that this was because there had never been a character who combined strength with femininity. Challenged to come up with an answer himself, Marston created Wonder Woman, who wielded a golden lasso that made all who are encircled by it tell the truth.

The New Truth Machines

The polygraph turned out to be rather more fallible than the lasso of truth. Today, brain-scanning techniques promise to succeed where it failed. These new technologies appear to offer the tantalising possibility of getting beyond the external signs of lying to the lie itself, written in the brain's neuronal activity.

The two main brain-scanning technologies used for lie detection are known as EEG (electroencephalography) and fMRI (functional magnetic resonance imaging). EEG measures electrical activity in the brain caused by the firing of neurons, via multiple electrodes placed on the scalp of the subject. During a typical EEG-based lie detection test, the subject – or suspect – is shown a series of images and words that may or may not relate to the 'crime' of which he or she is accused. According to Peter Rosenfeld of Northwestern University, who has done the most to develop this technique, when somebody recognises a stimulus, they involuntarily emit a particular type of brain wave (the P300) which the administrator of the test can detect. In theory, no matter how much the suspect denies recognising the name of a fellow bank robber or the face of his victim, their P300 will blurt out the truth. This kind of technique is sometimes called the 'guilty knowledge' test.

When breathless articles about the end of lying are published, however, they invariably focus on fMRI, just as eighty years ago they trumpeted the polygraph. Functional MRI, invented in the early 1990s, has primarily been used as a research tool to better understand how the brain does its work. The technique produces images of the brain in action, which in an image-obsessed age is bound to attract attention. Not that fMRI isn't worthy of it. Unlike the polygraph, it is a genuinely revolutionary technology, which has transformed the field of neuroscience.

To take an fMRI scan, a person must be lying down inside a machine that is, basically, a very large, very powerful magnet. Once in the scanner, they can be asked to perform a variety of tasks, such as listening to music, answering questions, or pressing buttons in response to images shown on a screen above them. As they do so, the technology detects which areas of the brain are more active than others. When neurons fire they consume more oxygen, which leads to an increase in the flow of oxygenated blood to the active region; this causes distortions in the local magnetic field which can be measured by the machine. These changes can then be translated into images, using highly involved – and sometimes controversial – statistical methods. The process is nuanced and complex, but the end result is attractively simple: pictures of the brain with areas of relatively high neural activity mapped in brightly coloured blobs. The theory behind the use of fMRI for lie detection is that the extra cognitive effort demanded by lying can be traced in neural activity, so when a person is asked a series of questions, and answers one of them deceptively, the lie – or rather the moment when they lied – can be picked out in red and blue.

As America battles terrorism and fights wars, the Pentagon's Defense Academy for Credibility Assessment has been a generous patron of research into deception-detecting technologies. There is much talk about the potential for civilian applications, too. It's been suggested that schools will use scanners to check for plagiarism, that airports will ask people to have their brains screened along with their baggage, that employers will have a new way of checking out job applicants, and that immigration agencies will check the validity of a visitor's thoughts as well as their passport. At least two American companies, Cephos and No Lie MRI, already sell fMRI scans to individuals who want to prove their innocence, or to vet potential life partners, and they are lobbying hard to get fMRI deception tests accepted as evidence in court. Law professors and ethicists are beginning to consider the tricky questions these new methods pose, such as whether the results of brain scans should stand as evidence, and, if so, whether they should be classified as something akin to a DNA sample, or as testimony.

EEG and fMRI lie-detection tests have produced some encouraging results under laboratory conditions. Ruben Gur, a professor at the University of Pennsylvania who researches into fMRI lie detection, showed me the results of his scans, flicking between the 'true' and 'false' answers to demonstrate the stark differences in brain activation shown up by the machine. It is likely to be a long while before such tests will be more reliable than human judgement, however. Neither EEG nor fMRI have been field-tested in the real world, where a thousand complications intrude. For example, the guilty knowledge test may not work if the suspect was too high on drugs or drink at the time of the crime to recall very much about it. The investigator has to know the concealed information he is looking for, and there are only certain circumstances in which recognition is enough to establish guilt. Another limitation of such tests is that they require full co-operation: even once the subject is inside an fMRI machine, if he moves his head during the test then the data is useless. (This at least postpones the murky ethical question of whether a suspect should ever have his mind read against his will.) Furthermore, nobody is sure whether fMRI can reliably distinguish between a lie and a true memory that is effortful or painful to recall.

And what if the suspect doesn't know whether or not he's telling the truth?

On 8 July 1997, a US Navy officer called Bill Bosko returned to his apartment in Norfolk, Virginia, after a week at sea, to find his wife murdered in their bedroom. She had been raped and repeatedly stabbed. Michelle Moore-Bosko was nineteen years old. The pair had only recently married, after Michelle had run away from her parents' home to wed in secret.

Soon after arriving at the crime scene the police arrested Bosko's naval colleague Danial Williams, who lived across the hall. After eight hours of interrogation, Williams confessed to the rape and murder of Michelle, describing to investigators how he had beaten her with his fist and a shoe before raping her. Williams' confession sparked a series of arrests as police became convinced that he had acted in concert with several other men, including his roommate, Joseph Dick, and two other sailors, Derek Tice and Eric Wilson. The other three men also confessed under interrogation, and later pleaded guilty at trial in a deal to escape the death penalty. Dick publicly apologised to the victim's family. 'I know I shouldn't have done it,' he said, just before the judge gave him a double life sentence. 'I have got no idea what went through my mind that night – and my soul.'

The case was not straightforward, however. Puzzlingly, investigators never found DNA or fingerprints connecting any of the suspects to the crime. Then, while the men were awaiting trial, it emerged that a convicted rapist called Omar Ballard had written to a friend claiming that he had killed Michelle. When police took a sample of his DNA it proved to be a match with that found at the scene of the murder. (Ballard eventually pleaded guilty in court and said that he had acted alone.) Despite this new information, Norfolk police and prosecutors continued to pursue their case against Tice, Dick, Wilson and Williams. After the men were found guilty, suspicions grew that a major miscarriage of justice had occurred, and in 2005 the Innocence Project, a non-profit group that works to clear people who have been wrongfully convicted, took up the cause of the 'Norfolk Four'. It assembled an impressive collection of legal and forensic experts who believed the men to be innocent.

When the veteran FBI man Larry Smith first reviewed the case materials he was inclined to give Norfolk's police detectives the benefit of the doubt. After all, why would four men confess to a crime they didn't commit — especially a crime as heinous as this? But the more he read, the more he became convinced of their innocence. There was no physical evidence linking any of the convicted men to the crime, and nothing in their backgrounds to suggest they might be prone to outbreaks of frenzied brutality. The convictions were based entirely on the men's confessions, which had been extracted by interrogators using lies and threats, and were riddled with contradictions and implausibilities[6]. 'The confession should not be the end of the investigation,' Smith told *Time* magazine. 'You should corroborate the facts and circumstances of the confessions with the crime scene.'

In this case, all the facts about the crime scene suggested a conclusion different to the one reached by the jury. Smith and twenty-five other ex-FBI agents wrote to Virginia governor Tim Kaine asking him to grant pardons to the four men. 'In rare cases,' they wrote, powerful interrogation techniques 'can produce false confessions.' In the last months of his term, Kaine issued conditional pardons to the three men still in prison (Eric Wilson, who had been convicted of rape only, had already been released after serving over eight years of his sentence, and wasn't pardoned). The men were allowed to leave prison but their convictions remained; they were placed on parole for twenty years, and required to register as sex offenders wherever they went.[7] Kaine confessed to struggling with the decision. 'They're asking for a whole series of confessions ... to all be discarded,' he told a radio show in 2008. 'That is a huge request.'

Kaine wasn't alone in finding it almost impossible to believe that somebody would confess to a crime they hadn't committed. Saul Kassin, a professor of psychology at John Jay College of Criminal Justice in New York, is an expert on the psychology of false confessions. Wherever he gives lectures on the subject he hears the same response from audience members: 'Well, I would never do that. I would never confess to something I didn't do.' People apply the same logic in the jury room, he says; a confession is an overwhelmingly powerful piece of evidence. Analysis of hundreds of trials shows that a conviction is far more likely to be made when a confession is involved, even when jurors believe the confession was coerced, and even when they say that the confession was not a factor in their judgement. 'I don't honestly think juries stand a chance in cases involving confessions,' says Kassin. 'They're bound to convict.'

A confession can influence a trial without even reaching the courtroom, by tainting other evidence. In an experiment conducted by Kassin and fellow psychologist Lisa Hasel, students were invited to participate in what they were told was a study of persuasion techniques. The experimenter told the subjects she needed to leave the room to get some supplies and asked them to wait until her return. As they did so, another person came in and stole a laptop that was lying on a desk. The 'thief' was in view for about thirty seconds.

When the experimenter returned she feigned shock at the theft, and the participants suddenly found themselves witnesses in an investigation. They were shown a line-up of six suspects – none of whom was the person who made off with the laptop – and asked to identify the culprit. Some did, some didn't. Two days later, they were invited back for more questioning. Different witnesses were given different information by the experimenters about who had confessed, and their subsequent responses demonstrated the extraordinary extent to which knowledge of a confession can distort a person's recollection. Of the people who had identified a suspect from the original line-up, sixty per cent changed their mind when told that one of the others had confessed. Of those who originally identified none of the suspects as having been the criminal, half changed their mind when told that one of them had confessed, and agreed that it was him. Those who were told that the person they had (wrongly) identified had confessed found their confidence in their own recollections soaring. Suddenly, their memory of the episode became crystal clear; previously obscure details came sharply into focus.

If eyewitnesses are so easily influenced by being told about a confession, we can at least be confident in the steadfastness of scientific evidence – can't we? In 2006 a cognitive psychologist at University College London called Itiel Dror took a group of six fingerprint experts, showed them sets of fingerprints, and asked them to determine whether they were matches or not. After making their judgements, the participants were given new information: either that the prints came from a suspect who had confessed or that they came from a suspect who was known to be in police custody at the time the crime was committed. Four of the six experts changed their judgements based on this new context.

Confessions are the nuclear weapon of evidence. Yet we know with certainty that they can be false. Advances in DNA evidence have helped the Innocence Project exonerate over 250 wrongly convicted people – a quarter of whom had confessed to their crime. For a few, confessing to a crime they didn't commit is a way of gaining attention and fame: in 1932, hundreds of people admitted to kidnapping the baby of the aviator Charles Lindbergh.

Most of those who make false confessions, however, do so under the intense strain of a police interrogation. The police, who in high-profile cases are themselves under great pressure to secure convictions, are skilled at making the accused feel as though they're better off confessing. They might promise leniency or threaten tougher sentences, as in the case of the Norfolk Four. If a browbeaten suspect comes to feel that a conviction is inevitable, a confession can seem like their least worst option.

Advocates for fMRI lie detection might argue that in such cases the technology can come into its own, by enabling us to disregard the suspect's false story. But if Joseph Dick had been subject to any kind of lie detection test, the result would probably have been taken as evidence that he was guilty. To understand why, we need to grasp just how deceptive our memories can be.

During the 1980s a psychologist called Elizabeth Loftus would stand before juries and explain to them that just because an intelligent, sane, trustworthy person swears they remember something, that doesn't mean it happened.

One of Loftus's earliest published papers was based on work done for the Department of Transportation, which funded research into car accidents. She showed videos of vehicle collisions to her subjects then interviewed them about what they had seen, asking the same question but using different verbs. If she asked people how fast they remembered the cars were going when they 'smashed' into each other the estimates she received were of significantly higher speeds than if she used the word 'contacted'. Her questions were skewing the answers.

Loftus became intent on showing that the way we intuitively think of memory, as a form of information storage, is deeply inadequate, and that this has implications for the way we run our legal systems. In an investigation into the reliability of eyewitness accounts, she showed participants a video depicting a killing in a crowded town square. They were then given written information about the killing, but misled about what they'd seen. A critical blue vehicle would be referred to as white, a clean-shaven man as having a moustache. Afterwards, those who had been given the misleading information would express certainty that they had seen a white car and a moustachioed man.

Defence lawyers who had heard about Loftus's work invited her to give expert testimony on their behalf. They often needed to undermine the confidence of a jury in a witness report in a way that didn't involve attacking the witness's personal credibility; to show how witnesses could be led astray by police investigators, who would (often innocently) drop into the witness's mind suggestions which would later harden into memories. *Was it a blue car you saw? Was the man wearing a grey jacket? Is this the guy?*

In the late 1980s there was a spate of widely publicised court cases in North America centring on people coming forward to claim that they had been abused as children, usually by family members. Recovered Memory Syndrome — the idea that memories of childhood abuse are often repressed by the conscious mind and resurface only after extensive therapy — was fashionable in the therapeutic community, many of whose practitioners pursued, with missionary zeal, the task of digging up such memories from the psyches of their patients. Patients were told that the cause of their current unhappiness might be long-buried memories of abuse, and in lengthy therapeutic sessions, often under hypnosis, they would begin to recall the details of the offence. Loftus strongly suspected that many of the memories being 'recovered' were false, even when those claiming to have been abused sincerely believed in them. If she couldn't prove they were fictions, she wondered if she could show that fictions can become memories — and far more easily than most people suppose.

In 1995 Loftus recruited twenty-four participants and presented them with several stories from their early childhood which she and her collaborator had gathered from interviews with the participants' relatives. Amongst the true stories, she planted a false one. This fictional story was checked out with the relatives too, to ensure it was both false and plausible. The common theme of the false memories was getting lost in a shopping mall when out on a trip with their parents, and being rescued by a kindly stranger. Here, for instance, is the memory created for a twenty-year-old Vietnamese-American woman who had grown up in the state of Washington. It involves a trip to the local K-Mart with her mother and her siblings, Tien and Tuan:

> You must have been five years old at the time. Your mom gave each of you some money to get a blueberry Icee. You ran ahead to get into the line first, and somehow lost your way in the store. Tien found you crying to an elderly Chinese woman. You three then went together to get an Icee.

The participants were first sent a written description of the four events. Then they were asked to write down which events they remembered, and to include any details that came to mind. After this, they were interviewed twice over the course of a week and gently prompted to recall memories of all four events, including the fictional one. When it was revealed that one of the memories was fake, they were asked to guess which one. Five people recalled the 'lost in the mall' story as a real memory, and would recount it using details that weren't contained in the original. One participant described the man that rescued him: 'He was wearing blue flannel . . . He was kind of bald on top. He had a ring of grey hair. He had glasses.' Presented with blind spots in our memories, we readily create — or confabulate — new ones. The Vietnamese-American woman vividly recalled running down the K-Mart's slippery aisles under long white lights. Another participant, after being debriefed at the end of the study, found it so hard to believe her memory was false she had to call her parents to check; both confirmed the episode never took place.

Elizabeth Loftus, and researchers inspired by her work, went on to find many more ways to demonstrate the disturbing malleability of our memories.[8] In a series of increasingly bold experiments, participants were induced to falsely remember accidentally spilling a punch bowl on the parents of the bride at a wedding; taking a trip in a hot air balloon; being the object of a vicious animal attack; almost drowning, and witnessing satanic rituals. After critics suggested to Loftus that she hadn't quite proved such memories were false, she managed to persuade her subjects that they had met Bugs Bunny at Disneyland (Bugs Bunny is a Warner Bros character). When it was argued that she hadn't shown it was possible to implant memories of *abusive* experiences, her team convinced another group of subjects that, during a Disneyland trip, a drug-addled Pluto had licked their ears with his large fabric tongue.

Loftus and her fellow experimenters used mild and subtle techniques to implant memories. None of her participants was engaged in long conversations, or subjected to hypnosis, or faced anything like the fierce, relentless pressure of a high-stakes police investigation. Under those circumstances, it is hardly surprising that a person's memory becomes prone to the most extravagant manipulations.

* * *

One of the expert witnesses called to testify at the trial of the Norfolk Four was Dr Richard Ofshe, a social scientist from the University of California and a friend of Elizabeth Loftus. Years before, Ofshe had carried out one of the most dramatic experiments in memory ever conducted, in the course of advising the prosecutors of a man accused of sexually abusing his daughters.

Paul Ingram, of Olympia, Washington State, could hardly have been a more upstanding member of his community. At forty-three years old, he was a happily married father of two daughters and three sons, the deputy sheriff of Thurston County, and chairman of the local Republican Party. A tall man who wore oversized glasses and a brown moustache, Ingram was a strong believer in authority, a devout Christian and a stickler for rules. He and his family were active members of the Church of Living Waters, a fundamentalist Protestant congregation whose members experienced heightened states of religious fervour during worship, speaking in tongues and laying on hands to the sick. In his job, Ingram was known as a strict enforcer of traffic regulations who nonetheless acted with formal courtesy and consideration towards those he awarded tickets.

In 1988 Ingram's elder daughter, Ericka, then twenty-one and still living with her parents, attended a 'Heart to Heart' Bible camp, an annual retreat for older girls organised by the church. The star speaker that year was a Californian woman named Karla Franko, who had become a church minister after a career as an actress and stand-up comic. An attractive, charismatic figure, on whom the glitter of celebrity had been bestowed, in the eyes of the girls, by appearances on minor TV shows and commercials, Franko believed herself to possess God-given gifts of healing and spiritual discernment, and she conducted emotionally charged sessions at the camp, during which painful memories resurfaced, fears were confessed, and tears shed.

At the end of the weekend, as the rest of the campers were boarding buses ready to take them back to the church, Franko came across Ericka Ingram sitting on the stage of the conference centre, sobbing. A few friends surrounded her, though they had no idea why she was upset. Franko prayed over her. As she did so she felt the Lord prompting her with information about Ericka's plight. 'You have been abused as a child, sexually abused,' the minister told Ericka. As her charge continued to weep, Franko received another divine prompting, and told Ericka that her father had been the abuser. Ericka was too overcome to say a word.

Shortly after returning from the retreat, Ericka and her younger sister, Julie, eighteen, moved out of the Ingram home. Six weeks later she told her mother that she had been repeatedly molested by her father. Sandy, Ericka's mother, immediately confronted her husband with the accusations. Paul claimed to have no idea what to make of them. Julie supported her sister's story, also claiming to have been molested by Paul. When word reached the sheriff's office, Paul was arrested.

BORN LIARS

In the febrile atmosphere of 1980s America, the concept of Recovered Memory Syndrome mingled with fundamentalist Christian doctrines stressing the Devil's active presence in the world to produce a potent, unpredictable force that tore through families and entire communities. Court cases based on these memories became a regular feature on local news bulletins, and a common theme of these stories was the involvement of satanic ritual. The inhabitants of many small towns began to wonder if there weren't dark forces at work just beneath the placid surface of their own community.

This was by no means an exclusively American phenomenon. In 1990, nine children from the Orkney Islands were seized from their homes in the middle of the night, bundled into a plane and flown to the Scottish mainland, after social workers reported that they had uncovered a devil-worshipping paedophile ring. The only evidence ever found for this was from the testimony of the children in subsequent interviews. The judge who threw out the original case said that the children were subjected to intense and aggressive cross-examinations designed to make them admit to abuse. In the late 1980s and early 1990s, more than a hundred children were removed from their families in Cleveland, Nottinghamshire, Rochdale, Bishop Auckland and Ayrshire, for similar reasons. Social workers 'uncovered' memories of children forced to eat faeces, drink blood and have sex with hooded adults. In none of these cases was any evidence found to support the allegations.

During interviews with detectives, Ericka and Julie Ingram expanded on their story. Their accounts of the abuse were strangely inconsistent and changeable, however. For instance, Julie had told her mother that the last time Paul had abused her was five years ago, but after the police informed her about statutes of limitations, she remembered that the last assault was only three years ago. As months passed and the girls were interviewed by a long succession of sympathetic lawyers, detectives and therapists, their recollections of the abuse became ever more vivid, detailed, and gaudily grotesque. Ericka described a large group of Satan-worshippers, including many well-known members of the community, who would don green robes, gather in barns and empty churches, and chant incantations around a fire as a priestess killed babies in acts of ritual sacrifice. The girls said they'd been cut, tortured, and nailed to the floor. Ericka said that when she was sixteen, and five months pregnant, the Satanists performed an abortion on her. The foetus was removed and, still alive, was placed on top of her, where it was cut into pieces and eaten by members of the congregation. Detectives grew suspicious of the daughters' outlandish allegations, for which they could find no corroborating evidence, despite strenuous and expensive efforts.[9] What kept the prosecution case alive was Paul Ingram's confession.

Following his arrest, the pressure on Ingram to confess was intense. During his first conversation with investigators, he denied the allegations, but the arresting officers

— Paul's own colleagues, men he knew and trusted — pressed him to consider how unlikely it was that his daughters were lying. Paul's confidence in his own memory — and his own character — soon began to weaken. After several hours of interrogation he still couldn't remember committing any abuse, but conceded the possibility he had made himself blind to it. Like the detectives, he didn't believe that his daughters were capable of lying about such things, and preferred to mistrust himself rather than them. 'There may be a dark side of me that I don't know about,' he said.

For six months Paul Ingram had almost no contact with anyone sceptical of the charges against him. He was kept in an isolated cell with the lights on nearly all the time (he was under a suicide watch) and interrogated by trusted former colleagues, all of whom appeared to believe the charges. His alleged crimes were spelt out in graphic detail. He was told by a police psychologist that he was probably repressing memories of his actions, and he was subjected to hypnosis in an attempt to 'recover' the hidden memories. The police department's chaplain urged him to confess, framing his predicament as a spiritual one in a way that Ingram must have found both moving and terrifying. 'If there's ever been a time that you were offered a choice between the Devil and God, it's right now,' said the pastor.

Eventually, the confessions started to flow. A ritual developed. During long interrogation sessions, Ingram would be told about specific crimes of which he had been accused, and return to his cell to 'pray on it'. This entailed going into a trance-like state (he had been urged by the pastor to visualise everything), after which he would return to describe his memory of the crimes in a calm, dreamy voice, using a curiously tentative syntax — 'I would've removed her underpants or bottoms to the nightgown,' he said, in the first of these sessions. The more he told, the more elaborate his recollections became: he described his participation in satanic rituals, including the time he cut the heart out of a live cat. He even confessed to the murder of a prostitute in Seattle in 1983, implicating himself in a well-known series of killings (Seattle police looked into it, but found nothing in Ingram's statement worthy of further investigation). The trouble was, Ingram's narratives repeatedly failed to match up with those told by his daughters, or with any other evidence.

To help build their case, the prosecutors decided to bring in a known expert on cults and mind-control: Richard Ofshe. A flamboyant man who sported a luxuriant grey and white beard, Ofshe had a reputation in the academic community for being arrogant, wilful, and brilliant. The Olympia policeman who picked him up from the local airport described the mysteries of the case to him: the lack of hard evidence, the conflicting stories, the girls' confusing testimony, the way that Paul Ingram's recollections combined gory imagery with a baffling vagueness about more prosaic details of time and place. The description struck a chord with Ofshe, who was also, coincidentally, becoming interested in the ability of coercive interrogations to extract confessions from innocent people. As soon as he interviewed Paul, Ofshe suspected that he was so confused, so desperate to help his interrogators and to protect his daughters from further pain, that he was 'confabulating' false memories of his supposed crimes. On the spot, Ofshe came up with an audacious method of testing his hypothesis.

'I was talking to one of your sons and one of your daughters and they told me about something that happened,' he told Ingram, as dumbfounded police officers, aware that Ofshe hadn't spoken to any members of Ingram's family, struggled to catch on. Paul had been accused, said Ofshe, of forcing one of his daughters to have sex with his son while he watched (the Ingram children had reported no such episode and later confirmed that it had never taken place). He provided Paul with a few suggestive details of the fictional incident – just as had happened in earlier interrogations – and asked if it was true. At first, Paul denied it, but Ofshe asked him to try and visualise the scene. Paul closed his eyes and after a few minutes announced that memories of it were beginning to return. Ofshe told him to go back to his cell and continue praying on it. When Ingram emerged the next day he presented Ofshe with a three-page written confession which described the imaginary event in detail, complete with dialogue.

The Dream of a Truth Machine

Recovered Memory Syndrome was founded on Freud's idea that the mind represses memories of events too awful to be allowed into consciousness. It was a theory that Freud abandoned late his career, when he came to believe that such repressions were more likely to involve forbidden fantasy and wishes rather than real incidents. Even when still in thrall to the theory, however, he seemed to intuit its fatal flaw. In this passage from 1899 he anticipated much contemporary research into the nature of memory:

> It may indeed be questioned whether we have any memories at all from our childhood: memories relating to our childhood may be all that we possess. Our childhood memories show us our earliest years not as they were but as they appeared at the later periods when the memories were aroused. In these periods of arousal, the childhood memories did not, as people are accustomed to say, emerge; they were formed at that time.

This description of memory tallies with the experimental evidence of Elizabeth Loftus, and with the findings of modern neuroscience. Remembering is an act of creative reconstruction rather than simple replaying. Every time a memory is recalled it is re-formed, and in the process it becomes mingled with the stories of others and shaped by our own anxieties, desires and imaginings. As the neurologist Antonio Damasio puts it, the brain carries 'no hard copies'.

Ofshe told Paul he had made up the scene, and repeatedly tried to get him to admit his confession was fictional. But Ingram would not shaken from his conviction that it was real. Ofshe wrote a report for the court, arguing strongly that Ingram's confessions were invented, but it came too late to influence the trial. Despite it becoming increasingly apparent to most observers that the allegations had no basis in reality, Ingram pleaded guilty to six counts of third-degree rape. Ofshe called Ingram, imploring him to withdraw his guilty plea, but Ingram held firm. Months later, after the interrogations had ceased and he was moved to a different prison, Ingram concluded that his visualisations had not been real memories after all. But by then it was too late; he was sentenced to twenty years imprisonment. Despite several legal appeals, at which Ofshe, Loftus and others testified on Ingram's behalf, and the campaign of a support group dedicated to getting the case reopened, Ingram served the majority of his sentence. A confession, once made, is almost impossible to retract.

We have long dreamed of a technology that can cut through the messy, confusing uncertainties of human behaviour and take us straight to an authentic source of truth. The polygraph rose to prominence when we started thinking of the body as the site of truth; these days we tend to look for truth in the brain. But, as Sartre's story about the soldier who unwittingly betrays his colleague reminds us, the truth doesn't reside inside any one person — it's out there in the world, and it can only be established by the gathering of evidence, and the painstaking assembly of multiple points of view. As individuals, we are thoroughly unreliable witnesses, even to ourselves.

Some legal scholars make the reasonable argument that even if the results of fMRI lie detection tests are not entirely dependable they should still be admissible in court. After all, unreliable evidence, such as the testimony of character witnesses, or circumstantial evidence, is regularly introduced as part of a larger picture put together by lawyers. As one scholar puts it, 'Although slight evidence ought not to be good enough for scientists, it is a large part of the law.' But the likelihood is that the results of an fMRI lie detection test will always be assigned more credence than they deserve; a jury faced with such evidence will, to borrow Saul Kassin's phrase, feel 'bound to convict'. Perhaps we are too in love with the dream of a truth machine to allow it to become a reality.

'It didn't cross my mind that I was lying,' said Joseph Dick, long after recanting his confession to the murder of Michelle Moore-Busko. 'I believed what I was saying was true.' Even knowing what we know, it is almost impossible to comprehend that a man could falsely believe he has committed a murder he didn't commit. But then, our capacity for self-deception is far greater than we imagine.

I Me Lie

Why we're designed to deceive ourselves

I thus drew steadily nearer to that truth, by whose partial discovery I have been doomed to such a dreadful shipwreck: that man is not truly one, but truly two. I say two, because the state of my own knowledge does not pass beyond that point. Others will follow, others will outstrip me on the same lines; and I hazard the guess that man will be ultimately known for a mere polity of multifarious, incongruous and independent denizens.

Henry Jekyll's Full Statement of the Case,
The Strange Case of Dr Jekyll and Mr Hyde
Robert Louis Stevenson

Imagine that I blindfolded you and walked you into a strange room in which there is a llama, an umbrella and a cactus. As soon as your blindfold is removed, you'd become instantly aware of the shape and dimensions of the room and its contents. You might take the llama for a goat at first, but that would probably be the extent of your confusion. You might be wondering why you're here – but you wouldn't exert any conscious mental effort establishing where or what 'here' is. You'd just look around.

But if you were to watch a recording of what your *eyes* actually see when the blindfold is off, you'd be shocked. It would resemble a bootlegged DVD of *The Blair Witch Project* on which somebody has spilt beer and then stuck in a toaster – shaky, blurred, black and white, and with a hole in it. In fact, make that two bootlegged DVDs, each of them showing a slightly different movie: if you cover one eye and then quickly switch your hand to the other, you'll remind yourself that each eye has a different field of vision. Even presuming you have perfect eyesight, the only part of the picture full of detail and colour would be a small area in the middle; to the right and left of it the screen would lose resolution steeply, becoming a greyish blur.

Our natural feeling is that our minds are like a mirror on which light falls – that we simply perceive the world as it is. For a long time, philosophers and scientists thought along similar lines. In the late eighteenth century Immanuel Kant introduced the idea that there is a stage between what our eyes and ears pick up and what we perceive; that while we depend on sensory data for our knowledge, we make sense of its profusion and confusion by relying on in-built mental categories. But it took science some time to catch up with Kant; in classical physiology up until the twentieth century, visual images fell upon the optic nerve, and that was that. Freud suspected that the functions of *receiving* sensory signals and *registering* them were separate, though he had no strong evidence for it at the time. We now know that the brain does indeed do a lot of work to make reality comprehensible — that the world as scanned by our eyes is rather different from the world we *see*. As the neuroscientist David Eagleman puts it, your brain 'serves up a story to you'. In a sense, deception begins the moment you open your eyes.

When the blindfold comes off, a huge amount of cognitive filling and smoothing gets under way. The brain seamlessly merges both fields of vision. The image that falls on your retina is in two dimensions; the third is added later. There is a blind spot in each eye; the brain fills in for it (this is a mundane problem of furniture arrangement: the optical nerve has to attach to the retina somewhere and it takes up space that would otherwise be filled with receptors). Your eyes don't have enough neuronal receptors to capture a whole scene properly, so your pupils dance frantically around as they try to bring the sharper region of focus to bear on every part of the room, a movement known as the saccade. Yet you have the illusion of continuous, coherent vision. Cognitive scientists have given this latter phenomenon the lyrical name of 'confabulation across saccades'.

The brain doesn't just tidy up what the senses record; it does something more creative than that. Larry Fitzgerald of the Arizona Cardinals is one of the best catchers of the ball in America's National Football League. As a wide receiver a large part of his job is to pluck passes out of the air, and he does it with acrobatic agility and perfect timing. He also does it with his eyes closed. Photographs that capture the moment he seizes the ball reveal that he does so without looking at it. His many admirers, already in awe of his ability, are baffled; it's a coaching truism that a player must keep his eye on the ball at all times. Fitzgerald himself can't explain it.

Joan Vickers, a cognitive scientist who studies the eye movements of sportspeople, hypothesises that Fitzgerald is using 'predictive control', a skill we all have, but one that Fitzgerald has honed through years of experience of the game. As the ball approaches him, he takes a mental snapshot of it, which his subconscious then instantly compares to a vast library of memories drawn from years of playing and observation. As a teenager Fitzgerald worked as a ballboy for six seasons, and Vickers thinks that the thousands of passes he witnessed from the sidelines left him with a catalogue of impressions most athletes take years to accumulate. By matching his snapshot with the memory of all these other passes, Fitzgerald's brain is able to conjure up a picture of where the ball will go. He can then work out how to put himself in position to catch it — without looking.[10]

Though Fitzgerald has an exceptionally refined skill in this regard, he's using a feature of the brain that we all share. In the words of Chris Frith, a cognitive neuroscientist, the brain 'actively creates pictures of the world'. Rather than trying to interpret every new thing it sees as if encountering it for the first time, the brain makes a series of working assumptions about what a chair looks like, or a person, and where that ball is going to be, then makes predictions — best guesses — about what's before us. It compares its expectations with the new information coming in, checks for mistakes, and revises accordingly. The result, in Frith's striking formulation, is 'a fantasy that collides with reality'.

Our pro-active, interventionist cognitive system works extremely well most of the time — it has to, otherwise we couldn't have survived as a species. But it can be fooled. The cognitive psychologist Gustav Kuhn recorded people's eye movements while they watched a video of a magician performing the Vanishing Ball illusion, in which a ball thrown into the air seems to disappear mid-flight. The magician tosses the ball straight up into the air and catches it a few times. On the final throw, he only pretends to toss the ball, secreting it in the palm of his hand. As he does so, he looks to the sky, as if tracking the rise of the ball into thin air. This last detail is significant. Half the spectators were shown a version of the trick in which the magician looked at his hand instead of skyward on the final throw, and most of them spotted the trick. The spectators who succumbed to the illusion were being led by the movement of the magician's head and eyes.

These participants reported that they'd actually seen the ball leave the top of the screen. The eye-tracking analysis, however, showed that on that final, deceptive throw, their eyes didn't even go to the top of the screen but stayed fixed on the ball. In other words, they had such strong expectations of where the ball was going to be that they hallucinated it.

Magicians, architects and artists have known about how to exploit the quirks of our perceptual system for millennia. The platform on which the mighty pillars of the Parthenon stand is not straight, but curved; its architects knew this is the only way to obtain the *effect* of a straight line. When magicians misdirect us away from their method and towards their effect, it's our attention they're manipulating, not our gaze. These bugs can occasionally cause disasters, when the brain directs our attention to the wrong things, overriding the reports of the senses. Time and again, under conditions of high visibility, and with no evidence of mechanical failure, drivers and pilots crash into obvious obstacles. In an experiment using a flight simulator, commercial airline pilots were asked to land a Boeing 727. On some approaches, the image of a small aircraft was unexpectedly superimposed onto the runway. Two out of eight pilots blithely continued with the landing manoeuvre as if the runway was clear.

So far we've talked only about vision, but the principles of cognitive self-deception apply elsewhere. We are deceived about our own bodies, for instance. Although we're rarely aware of it, we are constantly monitoring information about the position of our bodies, and unconsciously making adjustments. When you lift your left arm you subtly shift some weight to the right side of your body to maintain balance and avoid listing to one side. The sensory feedback we receive about our muscles, joints and skin is known as proprioception, but most of us barely know it exists, because the brain makes our normal movements feel effortless.[11] We vastly underestimate the mental sophistication and effort required just to stand still, or pick up a fork, let alone walk along a crowded street without colliding with people.

Our experience of *when* things are happening is partly illusory too. If you're touched on your nose and your toe at precisely the same moment, the signal from the toe will reach your brain one tenth of a second after the signal from the nose, because it has further to travel along the body's nerve fibres to the brain. But you will experience the touches as simultaneous, because the brain puts the first signal – from the nose – on hold while it waits for any other signals to arrive. When the toe signal arrives, you get the feeling of 'now'. We all live at a slight lag from reality, and tall people experience a slightly longer lag from reality than short people, simply because the distance from toe to head is greater, which means the brain takes longer to check on all the signals. David Eagleman recounts that in the early days of television broadcasting, engineers worried about the problem of keeping audio and video signals synchronised. Then they accidentally discovered that they had around a tenth of a second's grace; as long as the signals arrived within this window, viewers wouldn't notice a thing. Their brains would automatically resynchronise the signals.

The world we perceive is also shaped by our desires. In 1947 Jerome Bruner and Cecile Goodman found that children consistently judged coins to be bigger than identically sized cardboard circles. The monetary value of the coins was influencing how big they perceived the dimensions to be. Tellingly, children from poor families perceived the coins to be bigger than children from affluent families. In a more recent study, psychologists from New York University asked students to estimate the distance between their own position and a full bottle of water on the table at which they were sitting. Beforehand, they fed some of the students a diet of pretzels to make them thirsty. The thirsty students judged the bottle to be closer than the other students did. Another study revealed that hills appear steeper to us than they actually are, and that this tendency is exaggerated when the observer is old, unhealthy, or wearing a backpack. This is self-deception rather than simple misjudgement. When participants in these studies are asked to judge the hill's incline by adjusting the slant of a movable board with their hands (without looking at their hands) they got it right. Psychologists call this phenomenon 'wishful seeing'.

Imagination, said Coleridge, is 'the living power and prime agent of all human perception', a sentiment echoed by Charles Darwin when he asserted that there could be no true *observation* of the world without *speculation*. Beginning at the most fundamental level, we are engaged in a continual negotiation between our expectations and desires about the world, and the world itself, between imagination and reality. Why does our brain deceive us about so much? Partly because it needs to fill in the gaps left by our sensory organs, but also because without an automatic ability to interpret and organise the incoming chaos of signals we would drown in them, becoming slaves to our impulses. Some brain-damaged people cannot help but act on everything they see. If they see a glass they must drink from it; if they see a pen they must write with it. Through the use of what Frith calls 'controlled fantasy' our brain screens out what it deems irrelevant and helps us to establish what's important to us – amidst all the noise and chatter at a party your name leaps out at you.

For the brain, truthfully depicting reality accurately comes second to survival. Of course, the two objectives are very much aligned, but not completely. We're less likely to kill ourselves attempting that hill if we think it's steeper than it is, and we're more likely to make an effort to reach something desirable if it seems nearer than it is.

Choice Lies

In 1983, Benjamin Libet of the University of California asked participants in an experiment to make a movement at an arbitrary moment decided by them (they were instructed to flex their wrist 'freely and capriciously'), and to note the precise time, using a specially designed clock, at which they decided to make their move. As they did so, Libet monitored their brain activity. He found that the brain prepares the body to move several hundred milliseconds *before* the person consciously decides to move. The person's conscious intention seemed to be, literally, an afterthought.[12] We like to think that we deliberate about what to do, then do it. But Libet's experiment, and others that followed, suggest that most of the time we act first and invent reasons, feelings and motivations afterwards.

In another, rather eerie experiment, designed by the psychologist Daniel Wegner, you participate with a companion who is apparently doing the same experiment but who is actually an assistant of the experimenter. You and your companion sit at a computer screen and both of you place a finger on a shared, specially designed mouse. There are lots of objects on the screen, and through earphones someone tells you to move the on-screen pointer towards one of them. You have the thought, and then you move the mouse. If your companion moves the mouse as you are having the thought, but *before* you have actually moved your arm, then you will believe that you moved the mouse. You'll feel as if you chose to do something that somebody else did for you (this illusion works if the interval between having the thought and the mouse moving is about one and a fifth seconds or less).

Wegner believes that our feeling of free will is nothing but a trick of perspective − a deception practised by the brain. A conscious 'decision' is merely a story we tell ourselves to explain what has happened *to* us, or what our bodies have already executed. This is a deeply contentious position, although many neuroscientists agree with him. There is certainly a huge amount of experimental evidence that our unconscious brain guides and determines many of the everyday decisions we think of as conscious ones. When you choose a brand of toothpaste or reject someone for a job you may be doing so for reasons of which you're completely unaware − the unconscious associations you have with a brand name, the job candidate's gender. What's certain is that you'll spontaneously come up with a plausible reason: the toothpaste's plaque-reduction system, the interviewee's lack of experience.

Two cognitive scientists from Sweden named Lars Hall and Petter Johansson devised an experiment that relies on a card trick they were taught by a professional magician. The researcher holds up two photographs, each with a different face on it, and asks the subject to choose the one she finds more attractive. The researcher lays both pictures face down and slides the chosen photograph over to the subject – except he doesn't. Using a sleight-of-hand technique he covertly swaps one picture for the other, so that the picture the participant ends up with is the one she *didn't* choose.[13] You might expect the subject to take one glance at the photo in her hand and protest to the researcher that this isn't the man she chose, and indeed in some cases that's exactly what happened. But in most trials, the participants didn't appear to notice. This alone would make the experiment interesting. The most telling part, however, came when the subjects who had accepted the 'wrong' card were asked how they had made their 'choice'. They unhesitatingly offered up elaborate explanations of what had attracted them to that person's eyes, hair, or bone structure.

One classic experiment was conducted in a park in British Columbia, Canada. A female assistant with a clipboard approached young men in the park and asked them to take part in a survey on creativity. After writing down their answers, she suggested that maybe they might like to discuss the results with her later, and wrote down her number for them. The researchers tallied how many of the men called her later and asked her out. The clever part of the experiment was that the researchers varied the situation the men were in when approached. Half of them were on a terrifying footbridge spanning a deep gorge. As these men talked to the woman they were holding tight to the flimsy handrail as the bridge swayed in the breeze. The other group of men were sitting safely on a park bench. The question the researchers were interested in was, which group of men would be more attracted to the woman?

You might wonder why on earth it should make a difference whether they were approached on the bridge or the bench; after all, it's the same woman. Yet sixty-five per cent of the men on the bridge called to ask the woman on a date, compared to thirty percent of the men on the bench. The reason for this is that the brain can pursue its mission to explain with a little too much zeal. When the men on the bridge took the woman's number, their hearts were pumping rapidly, they were perspiring, and a little short of breath. They would have recognised to some extent that these symptoms were down to their physical situation, but even so, they misattributed some of their arousal to attraction to the woman. The sense-making part of their brains had gone into overdrive and created a surfeit of explanation for what was going on. As a result the men became much more likely to tell themselves they had a crush on the woman, and more likely to call her afterwards. So there you are: if you want to ask a stranger out, wait until they're in physical danger and seize your moment.

Like our perception of the physical world, our perception of why we do things is a fantasy that collides with reality. This description would have made sense to Freud, of course, who believed that we are deceived about the nature of reality because we fundamentally deceive ourselves about who we are. We fantasise that we know what we want out of life when in reality we are divided into warring factions, each wanting something different. Amongst academic psychologists at least, Freud's ideas fell deeply out of fashion after he died. His arguments were based more on intuition than evidence, and his gothic vision of the unconscious as a realm of repressed sexual desires remains deeply idiosyncratic. But in recent decades, neuroscientists have concluded that he got at least two very important things right: our psyche *is* deeply divided, and our conscious actions *are* deeply influenced by sophisticated mental processes of which we remain unaware, day by day. All of us are engaged in an act of creative self-deception to maintain the fiction that we know why we do the things we do.

The Lie of 'I'

In 1960 a young graduate student called Michael Gazzaniga joined the laboratory of the great neurologist Roger Sperry. Gazzaniga was overjoyed to have landed a job under Sperry, who was the first to discover that the brains of some animals, including ours, are split into two systems, left and right, each with different responsibilities. If you stare at a fixed point in space, like a dot on the wall in front of you, everything to the left of the dot is projected to the right half of your brain, and vice versa. Each hemisphere receives nerve transmissions from the opposite leg and arm and picks up sound from the opposite ear. Nobody knows why the signals cross over – the official scientific explanation is pretty much, *they just do* – and in the normal brain it doesn't make much difference where the information lands because the connecting pathways between each half-brain are intact.

In 1961 Sperry got a call from a former colleague, the neurosurgeon Joe Bogen, who told him that he was about to perform a radical new operation on a patient suffering from epilepsy. Epileptic seizures always start in one part of the brain and then spread to the surrounding tissue. A minor seizure can spread to the entire brain, causing the person to lose consciousness, fall to the floor and writhe uncontrollably. To stop the seizure spreading from one half of the brain to the other, Bogen proposed a severing of the thick bundle of nerve fibres, known as the corpus callosum, that connects the two hemispheres. Sperry sent his protégé Gazzaniga over to Bogen's lab, to perform tests on the patient before and after the operation.

Given that nobody was quite sure what the corpus callosum was responsible for, or how the two halves of the brain interacted, Bogen's proposed operation was risky. But he knew Sperry had performed this operation on animals with no apparent ill effects, and he knew that his patients, some of whom suffered from severe, life-ravaging epilepsy, were desperate to try something. William Jenkins, a smiling, chipper forty-eight-year-old, had volunteered to be first to undergo the operation. Bogen had first met him when Jenkins was admitted to the emergency room of Bogen's hospital in the middle of a severe fit. Jenkins suffered frequent, punishing convulsions and dangerously sudden losses of motor control, which effectively prevented him from living anything close to a normal life, and he had been told there was no cure for his condition. He knew that Bogen's solution was something of a leap into the unknown, but he and his wife told the surgeon that they were eager to go ahead. 'You know,' said Jenkins, 'even if it doesn't help my seizures, if you learn something it will be more worthwhile than anything I've been able to do for years.' In February 1962, after practising the operation half a dozen times in the morgue, Bogen severed Bill Jenkins's corpus callosum.

It worked. Jenkins recovered strongly from the surgery and was soon feeling something like his old self again, his seizures greatly alleviated. But were there really no side-effects? Gazzaniga asked Jenkins to stare at a spot on a screen while he flashed images just to the right or just to the left of it. The images came and went quickly enough that the patient couldn't move his gaze, so when a picture of a hat was flashed just to the right of the spot, it was processed by his left hemisphere. When Gazzaniga asked, 'What did you see?' Jenkins had no difficulty in identifying the hat. But if the same image was flashed on the left side of the spot, he didn't know what to say. The image was being processed by the right hemisphere, which doesn't have the power of speech.

It's not as if the right brain hadn't seen anything. Gazzaniga showed Jenkins a card with several images on it, and asked him to point *with his left hand* to the image that he had just flashed up on the screen. He had no difficulty doing so. The right hemisphere knew the answer — it could point — but was unable to communicate verbally. Normally, Gazzaniga realised, it could call out to the left hemisphere via the corpus callosum for help in finding the right word. But without it, nothing emerged from the patient's mouth. In another experiment, Gazzaniga blindfolded Jenkins and asked him to hold an object like a comb or a coffee cup in his left hand. If he held it in his right hand he had no trouble identifying it. When transferred to the left hand, he was literally at a loss for words.

Gazzaniga had fallen upon an insight he was to explore and develop for the rest of his career: we are not one, but two. The brain's hemispheres, left and right, operate as separate intelligences housed in one body. The left side deals with analytical and logical thinking and has the gift of language; anything to do with speaking or writing is dealt with here. The right side is illiterate and mute, but has its own magical powers.[14] It is much better at identifying *patterns* — at recognising categories, objects and faces, and enjoying music or art. The two systems work closely together, but are independent. With the messenger cut out, the inner division of the mind into two different entities was laid bare. Henry Jekyll had been on to something.

Gazzaniga went on to discover much more about how

the parts of a split brain relate to each other. For instance, when they are no longer joined up directly, they can find new ways to co-operate. In one of Gazzaniga's experiments, a split-brain patient is asked to reach into a closed bag with his left hand, feel the object inside, and say what it is. The object is something easy to identify, like a pencil, but because the right brain is mute, the patient can't say the answer. The right hemisphere hits upon a cunning plan. As we've seen, most tactile sensations are cross-wired. But there is an exception: pain stimuli go to both hemispheres. The patient holds the pencil in his left hand with the point pressed hard into his palm. This sends a pain signal shooting into *both* parts of the brain. So now the left knows something, at least — there is a sharp object in the bag. Using this hint, it begins to guess. The patient speaks: 'A pin, a needle, a pen?' The right hemisphere, which possesses the answer, helps out: it signals when these guesses are getting warmer by smiling or nodding. Very soon the patient announces the correct answer. It's a stunning example of neural teamwork. Even with the internal connection cut, the two hemispheres find a way of communicating by going via the outside world.

The brain's hemispheres can also fall out with each other, and violently. Some split-brain patients suffer from a condition known as 'alien hand syndrome'. One hand, usually the left, takes on a life of its own, and a bizarre Punch and Judy show ensues. The neurologist Victor Mark of the University of North Dakota interviewed one such patient. When asked how many seizures she had recently experienced, her right hand held up two fingers. Her left hand then reached over and forced the fingers on her right hand down. After some back and forth she gave up and let both have their say, displaying three fingers with her right hand and one with her left. When Mark pointed out the discrepancy, she commented that her left hand frequently did things on its own. A fight ensued between the two hands, at the end of which the woman burst into tears.

Many similar cases have been recorded. The alien hand might pick up a ringing phone but then refuse to pass it to the other hand, or grab a shirt picked out by the other hand and place it firmly back on the rack. It often seems to be on a mission to disrupt the person's conscious intentions, dumping a glass of water into a bowl of cereal, unbuttoning a shirt that the right hand is in the process of buttoning, removing a cigarette the person has placed in his mouth with his right hand. One man recalled seizing his wife with his left hand and shaking her violently, while with his right hand he tried to come to his wife's aid. In several cases, the alien hand has reached for its owner's neck and tried to strangle him.

Hard as it is to conceive of, some scientists think it likely that left and right hemispheres, speaking and mute, are each conscious entities in their own right, with their own thoughts and moods.[15] This central division is made up of further divisions into hundreds of independently functioning, non-conscious modules, all capable in different ways of initiating behaviour or generating an emotion. They aren't necessarily designed to cohere. The brain wasn't built to a master plan, but has picked up different functions over millions of years, yoking them together imperfectly as it goes, like a royal palace that has been added to, altered and extended in different architectural styles, with the result an imposing but untidy sprawl that somehow works as a single building. It shouldn't be a surprise, then, that the brain's agents are sometimes at cross-purposes. Although the fully functioning brain does a pretty good job of maintaining the internal flows of information and keeping order, there is no all-seeing, all-powerful chief executive or president tasked with ruling over Jekyll's society of 'multifarious, incongruous and independent denizens'.

We are familiar with the sense of internal conflict; most of us know the battle between desire and conscience all too well. In Ovid's *Metamorphoses*, Medea describes herself as being torn apart, 'desire and reason are pulling in opposite directions'. In his novel *Solar*, Ian McEwan describes a mind in decision-making mode as a parliament or debating chamber: 'Different factions contended, short- and long-term interests were entrenched in mutual loathing. Not only were motions tabled and opposed, certain proposals were aired in order to mask others. Sessions could be devious as well as stormy.' But, most of the time at least, I don't *feel* like an assembly of different selves (whatever that would feel like). I feel like me, and you feel like you, or at least I assume you do. Split-brain patients feel this way too. They have no sense of themselves as anything but whole. Even those suffering from alien hand syndrome only see the effects rather than sensing the cause. How is it that each of us feels like one person, with one mind, when in reality we are divided? More than ten years after his momentous encounter with William Jenkins, Michael Gazzaniga made another breakthrough that helps to explain how we keep it all together.

Varying his original experiment, Gazzaniga started to flash two pictures up at a time, one on each side of the dot. To one patient, a fifteen-year-old boy, he flashed a picture of a chicken's claw on the left, and on the right, a house and car covered in snow. He then showed the patient a card with various pictures on it and asked him to choose one to go with the pictures he'd just been shown on the screen. Each of the patient's hands pointed to different images, as if sent out on competing missions by different sides of his brain. The patient's left hand pointed to a shovel (which went with the snow scene) whilst his right hand pointed to a chicken (which went with the chicken claw). Gazzaniga asked the patient why he was pointing to these two pictures. He suspected that the patient would have some difficulty explaining what was going on with his left hand. After all, the only part of his brain able to issue a verbal response was the left hemisphere, responsible for the right hand, and his left hemisphere was oblivious to the earlier image of a snow-covered house. But the patient didn't say, 'I've no idea why my left hand is pointing to a shovel.' He said, without any hesitation, 'Oh that's easy. The chicken claw goes with the chicken, and you need a shovel to clean out the chicken shed.'

Gazzaniga was quietly awestruck. He realised that the left-brain, though ignorant of why the left hand was pointing to the shovel, had simply invented a plausible reason after the fact. When Gazzaniga flashed the word WALK to the right hemisphere of another split-brain patient, the man got up from his seat and started walking away. When asked why, he (or at least, his left hemisphere) smartly replied that he was 'just going to get a Coke'. Another was flashed the word LAUGH and started to laugh. Questioned, he replied, 'You guys come up and test us each month. What a way to earn a living!'

Of course, the examples above are drawn from case studies of people with rare brain conditions. But the startling suggestion made by Gazzaniga is that they simply reveal, in a particularly clear and dramatic way, the way our own minds hastily fabricate stories, or what he calls 'confabulations', to make our own choices intelligible to us. Earlier we met patients who had been diagnosed as chronic confabulators. The term is used more generally here, but the principle is the same. Confabulations spring from the language circuitry in the left hemisphere, which Gazzaniga goes so far as to call 'the interpreter module' because, as he sees it, its job is simply to interpret actions and emotions that have been generated from elsewhere in the brain. The interpreter module – which equates closely to the conscious mind – blithely concocts *post hoc* explanations for whatever we do or feel, even when it has no access to the causes or motives of that behaviour. The student on the bridge felt physiologically aroused; his interpreter module told him it was because he was attracted to the girl.

If Freud anticipated the neuroscientific vision of a brain engaged in the ongoing work of self-deception, he himself was influenced by the Romantic poets, who were fascinated by the mind's struggle to create and recreate the world, and the self, anew. Earlier I quoted Coleridge. Here is a fuller version of what he said:

> The primary imagination I hold to be the living power and prime agent of all human perception, and as a repetition in the finite mind of the eternal act of creation in the infinite I AM.

The philosopher Arthur Schopenhauer, a contemporary of Coleridge and himself a great influence on Freud, argued that our sense of self is an artfully constructed fiction:

> We know, it is true, something more of the course of our life than of a novel we have formerly read, but not much more. The principal events, the interesting scenes, have been impressed upon us; for the rest, a thousand events

have been forgotten for one that has been retained . . . It is true that, in consequence of our relation to the external world, we are accustomed to regard the subject of knowing, the knowing I, as our real self. This, however, is a mere function of the brain, and is not our real self. Our true self, the kernel of our inner nature, is that which is to be found behind this, and which really knows nothing but willing and not-willing.

The modern philosopher Daniel Dennett, whose ideas have been shaped in part by the discoveries of cognitive neuro-science, echoes Schopenhauer when he suggests we think of our conscious self as a virtuoso novelist, engaged in drafting and redrafting a story in which we are the central protagonist – the 'chief fictional character'.

A novel, if it is to work, requires some kind of dramatic conflict. The interpreter's job of providing a unified front for the mind's jostling factions is not always easy, and our strongest emotions are generated by the struggle to do so. For Freud, the drama of the psyche arises from the labouring of the ego to repress the knowledge of the uncon-scious. For an American psychologist whose theory of self-deception was almost as influential in the second half of the twentieth century as Freud's was in the first, it comes from the effort of persuading ourselves that we were right all along.

Cognitive Dissonance; the Infinite I Am

Leon Festinger used to pay people to lie. In one experiment, he asked participants to spend an hour performing a series of deliberately boring tasks, such as turning pegs in a pegboard. Unsurprisingly, nobody enjoyed the experience. The participants were then paid either one dollar or twenty dollars to tell a waiting participant that the tasks were fabulously interesting and fun. Almost all agreed to lie about their experience. Later on, they were interviewed. Those who had been paid one dollar to spin a story rated the tedious task much more enjoyable and satisfying than those who were paid twenty dollars. The less-highly paid subjects had come to believe their own lie.

Festinger's explanation was that it's easier to justify lying for twenty dollars than it is for one. Most people like to think of themselves as decent and honest, and after telling their lie, the people who got paid one dollar were left with two incompatible beliefs in their heads: 'I am a good person', and 'I just sold my integrity for a buck'. Unwilling to jettison the former belief, and unable to pretend that the new dollar bill in their wallet was a twenty, they smoothly manoeuvred their memories into alignment with their actions. The participants who got paid more experienced less of what Festinger called 'cognitive dissonance'. They were simply able to say to themselves, 'Yes, I lied, but twenty dollars is a lot of money. I did the right thing.'

Festinger was born in New York in 1919 to Jewish parents who had emigrated to America from Russia. A short, bespectacled man possessed of an intense, prickly manner, he held a rather pessimistic view of human nature. He admired the writings of Jean-Paul Sartre and Albert Camus, who observed that humans are creatures who spend their whole lives trying not to admit that their existence is absurd. In the late 1950s, Festinger developed his own ideas about how we manage to turn a blind eye to this unwelcome insight, the most famous of which was his theory of cognitive dissonance.

Benjamin Franklin once described the cunning way he had won over a difficult political opponent. Having heard that this man had in his library a copy of a rare and fascinating book, Franklin wrote him a note asking if he might borrow it. He received the book immediately, and about a week later sent it back with a note expressing deep gratitude. When they next met, the man was full of civility and warmth, and expressed a readiness to help Franklin out in any way he could. The two remained friends until death. Franklin later observed, 'He that has once done you a kindness will be more ready to do you another, than he whom you yourself have obliged.' In Festinger's terms, Franklin's adversary had found himself with two cognitions after lending the book: he was an opponent of

Franklin, and yet he had done him a favour. The way he resolved his dissonance was by telling himself he actually liked Franklin.

In Festinger's view, we constantly struggle to avoid cognitive dissonance in order to maintain our sense of who we are. Whenever we end up with contradictory ideas about the world, the anxiety generated gives us a strong hint that we need to change our behaviour, or our beliefs, to avoid the absurdity of thinking two different things at once. Usually, it's easier to change our beliefs. Faced with information that suggests we are wrong about something, we will try everything else first — making up reasons, blaming others, denying there's an issue at all — before changing our minds. If smokers want to quit but can't, they'll find justifications for continuing — it really won't do me any harm, my life will be shorter but fuller. If you spend a lot of money on a ticket for a concert, you'll make more effort to persuade yourself it was enjoyable afterwards, even if you were bored. The tougher the initiation into a group, like a university fraternity, the more committed you will subsequently be to that group.

Festinger took a deep interest in the history of religion, and in particular the recurrence of sects or cults that prophesied a worldwide cataclysm on one particular date or another that would sweep away everyone except for the true believers. Only those who believed in the teachings of the group would then enjoy salvation and eternal happiness. Festinger noted that when the predictions of these groups proved false, as they invariably did, the group rarely disbanded or dispersed, at least not immediately. After the initial dismay, the cultists would *strengthen* in their conviction, defy the scorn of non-believers, and take to the streets to assert, with increased fervour, the righteousness of their cause.

In 1954, when Festinger was thirty-five and working at the University of Minnesota, he came across a newspaper report of a doomsday cult that was prophesying the destruction of the human race at the hands of aliens. The cult was based not far away, in Lake City, a Chicago suburb. Festinger decided that this was too good an opportunity to miss. He and a few colleagues went to Chicago and joined the group incognito, pretending to be believers. Later, he published an account of his time with the Chicago cult that was refracted through his study of apocalyptic movements from history, including – strangest of them all – the cult of Sabbatai Zevi.

* * *

On 31 May 1665, an unhappy thirty-nine-year-old man knocked on the door of a house in Gaza, asking for help. The master of the house was Abraham Nathan ben Elisha Hayyim Ashkenazi, commonly known as Nathan of Gaza. Nathan was a young Jewish mystic – a kabbalist. At just twenty-two, he had gained a great reputation for the sophistication of his spiritual visions, the beauty of his divinely inspired prophecies, and the restorative power of his eloquence. When his visitor introduced himself, Nathan must have felt a shock of recognition — and excitement.

Sabbatai Zevi was the deeply wayward third son of a prosperous merchant from Smyrna. A more sensitive, bookish soul than his brothers, who became successful businessmen like their father, Zevi underwent a rabbinic training, before studying the kabbalah. It soon became clear, however, that no established school of religious thought could accommodate this bright but eccentric young man. Zevi had a temperament that would today be diagnosed as manic-depressive or bi-polar; after periods of wild exultation and hyperactivity he would sink into deep gloom and inaction. His mood swings became more frequent and more extreme as he grew older, and during his wild phases he committed terrible blasphemies and transgressions. He spoke the forbidden name of God, pronounced himself 'married' to a Torah scroll, committed unspeakable sex acts, and even declared himself the Messiah. For these and other crimes he was expelled successively from Smyrna, Salonika and Constantinople. When he was feeling placid-minded and normal, Zevi wondered if he wasn't diabolically possessed. But then he would be seized by his dark exuberance once again.

In the spring of 1665 Zevi's wandering journey took him to Gaza, and to Nathan, whose help he sought in exorcising his demons. Nathan of Gaza was the son of a distinguished rabbinical scholar and kabbalist from Jerusalem. After completing the first stage of his religious education, he took up the study of kabbalah in Gaza, where he settled with his new wife. Nathan was a gifted student, possessed of a highly original and inventive mind; as one historian of the period puts it, he combined 'intellectual power and capacity for profound thinking with imagination and strong emotional sensitivity'. Rather than being content with learning, Nathan developed his own ideas and ideology. By the time he met Zevi he was well on his way to developing a radical, all-encompassing system of thought, rooted in kabbalism but unique to him. It was the kind of worldview that explains everything, and accommodates anything. Nathan had first come across Zevi in Jerusalem, and had not thought much of his claim to messianic status. But in Gaza, during a fast, he had experienced an overpowering vision, lasting twenty-four hours, in which, as he later told it, he beheld the Messiah in the person of Sabbatai Zevi. And now here was Zevi, knocking at his door. What clearer sign could there be?

* * *

The Chicago cult had two leaders. Dr Thomas Armstrong, a physician who held a senior post at a nearby college, had a long-standing interest in the occult and in flying saucers. He was the group's spiritual authority. Marion Keech, a housewife, was its prime mover and organiser. In the autumn of 1954, Marion was at home when she received her first message from the spacemen. It came in the form of a high-density vibration that guided the pen in Marion's shaking hand across the paper in front of her. The news it scrawled out was not good: 'The uprising of the Atlantic bottom will submerge the land of the Atlantic seaboard; France will sink . . . Russia will become one great sea.' America would not be spared. Eventually the whole world would be submerged, 'for the purpose of purifying it of the earthlings, and creating the new order'.

After this first message more followed, in quick succession. The spiritual beings communicating with Marion revealed themselves to be called The Guardians. Their ruler was a God named Sanander. The Guardians gave Marion the exact time and date of humanity's impending destruction. At midnight on 21 December, only those who believed in Sanander would be saved.

Luckily, Marion knew just who to speak to about this. She had met Dr Armstrong at the local flying saucer club, where local people met to discuss the possibility of alien visitations. As soon as Marion told Dr Armstrong about her message, he understood the gravity of the situation. They agreed to tell the others from the club and to make preparations for the alien landing. Within a week or two they had gathered a group of around thirty believers, including several undercover social scientists.

In the weeks leading up to the flood date, Festinger and his colleagues were impressed by the solidarity and commitment of the group, which only seemed to grow stronger the more they were criticised or ridiculed by outsiders. The members endured fallings-out with family and friends, and threats from their neighbours to have them declared legally insane. Dr Armstrong was fired from his post; his sister filed a motion to take away his two children. One cult member sold her house and moved in with her infant daughter to Mrs Keech's home. Others quit their jobs and threw away their belongings. What did it matter if the whole world was against them when the whole world was about to be swept away?

Festinger noted that the group didn't proselytise. Although it issued one press release, announcing the news of the apocalypse, it did surprisingly little to spread the word of The Guardians or to recruit new members. As the day itself approached, dozens of requests for interviews with local newspapers and TV stations were ignored or refused by Marion, and every other member of the group. The researchers later remarked that the group behaved towards the outside world 'with an almost superior indifference'.

* * *

After listening to Sabbatai Zevi explain why he had come, Nathan told him he didn't need curing – that he was indeed the Messiah, whose arrival on earth signalled the End of Days and the salvation of the Jews. Zevi, who was used to derision, laughed uneasily at the young man's joke, but Nathan made it clear he was serious. The two spent the next few hours engaged in intense theological discussion, at the end of which Zevi accepted his messianic mission.

Zevi began to feel intensely, manically happy. He rode

around Gaza on horseback, announcing to its inhabitants that he was the Chosen One. He had done this before, of course, in other towns. But now Nathan was at his side, exuding conviction and providing learned disquisitions on why God had picked this moment for the Messiah to arrive, and why he had chosen Zevi to save His people. Gaza's rabbis joined in the acclamation. Zevi, dispensing charm and regal condescension in equal measure, appointed ambassadors to summon the tribes of Jerusalem.

This was just the beginning. Over the next six months, Nathan wrote long, closely argued letters to Jewish communities all over the world, bringing news of the Messiah and explaining that a new phase of history was starting. For everything that Zevi did, Nathan provided elaborate rationalisations, acting as the interpreter module to Zevi's impulsive *id*. Zevi set off on a roadshow, starting in Jerusalem and heading northwards to Smyrna and Aleppo. Everywhere he went, he was hailed as the Messiah.

In previous decades the Jews had endured one of the worst periods of expulsions and pogroms in their history. They desperately wanted to believe that better times were at hand. Excited that their saviour had finally arrived, they turned out in vast numbers to see him, but rabbinical communities were split. Younger ones tended enthusiastically to embrace Zevi and Nathan's ideas; the more conservative rabbis held their peace and hedged their bets.

Zevi now started to act with his old, wild extravagance: blaspheming, eating pork, and urging others to break the law. If a rabbi protested, Zevi would lead a mob to threaten his home. In Smyrna, he took an axe to the door of a synagogue that refused to recognise him, forcing his way in. Once inside, he announced the date of Redemption: 18 June 1666.

* * *

In Lake City, Chicago, the night of the Great Event arrived. At Marion Keech's house, squeezing into her living room, the groups' members gathered: college students, house-wives, a publisher, a hardware-store clerk and his mother, and Dr Armstrong. Everyone awaited new messages from Sanander and his assistants; nobody was sure what form they would take, or what exactly was about to happen – The Guardians were frustratingly vague on the precise details of the pick-up.

That evening, everything was laden with significance. When the phone rang and a sharp, sardonic voice said, 'Hey, there's a flood in my bathroom, wanna come over and celebrate?' the group expressed delight at what was clearly a coded communication from The Guardians. The members rehearsed the passwords they had been given, in call-and-response with the group leaders: 'I left my hat at home', 'I am my own porter'. . . When a tiny scrap of tin was discovered on the living-room rug the group took it as a message to remove every last piece of metal from their bodies. The women frantically tore out clasps from their brassieres, and one of the men – actually one of Festinger's researchers – had to be removed to the bedroom, where a panicked Dr Armstrong used a razor blade to cut out the metal zip from his trousers.[16]

As their time left on this earth became a matter of minutes, the group sat in silence, coats in laps. There was nothing left to say or do. Here is Festinger's description of the passing of midnight:

> In the tense silence two clocks ticked loudly, one about ten minutes faster than the other. When the faster of the two pointed to twelve-five, one of the observers remarked aloud on the fact. A chorus of people replied that midnight had not yet come. Bob Eastman affirmed that the slower clock was correct; he had set it himself only that afternoon. It showed only four minutes before midnight.
>
> These four minutes passed in complete silence except for a single utterance. When the [slower] clock on the mantel showed only one minute remaining before the guide to the saucer was due, Marion exclaimed in a strained, high-pitched voice, 'And not a plan has gone astray!' The clock chimed twelve, each stroke painfully clear in the expectant hush. The believers sat motionless.

Nobody said anything at first, but over the next minutes, and then hours, 'an atmosphere of despair and confusion settled over the group'. Dr Armstrong and Mrs Keech exhorted everyone to keep faith, but as the group offered, then discarded, explanation after explanation for what had just failed to happen, they started to lose their composure.

In Festinger's words, 'The group seemed near dissolution.' At 4.45 a.m., Marion Keech's hand shook into action and wrote out a message from above: 'The little group, sitting alone all night long, had spread so much light that God had saved the world from Destruction.' It was an elegant explanation, but it didn't quite break the gloom; one group member silently rose, put on his hat and coat, and left.

* * *

Throughout the winter of 1665–6, the Jewish world was in turmoil. From Frankfurt to Amsterdam, Prague to Constantinople, Jews prayed and fasted and took constant ritual baths in preparation for the End of Days. Many sold their possessions and went on pilgrimages to the Holy Land, hoping to catch a glimpse of Zevi. Poems were written, books printed, public processions organised. Something approaching mass hysteria broke out across the European continent. In Poland, there were riots in every major city.

Next, Zevi took his biggest step yet: he ventured to Turkey where, it was announced by Nathan, he would take the crown and make the Sultan his servant. His ship reached Turkish waters in February 1666. The Turkish authorities, who had heard about the disruption caused by Zevi in Europe, were taking no chances. They promptly detained Zevi's ship, put him in chains, and brought him ashore, where he was held in honourable captivity and allowed to receive visitors. Nathan rationalised this potentially embarrassing development to fit his theory, explaining that the Messiah's imprisonment was symbolic of his inward struggle with evil forces. Zevi maintained his pretensions from his prison in Gallipoli, convincing delegations of Constantinople Jews that the date he had set still stood.

June 18 1666 came and passed. In September, Zevi was summoned before the Council of Constantinople in the presence of the Sultan, who listened to the proceedings while hidden in a latticed alcove. Zevi was given a simple choice: convert to Islam, or die. He immediately opted for the former. He wore a turban, assumed the name of Aziz Mehmed Effendi and accepted the title 'Keeper of the Palace Gates', which came with a small government pension.

* * *

Marion received another missive from above, asking her to publicise the explanation. She called a local newspaper, and told them she had an urgent message. The whole group followed Marion's lead. They took turns to telephone the press and wire services, radio stations and magazines to spread their explanation of why the flood never came. This continued in the days that followed. Having shunned all attention prior to the appointed hour of The Great Event, the group now energetically sought it out. They also started to proselytise. Whereas before, potential recruits had been dealt with casually or turned away, now all visitors were enthusiastically received and engaged in discussion. The conspirators had become missionaries.

It was a strange paradox. Only when the group's dogma had been exposed to maximum ridicule – when the whole basis of their commitment to the cult proved to be an illusion – did they want to tell the world about it. Only when they had been proved indisputably wrong did they want to make arguments. It sounds crazy, but Leon Festinger didn't think the Lake City cultists were mad; he thought they were human.

Festinger published an account of his fieldwork in a book entitled *When Prophecy Fails*,[17] in which he argued that the more difficulty, embarrassment or pain people go through to get something, the more determined they will be to cherish it. The Lake City group had gone too far out along the branch, suffered too much scorn, and surrendered too much of their previous lives to retreat. Four hours after the flood had failed to come, Dr Armstrong told one of the researchers, 'I've had to go a long way. I've given up just about everything. I've cut every tie. I've burned every bridge. I've turned my back on the world. I can't afford to doubt. I have to believe.' He and the others knew that they weren't the kind of people to do things like this without good reason. So now reasons would be found. Reasons, and affirmation: to assuage their doubts, the cultists suddenly needed to see their beliefs reflected in other people. At the end of *When Prophecy Fails* Festinger concludes that it is precisely when the strongly held beliefs of a group have been challenged that it most feels the need to stick together, and to search for psychological reinforcement in numbers. He points out that the Christians' Messiah was not supposed to suffer pain. When Jesus cried out from the Cross his followers must have felt distressed, and perhaps suffered a momentary shock of doubt – before setting out to spread the word. At midnight on 21 December 1954, no space-craft came down to Lake City. The Atlantic sea did not rise up, nor did the heavens open. Denied affirmation by callous reality, the Lake City cultists sought it elsewhere – in other people.

The original meaning of confabulation is, roughly speaking, 'to make up stories together' (it derives from Latin: con, 'together' and fabula, 'fable'). Implicit in Festinger's study was the idea that all religions are gigantic confabulations which spring from the biggest dissonance of all: we want to believe the world makes sense, but it doesn't make sense. Indeed, all human culture, our symbols, myths and rituals, might be seen as a way of reconciling our inherent drive towards sense-making with the randomness of birth, death, and everything in between.

Festinger's logic is powerful, though ultimately it feels a little tinny as a way of explaining – or rationalising – the grandeur, beauty and *mystery* of our rationalisations, if that's what they are; the Lake City cult is not a simple analogue for the religion that inspired Chartres cathedral or the music of Bach. Perhaps, also, the logic can be reversed. Festinger argued that people seek the affirmation of others in order to make their fragile theories about the world seem more robust, but isn't it also possible that we make up our stories as a reason to reach out to others — that our lies form pathways to love?

* * *

When the news of his meek submission to the Sultan reached them, Sabbatai's followers were devastated. The euphoria that Nathan's letters somehow managed to sustain past 18 June now evaporated, leaving embarrassment and denial; the rabbis insisted that the affair had never taken place at all. Nathan of Gaza, however, was ready with yet another finely wrought explanation: while giving the appearance of submitting to the apostates, the Messiah had merely found it necessary to sink deep enough inside the realm of evil that he might explode it from within. The shame of apostasy was his final sacrifice.

Sabbatai Zevi died in 1676, still a servant of the Sultan. Nathan, who declared Zevi's death a mere 'occultation', died four years later. For years afterwards, Sabbatai's followers kept the faith. Unwilling to accept that their saviour had been a fraud or that the ideas they believed in so passionately were nonsense, they clung to the figure of Zevi, and to each other. They even created a new form of worship, based on the principle of pretend-apostasy. In Turkey, a Sabbatean sect called the Donmeh remained active and influential until well into the twentieth century. In public, they affiliated themselves with Islam; in private they celebrated Passover.

I Am Nice and in Control

The benefits and the dangers of self-deception

> *The faculty of self-deception, essential*
> *requisite for anyone wanting to guide others.*
> Giuseppe Tomasi di Lampedusa

People can persuade themselves they're good whilst performing the worst acts imaginable. Suicide bombers kill hundreds of innocent people and yet die convinced they are going to heaven. Members of the Sicilian mafia regard themselves as good Catholic men, murdering during the week and worshipping on Sunday. (The Catania boss Nitto Santapaola was so devout he had a small chapel constructed in his villa; he also once ordered four kids to be garrotted and thrown in a well.) Even the doctors who oversaw the gas chambers at Auschwitz convinced themselves that they were remaining true to the Hippocratic Oath – that by helping to exterminate Jews they were curing the *Volk* of a malignancy.

These are rare and extreme examples, of course, but

most people have a tendency to throw a flattering light on their actions. If a boss promotes an incompetent employee he happens to be attracted to, he will have little trouble reassuring himself she's the best person for the job; a middle-class socialist who sends her son to a fee-paying school will persuade herself she had no other option; a man who cheats at cards can convince himself that his opponents aren't worthy of fair play. 'So convenient a thing it is to be a reasonable creature,' said Benjamin Franklin, 'since it enables one to find or make a reason for every-thing one has a mind to do.'

Psychologists have noticed that we often combine opti-mism about our own motivations with a tendency to see ourselves as slightly more capable than we really are. This is sometimes referred to as the Lake Wobegon Effect, after Garrison Keillor's vision of a town in which 'all the women are strong, all the men are good looking, and all the chil-dren are above average.' In a survey of college students, eighty-eight percent of respondents rated themselves as in the top fifty per cent of drivers; and in a survey of college professors, ninety-five per cent declared themselves to be doing above-average work. Other studies suggest that we tend to overestimate our physical attractiveness, our intelligence, and our fairness to others. Most people in relationships believe their relationships to be better than most others and – yes – most parents think their children are smarter and nicer than other kids.

It's not that people are simply making errors. They are

deceiving themselves. People do store accurate information about themselves and the world, but keep it concealed in their subconscious until needed — just as our mind screens out most of the information it receives from our senses until there's reason to pay attention to it. In an adult variation of the Peeking Game, the economists Dan Ariely and Michael Norton asked college students to complete intelligence tests, and allowed half of them surreptitious access to an answer key. Those students with the answers outperformed those without — they'd been peeking. That wasn't so surprising. What was significant was that they tricked *themselves* into believing they were as intelligent as their fraudulently achieved scores suggested. When offered a monetary incentive to accurately forecast their performance on a future test (without the answers) they over-inflated their predictions, having persuaded themselves that their initial score was down to their unusually high intelligence. As a result they lost their money.

There is something amusing about this, and of course, self-deception is the source of much of our greatest comedy. From Malvolio to Mr Pooter, through David Brent to the X-Factor auditions, we love to laugh at the gap between the way people present themselves and the way they really are. Perhaps this is because we instinctively recognise that all of us need a little self-deception to get by.

Asked for a shorthand definition of sanity, you would probably say it had something to do with being free of illusions. When we think someone's in danger of going mad we say they're 'losing touch with reality'. For most of the twentieth century, this was an axiom of the mental health profession too. A report commissioned by the American government in 1958 concluded that, 'The perception of reality is called mentally healthy when what the individual sees corresponds to what is actually there . . . Mentally healthy perception means the process of viewing the world so that one is able to take in matters one wishes were different without distorting them to fit those wishes.' In 1988, Shelley Taylor and her collaborator Jonathon Brown published a paper which turned this wisdom on its head.

As a young psychologist Taylor worked with people who had suffered severe trauma or tragedy, such as rape victims or cancer patients. Interviewing them wasn't easy; Taylor describes it as 'a wrenching way to make a living'. The worst part of it was that Taylor couldn't help but notice how some patients developed self-deceiving fictions about their future. She would hear a cancer patient state with utter confidence that he would never get cancer again, even as she knew from his medical records that he would almost certainly die of the disease. But Taylor gradually realised that the patients who maintained these unrealistically optimistic beliefs were the ones most likely to make the fullest return to mental health. They may have been telling themselves lies, but the lies worked.

This led her to investigate the role that self-serving

fictions play in the lives of the healthy and happy amongst us, rather than just the traumatised. She arrived at a startling conclusion: the normal human mind works with a pronounced positive filter on reality. 'At every turn,' Taylor writes, '[the mind] construes events in a manner that promotes benign fictions about the self, the world, and the future.' We routinely over-estimate ourselves and — because other people are the only standard which we have to go by — underestimate others.

What Taylor calls 'positive illusions' fall into three broad categories. The first is an exaggerated confidence in our own abilities and qualities. These 'illusions of superiority' are extremely sticky: although people are very willing to believe that other people are prone to them, they can't help but think they're different. Emily Pronin calls this the 'bias blind spot'. She gave a group of psychology students a booklet describing eight common self-deceptions (or cognitive biases) and, after they'd read it, asked them to rate how susceptible they were to each bias compared to the average person. Each rated themselves as less affected by biases than other people. The strange, recursive loop of self-deception doesn't stop there: in a follow-up study Pronin explained to the subjects how and why they might have displayed this bias, but despite this they still insisted *their* self-assessments were objective, while the self-assessments of others would probably be biased.

The second class of positive illusion is unrealistic optimism; our over-confidence extends to feelings about how we will fare in the future. When students are asked to envision what their future lives will be like, they say they're more likely than their classmates to graduate top of the class, get a good job, high salary, and give birth to a gifted child — and less likely to have a drinking problem, get divorced, or suffer from cancer. In the short term, we tend to over-estimate how likely we are to lose weight, give up smoking, or complete difficult tasks. In one study, subjects predicted how quickly they (or others) would complete various work projects, and whether they would meet their deadlines. They were over-optimistic about themselves, and over-pessimistic about others. The reason for this seemed to be that their own good intentions loomed much larger in their minds than rational assessment of their own past behaviour. Our inflated sense of potential is underpinned by our tendency towards self-absorption.

The third category is an exaggerated sense of control. We're prone to imagine that through our physical dexterity we can affect things we patently can't — when rolling the dice in a game of craps, people throw harder when they want high numbers and softer for low numbers — and we tend to think our decisions are shaping the world even when they're not. In one experiment, a group of successful professionals were placed in front of computer screens on which a line flickered up and down in imitation of a stock market index like the FTSE 100. The subjects were asked to press a series of buttons which, they were told, may or may not affect the progress of the line. Afterwards they were asked to estimate their effectiveness at moving the line. Many of them were convinced that they had made the line go up. In reality, the buttons had no effect whatsoever on the line. (The subjects in this test were all traders at an investment bank.)

When bad things happen we're much less likely to take responsibility for them. To illustrate how reluctantly people assume blame, Shelley Taylor quotes from drivers' explanations to police:

'As I approached an intersection, a sign suddenly appeared in a place where a stop sign had never appeared before. I was unable to stop in time to avoid an accident.'

'The telephone pole was approaching. I was attempting to swerve out of its way when it struck my front end.'

In the pithy summary of psychologist Eliot Aronson – a disciple of Leon Festinger – the average person will go a long way to persuade themselves that 'I am nice, and in control.' Anthony Greenwald compressed this even further when he coined the word *beneffectance* to describe the normal human tendency to interpret reality so as to present ourselves as both beneficial and effective. Whenever either of these propositions are thrown into question, we are good at inventing stories that resolve the inconsistency between our actions and our self-image. Most of the time we're not aware of doing so.

This isn't necessarily a bad thing. It makes it easier for us to interact and cooperate with other people if we assume that we are conscious, reasoning, reasonably nice people, and that most other people are like us (just slightly less so). If I weren't able to deceive myself about my ability to control my destiny I'd become petrified by self-doubt. The philosopher William Hirstein has proposed that the opposite of self-deception is not self-knowledge, but obsessive-compulsive disorder: 'Whereas the self-deceived person might say to himself "It'll be OK if I don't brush my teeth tonight," the person with OCD will get up and brush his teeth again and again. The nagging thought, so easily suppressed by self-deceivers, rages out of control in OCD, cannot be ignored, must be acted on.'

There is good reason to think that our over-confidence is a trait that provided a survival or reproductive advantage and was therefore spread by natural selection. A degree of unrealistic optimism about ourselves would have helped us survive in the treacherous ancestral environment, and confidently impress potential mates. Now that we live in centrally heated houses rather than caves, we still rely on illusions to carry us through life. We imagine that having children will make us happier even though empirical studies suggest this is, at best, uncertain (anticipating our own happiness isn't the only reason we have children, of course, but it certainly smooths the decision). We fall in love with a person we believe is uniquely suited to us, and this helps us stick with them for long enough to raise those children. We believe that though our lives on this planet will end, we will live on in another form, and — somewhat paradoxically — that helps us to live longer. Without the ability to fool ourselves we would be sadder, limper, less dynamic creatures, unwilling to meet or rise to challenges. As Shelley Taylor puts it, positive illusions are 'the fuel that drives creativity, motivation and high aspirations'.

There is a group of people with no positive illusions, who get closer to the truth about themselves, who have a more realistic perception of their abilities, of how the future will pan out and of the amount of control they have over things. Philip Larkin described them as 'the less deceived'. Psychiatrists call them clinically depressed. In various studies, depressed people have been shown to have a firmer grip on reality than most. They don't have an exaggerated belief in their own competence or goodness, or remember the past with a deceptively warm glow, or over-estimate their agency in tasks of control. *Severely* depressed people can live with negative illusions about themselves. But the moderately depressed, in Taylor's words, 'appear to have more accurate views of themselves, the world, and the future than do normal people'. Psychologists call this phenomenon 'depressive realism'. Prior to the emergence of this category of disorder most researchers and clinicians focused on how the depressed person distorts reality. As it turns out, they're not distorting it enough.

It appears that most of us need a cushion of self-deception to protect us from the harsh edges of reality. In the words of the social psychologist Roy Baumeister, we have an 'optimal margin of illusion'.

The actual margin fluctuates from day to day. In Joni Mitchell's song 'Both Sides Now', our oscillations from illusion to reality and back again are described in exquisitely bitter-sweet poetry. In the first verse, clouds are ecstatically celebrated as 'rows and floes of angel hair', 'feathered canyons' and 'ice-cream castles in the air'. By the second verse they have lost their lustre – they block the sun, drop rain and snow and generally get in the way of the singer's life. Love is either 'moons and Junes and Ferris wheels' or 'just another show' made for someone's cheap amusement. On the one side lies glorious illusion, on the other, mundane and dispiriting truth. At the end of the song, the singer reflects that though she's looked at life from both sides, it's the illusions that persist: 'I really don't know life at all'. Apart from being a beautiful song, it's an unnervingly acute description of the normal human relationship with reality.

The Self-Deceptive Habits of Highly Effective People

Although positive illusions are very common, some people have a larger dose of them than others. As an undergraduate, the psychologist Joanna Starek had been a competitive swimmer, and she often wondered why it was that two swimmers of similar physiological abilities could achieve very different levels of success. She guessed that the more successful athletes were the ones who were better at telling themselves they were better, even when some part of them knew they weren't.

Later, Starek and her research partner Caroline Keating decided to find out if there was something to this. They used a 'self-deception' questionnaire first created by two psychologists called Harold Sackeim and Ruben Gur (the same Gur who now researches fMRI lie detection). It consists of twenty rather pointed questions, including, 'Is it important that others think highly of you?', 'Have you ever doubted your sexual adequacy?' and even 'Do you enjoy your bowel movements?' Subjects can answer on a graded scale ranging from *not at all* to *very much so*. The idea is that nearly everyone, if they are being completely honest, will say yes to most of these questions – so the people who consistently reply with a firm 'no' are more likely to be habitual self-deceivers.

In the original experiment, Sackeim and Gur asked their subjects to fill out this questionnaire and then recorded them saying the words 'Come here.' They then played each participant a tape of lots of different people saying the same phrase, with the subject's own version mixed in somewhere at random. Afterwards, many said they hadn't been able to pick out their own voice on the tape. However, their physiological responses — pulse, blood pressure and perspiration showed spikes of activity at the moments when the subject's own voice appeared in the mix. It was clear, then, that some part of the participants *had* recognised their own voice, even if they hadn't consciously registered it. This is the essence of self-deception — the ability to hold two contradictory beliefs, but to allow only one of them into consciousness. The subjects who were unable to recognise their own voice were the ones who scored highly on the self-deception questionnaire.

Starek and Keating invited forty members (twenty men and twenty women) of the swimming team at a college in upstate New York to complete Sackheim and Gur's questionnaire. As an extra test, the swimmers were also asked to look through a stereoscope as pairs of words, in which one was designed to be positively or negatively charged for them, and one neutral (for example *fear-hear*, *lose-nose*, or *medal-pedal*), were flashed simultaneously to their left or right eyes. As we've seen, perception is to some extent the servant of our desires, and previous studies had shown that the brain will often deal with this potentially confusing double-vision by picking the word the subject *wants* to see. The more often the swimmers screened out the negative words and saw only the positive ones, the higher their self-deception score. When Starek and Keating matched the overall scores from both tests against the results of the swimmers in competition, they found a clear correlation between the tendency to self-deceive and qualification for national championships. The swimmers who were good at lying to themselves were consistently swimming faster in big competitions. In her subsequent paper, Starek noted that what she and other psychologists call 'self-deception' is called 'championship thinking' by sports coaches.

The link between self-deception and over-achievement isn't restricted to sport. It's been shown that people who are talented self-deceivers are more likely to be successful at school or in business than those who aren't. Sometimes people will persuade themselves and others that they believe in something that *will* be true, even if it isn't yet; a study of American students showed that the ones who dishonestly exaggerated their grade averages in interviews subsequently improved their grades up to the level they claimed at the time.[18]

Such overreaching doesn't just benefit those who enjoy it; it is an engine of economic growth and human betterment. In *The Theory Of Moral Sentiments*, Adam Smith describes 'a poor man's son, whom heaven in its anger has visited with ambition'. The man looks around him and admires the wealth and luxury of the rich, their palaces, carriages and retinue of servants. Regarding himself as naturally lazy, he thinks that 'if he had attained all these, he would sit still contentedly, and be quiet, enjoying himself in the thought of the happiness and tranquillity of his situation.' Enchanted by this distant idea, he devotes his life to the attainment of it. But the serenity he foresees is an illusion, a trick. He becomes wealthy, but he has to work so hard that he can never relax. 'Through the whole of his life, he pursues the idea of a certain artificial and elegant repose which he may never arrive at, for which he sacrifices a real tranquillity that is at all times in his power.' The man's self-deception has brought him real achievements however, and even more significantly, it has benefited society. 'It is this deception,' says Smith, 'which rouses and keeps in continual motion the industry of mankind':

> It is this which first prompted them to cultivate the ground, to build houses, to found cities and commonwealths, to invent and improve all the sciences and arts, which ennoble and embellish human life; which have entirely changed the whole face of the globe, have turned the rude forests of nature into agreeable and fertile plains, and made the trackless and barren ocean a new fund of subsistence, and the great high road of communication to the different nations of the earth.

The economic historian John V.C. Nye has argued that countries become economically stagnant when their business people become too rational and sensible. Every dynamic economy needs its share of what Nye calls 'lucky fools'; over-optimistic entrepreneurs who are prepared to take irresponsible risks. It's certainly true that without people prepared

to ignore the prevailing wisdoms, disregard public information and follow their instincts, many of our biggest inno-
vations and creative leaps forward wouldn't have happened.
Every year thousands of people with vaulting ambitions
start new companies in full awareness that the odds are
against them achieving the kind of world-changing success
of which they dream. Most fail, or settle for something less,
but a few of those companies become Apple or Starbucks
or Dyson. We write symphonies and novels that are unlikely
to be any good, and search for the secret of human life in
the knowledge that everyone else has tried and failed. Just
occasionally, somebody under such an illusion writes
Catch-22, composes the *Eroica* Symphony, or discovers DNA.
As George Bernard Shaw observed, 'Reasonable people adapt
themselves to the world. Unreasonable people attempt to
adapt the world to themselves. All progress, therefore,
depends on unreasonable people.'

Of course, exceptionally over-confident people are also
the ones most likely to leave behind some wreckage in
their wake. The psychologist Ellen Langer had her subjects
play a betting game in which cards were drawn entirely
at random and the players had to bet on whose card was
highest. Each subject played against both a well-dressed,
self-assured opponent (the 'dapper'), and a shabbily dressed,
boorish opponent (the 'schnook'). Her subjects took far
more risks against the schnook. They thought, 'I'm better
than he is, I can win this'. The game was pure chance,
and the participants knew it. But their high confidence

in one area ('I'm better than that schnook') irrationally spilt over into another ('I'll draw better cards'). This fluidity is a key mechanism of over-confidence and it helps to explain why, in 1990, the top executives at AOL and Time Warner decided that they could run each other's businesses (the merger proved to be one of the biggest blunders in business history) or why, in the decade leading up to 2008, many bank executives concluded that if they were competent at borrowing and lending then they would also be good at gambling on the capital markets.

This effect works both ways. Observers often assume that because somebody is good at something (say, public speaking) then they will probably be good at something else (say, governing). In organisations where it's not crystal clear who is contributing what — that's to say, most organisations — over-confident people tend to get promoted quicker and further. This is because they send out more 'competence cues': they talk louder, speak more assertively, make emphatic gestures — and we tend to assume these things mean they must be good at their job. A feedback loop is created: they get promoted, which makes them more confident, which spins them further up the hierarchy. Then these people hire and promote other people in their own image, until the boardroom table is populated by self-assured people who speak well and are possessed of a rock-solid — and often unjustified — confidence in the wisdom of their own decisions.

In time though, the over-confident and under-competent

get found out, don't they? Not necessarily. Over-confident people are more likely to take risky decisions, and as long as they're not insanely risky, there's a good chance some of them will pay off, especially if the conditions in which they're operating are favourable – a booming industry or rising market. In these situations, their failures are written off as bad luck and their successes attributed to innate brilliance. As a result, they acquire superstar status and the salary to go with it. Only if they're unlucky does something so catastrophic happen as a result of one of their decisions that they can't escape the blame. Such catastrophes can arise when two exceptionally over-confident sets of people collide with one another.

The Clash of Positive Illusions: Self-deception in Warfare

On the evening of 15 November 1532, the Spanish explorer Francisco Pizarro led a small band of weary men down a mountain in the northern highlands of Peru and into the town of Cajamarca. In the town square, he explained his plan. The Inca emperor, Atahualpa, was to meet them there the next day, ostensibly to open a negotiation over land and gold, and he would be surrounded by his vast armies. This, said Pizarro, would be the perfect moment to capture the emperor and hold him to ransom. Exactly what Pizarro's troops thought about this plan is unrecorded, but they were a long way from home and many miles from their nearest countrymen, so had little option but to set up camp in the square and try to get some rest before the next day. As night fell the Spanish saw something beautiful and terrifying: thousands of flickering lights surrounded the town, as if the night sky had been draped over the mountains. Each light was a campfire, lit to warm members of Atahualpa's army. In an attempt to keep spirits from breaking, Pizarro's brother Hernando told the men he estimated there were forty thousand Incas, though all knew there were at least twice that number. The Spanish numbered one hundred and sixty-eight. Not one of them slept that night.

In the morning, Pizarro ordered his troops to conceal themselves in forts around the square and wait for his command. From their hiding places they watched as a wide river of Inca soldiers advanced slowly down the mountain towards the town. After several long hours they heard voices raised in song, and hundreds of Inca warriors filed into the square, the sun glinting off their jewellery. Atahualpa himself was carried in on a litter lined with brightly coloured parrot feathers, bedecked with gold and silver plates and hoisted by eighty chieftains in ceremonial dress. The watching Spanish soldiers felt sick with fear, some urinating involuntarily. They could hardly have been more certain that they were about to meet violent deaths.

After a brief meeting with the Spanish priest, during

which Atahualpa angrily rejected a demand that he and his people should convert to Christianity, Pizarro gave the order to attack. The Spaniards sounded trumpet blasts, opened fire from their clumsy but noisy guns, and rushed out of their hiding places. Many of them were riding horses, which the Incas had never seen before. Stunned by the noise and the horrifying spectacle of half-men, half-beasts bearing down on them at tremendous speed, Atahualpa's warriors panicked, dropped their weapons and fled. As they did so, they ran into each other and piled on top of one another, making them easy prey to the Spaniards who ran them through with their swords. Amidst the bloody chaos, Pizarro captured the emperor. He held Atahualpa to ransom for eight months and extracted a staggeringly large haul of gold in return for his freedom. After taking delivery of it, he reneged on his promise and executed him. The Incas — who had been obeying Atahualpa's orders from captivity — were utterly reliant on the man they revered as a sun god. His death left them frantic and disunited, making subsequent Spanish victories much quicker and easier.

The battle of Cajamarca was perhaps the most astonishing upset in the history of warfare; at least seven thousand Incas were killed by fewer than two hundred Spanish fighters. It was decisive in the European conquest of the Americas, and thus a pivotal point in the biggest and most significant migration in human history. It was made possible by the superior technology of the Spanish — swords made of steel, clumsy but terrifying guns — and by their horses. But that it was embarked upon at all, given the wildly asymmetric nature of the contest, is a tribute to Pizarro's powers of persuasion; he had to convince his men that such a victory was remotely possible in order to stop them fleeing or rebelling when they glimpsed the extent of Atahualpa's army. And before that, he had to persuade himself.

From this side of history, Pizarro's optimism looks visionary. In the face of his adversary's overwhelming numerical superiority he saw something that nobody else could see — that a shock and awe strategy might enable his tiny band of *conquistadors* to overcome the massed ranks of Incas. But what if he'd been wrong?

Three hundred and fifty years later, at the Battle of Little Bighorn, General Custer, perhaps inspired by the legendary tale of Pizarro's victory, led his force of six hundred and seventy-five men into battle against three thousand Indians with a cry of, 'Hurrah boys, we've got them!' Custer's army was annihilated and the general himself was killed. In retrospect, Custer was a disaster waiting to happen. His sole talent was for recklessness; he had finished thirty-fourth and last in his class at West Point, and later was nearly expelled from the army on two occasions for misconduct. But when the Civil War came, what one officer called his 'desperate gallantry' caught the eye of the generals. He was promoted, found himself at the forefront of some dramatic victories, and capped a glorious war by receiving the Confederate flag of truce at Appomattox. In his own mind, he was a brilliant as well as fearless leader of men, rather than a man who had ridden his luck further than he had any right to expect.

Following the war, Custer's star waned. He was involved in botched campaigns against Native Americans. By the time that President Ulysses Grant ordered the army to deal with the Sioux and Cheyenne forces occupying land between the Yellowstone River and Montana's Bighorn Mountains, Custer was yearning to restore the shine to his reputation. On 25 June 1876, he waved away the suggestion that he arm his regiment with Gatling guns, disdained the pleas for caution from men who knew the terrain and enemy better than he did, ignored the carefully planned orders of his commanding officers, and led his men to their deaths.

The Duke of Wellington remarked that, 'There is nothing on earth so stupid as a gallant officer.' If Pizarro had lost his audacious gamble we might regard him as we regard Custer, or the hundreds of lesser known commanders who led small forces of men into the jaws of larger armies: as an irresponsible, delusional fool. Throughout military history there have been many more Custers than Pizarros, enough for a whole field of study to be devoted to their blunders – that of 'military incompetence'. Again and again, generals deceive themselves, and often their civilian masters, into thinking that unlikely victories are possible. Sometimes they are right; more often they are proved wrong. According to Norman Dixon, one of a handful of historians to apply a psychological analysis to military history, the tendency of military leaders to 'under-esti-mate the enemy and over-estimate the capabilities of one's own side' is a persistent feature of military disasters. Unrealistic over-confidence in rapid victory was a signif-icant cause of the second Boer War, the First World War, the Second World War, and the Bay of Pigs fiasco.

The problem is not just that a tendency to over-confi-dence seems to be built into normal human psychology; it's that military leaders are even more prone to it than the rest of us. Like Starek's championship swimmers, an exceptionally successful soldier is likely to be good at deceiving himself — it would help him perform well under stress, and to instil confidence in himself and others that victory is possible even in desperate situations. If he makes the odd mistake then, with luck, little harm is done. But when he's acclaimed by his peers, promoted to the senior ranks of command and involved in decisions about battles and wars, his natural over-confidence can cost hundreds or even thousands of lives

In democratic societies, the civilians in charge of the military may also be cut from this cloth; successful politi-cians are likely to be particularly talented self-deceivers. During his 2008 campaign for the presidency, Barack Obama remarked that, at some level, anybody who runs for president is a megalomaniac; you have to be at least half-crazy to think you should be in charge of the country, and that enough other people will agree for it to come true. Of course, if nobody convinced themselves of this, nobody would be president, but it leaves us with a ruling class that is unusually prone to excessive optimism. Indeed, Michael Handel, a scholar of military strategy, has suggested that when it comes to war, politicians are even more likely to self-deceive than generals, because politicians are often dealing with vague matters like an adversary's intentions or long-term policy rather than with 'hard' evidence like aerial photographs and tank and troop concentrations. Perhaps they are also even more likely to think of the contest in moral terms, as a battle between good and evil in which they are, invariably, on the side of righteousness.

Dominic Johnson, author of *Overconfidence and War; the Havoc and Glory of Positive Illusions*, has designed a scale of self-deception (see overleaf). Should the military only promote officers who don't appear to be over-confident, and should voters do the same with politicians? Not necessarily; a generous measure of self-deception, when combined with other qualities, can certainly make for a better leader. 'Force, and fraud, are in war the cardinal virtues,' said Thomas Hobbes, and a measure of self-deception helps with both. Deceiving yourself about your ability to win a fight enhances your combat performance; it also helps to bluff better, and thus to inspire confidence in

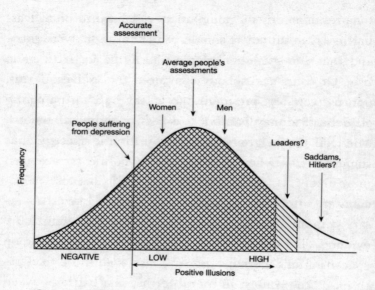

Conceptual scheme of variation in positive illusions among the population at large.

your troops and fear in your opponents. The most efficient way to see off a rival, or group of rivals, is to bluff them into backing down. If the bluff works, then one side may 'win' but both have been saved loss of life. When two sets of over-confident bluffers come into conflict, however, a catastrophic war is more likely, because both sides are over-estimating their chances of victory and will stop at nothing to prove themselves right. The biological anthropologist Richard Wrangham argues that this helps explain why there have been so many irrationally destructive wars in human history.

'Always remember,' said Winston Churchill, 'however sure you are that you can easily win, that there would not be a war if the other man did not think he also had a chance.' It's a warning our leaders tend to be inclined, by nature, to ignore. We are left with a troubling paradox: self-deception may be useful to the individual and even beneficial to the group, but deadly for the species as a whole.

'Everyone Started Lying': Saddam's Last Stand

> *The better part of war is deceiving.*
> Saddam Hussein

The 2003 Iraq war was a grisly example of two sets of illusions coming together to produce catastrophe. Much effort has already been expended in analysing the West's miscalculations; here I'm going to focus on the Iraqi perspective because, for all the mistakes made by the US and its allies, Saddam's were at least as significant.

After 11 September 2001, a steady drumbeat of pronouncements from the American government signalled that the US was preparing to disarm and overthrow by force a regime it had already declared its intention to remove. As we now know, Saddam didn't pursue a serious weapons of mass destruction programme after 1998. Yet he managed to convince everyone, including Western intelligence agencies, his neighbours in the region, and his own people, that he was doing so. If he had acted quickly, Saddam might have struck an agreement with the US and its allies, enabling him to stay in power. But he made no such attempt, and never backed down from his bluff, even when it was clear to everyone that the United States, under the second President Bush, was serious about removing him. Neither did Saddam do much to prepare his military for war; the swift collapse of Iraq's defences came as a welcome but baffling surprise to the invaders. He didn't even arrange his own escape: seven months after the invasion, the dictator was found hiding in a rabbit-hole near his family home. For over twenty-three years, Saddam had survived internal revolts, assassination attempts, two wars, destabilising defections, and concerted international efforts to remove him. Why did this master of self-preservation simply walk into the fire in 2003? The answer has much to do with the dynamics of deceit.

Following his capture, Saddam himself provided his interrogators with little insight about his pre-war calculations — he was too intent on presenting himself as heir to the great Arab heroes of the past. But we now have a much clearer idea of his thinking than we did at the time. After Baghdad fell, the US military scooped up many of the regime's most sensitive documents from government ministries and Saddam's palaces, including thousands of hours of recorded conversations between Saddam and his inner circle (Saddam had the Nixonian habit of taping all of his meetings and phone calls). As part of a 'lessons learned' exercise, the army handed over this vast dossier to a team led by Kevin Woods, a defence analyst, retired army officer, and former member of the US Joint Forces Command.

Woods also spent more than three months in Baghdad in the summer of 2003 talking to former members of the Iraqi army and government, who were by then in the custody of the coalition. He would sit down, put a map on the table and invite them to tell him everything. 'I'm not here to interrogate you,' he assured them. 'I'm here to get your story.' These were experienced, proud men who were keen to take this chance to let the world know about the sacrifices they and their troops had made in impossible circumstances, and most were happy to talk.[19] Over a period of more than five years, Woods pieced together their testimony with the documentary evidence to create a detailed picture of how Saddam's regime prepared – or didn't prepare – for war. Woods discovered that the world from the point of view of Saddam in early 2003 looked very different to the world as seen by the West.

When American soldiers entered Iraq, they were surprised and grateful that the Iraqis were not better prepared to defend themselves. For instance, the Iraqi army failed to blow up bridges across the Euphrates, enabling their enemies to advance at much greater speed than they would otherwise have done. After the fall of Baghdad, a senior Iraqi official was asked what he had imagined would happen when the coalition invaded. The official recalled that he and his colleagues had given little thought to it, being more concerned with potential threats from Turkey and Iran than any threat from America. It was a stunning insight into the delusional mindset of the whole regime, a mindset that had melded with that of Iraq's leader.

Most of the world viewed the 1991 Gulf War (Desert Storm) as a humiliation for Saddam. But faced with two contradictory cognitions – his army was devastated by the Americans and he was forced to withdraw from Kuwait, versus his self-perception as an invincible leader of the Arab world – Saddam chose to see it as a victory. After all, he and his regime had survived in the face of accumulated Western might. This belief was reinforced when the first President Bush lost his 1992 re-election attempt, a defeat for which Saddam took credit. In the face of America's renewed threats, Saddam remained sceptical and unperturbed. He reminded his advisers that even if the Americans were serious, this time they had only half the number of troops and fewer allies, even though 'Little Bush' wanted to go further than his father and occupy Baghdad itself. To Saddam, *America vs Iraq: The Sequel* would be a pale retread of the first, but with an even more glorious ending for Iraq.

Saddam's officials, rather than telling him the truth — that America seemed quite willing and more than able to remove him by force — told him what they knew he wanted to hear. He was reassured by his foreign ministers that America and Britain would never go to war without Russia and France, and by his generals that non-existent state-of-the-art weapons systems were coming along nicely. The military internalised Saddam's views, focusing more on threats from within the country and from their neighbours than from the US and UK. This delusion was sustained even after the invasion; the reason the army didn't blow up the Euphrates bridges was because they anticipated having to quell an internal rebellion after the war once the Americans had stopped or retreated. Saddam's personal secretary told Woods that even ten days after the US invasion, Saddam was sublimely confident of prevailing.

Admiral John Godfrey, Britain's head of Naval Intelligence during World War II, noted that when presented with two items of contradictory information, Nazi leaders were always 'inclined to believe the one that fits in best with their own previously formed conceptions'. Hitler's officers would deliberately distort and even invent evidence to confirm what he already believed. Stalin famously refused to believe that the Nazis were about to invade in 1941, despite the massive build-up of German troops on his border. Saddam's regime was beset by the weaknesses that Godfrey identified as 'wishfulness' and 'yesmanship'. Everyone knew the legendary story of Riyadh Ibrahim, the former health minister. During a low point in the Iraq–Iran war Saddam asked his ministers for candid advice. Ibrahim had the temerity to suggest that Saddam might consider stepping down temporarily, and resume his presidency once a peace deal was brokered. Saddam had him carted away immediately. The next day, pieces of the minister's chopped-up body were delivered to his wife. In the delicate words of one of Ibrahim's former colleagues, 'this powerfully concentrated the minds of ministers'. Twenty years after it happened this story continued to haunt those officials who considered telling Saddam anything he might not want to hear.

Nevertheless, at least one of them did so. Four years after the first Gulf War, a senior Republican Guard dared to challenge the regime's military orthodoxy. This is how he described the moment to Woods:

There was a big military science lecture and conference. Saddam attended along with most of the military leadership. Three of us were scheduled to make presentations. The central idea of my presentation was simple . . . our capabilities were weakening. The Americans' technological capabilities were growing . . . By 1995 we knew we were moving towards conflict and lacked the capability. I said we should change the picture of the whole Iraqi military. We need to change from a heavy mechanised force to a light infantry force. We should make simple light infantry formations and start fighting right away in a guerrilla war. Like in Vietnam – fight and with-draw. I was the first presenter and Saddam became very angry at my thesis. I was singled out as being a mental hostage of American thinking . . . Saddam was so mad at my presentation that the other presenters who were going to say something similar became too scared and changed their reports . . . It was around this time that everyone started lying.

Saddam had created a punitive environment; one in which the rational survival strategy for everyone was to lie about everything.[20] In the end he and his country became victims of the insidious symbiosis between deception and self-deception.

* * *

Robert Trivers alighted on evolutionary biology after studying, successively, mathematics, law and American history. Upon falling in love with Darwinian theory, he realised that nobody had yet arrived at a convincing evolutionary explanation of human social behaviour and set about remedying the oversight. In the early 1970s, while still a graduate student, he published a series of five brilliant papers that included radical new theories of altruism, parenting, and self-deception.

Trivers's theory was that human beings developed the capacity to deceive themselves in order to become better deceivers, and thus better competitors, in the Machiavellian arms-race of deception and counter-deception. Those who wanted to persuade a potential mate or ally of their good intentions would be better at it if they could deceive themselves without 'leakage' of knowledge or intent; and the most efficient way to simulate truth-telling would be to erase internal awareness of the deception. The best liars would be those who were better at lying to themselves because they would actually believe their own deceptions when they made them. They would be more likely to survive and pass on their genes; hence our gift for self-deception.

Trivers's theory is very plausible, and if it seems a little pat – it is, after all, a truism that the best liars are people who believe their lies – it offers a useful way of thinking about the relationship between deception and self-deception in organisations. Each begets the other. People tell their superiors what they think they want to hear, so as to avoid the perception of hesitancy, a lack of conviction, or disloyalty. The ones that are best at doing this get promoted. Their superiors become even more confident in their own convictions. As everyone in the organisation cleaves to the same script, everyone starts to believe it, even when it contradicts the facts. In organisations dominated by an over-confident and over-powerful leader, a virtually seamless alternative reality is formed.

There is an important distinction between illusions and delusions. The normal person might be an unrealistic optimist, but he or she is far from oblivious to reality. Most of us are capable of responding to new facts that dispel our illusions — even if it takes us longer to do so than it should. A person, or an organisation, can be said to be deluded when they manage to exclude all new information, however pertinent or dramatic, that threatens to undermine a cherished illusion. In Shelley Taylor's succinct summary, 'Delusions are false beliefs that persist despite the facts. Illusions accommodate them, though perhaps reluctantly.'

The historian Christopher Andrew has argued that one of the main purposes of an intelligence service in a one-party state is to reinforce the regime's misperceptions of the outside world. In Saddam's Iraq, every part of the national security apparatus conspired to shut out information that conflicted with Saddam's version of reality, thus creating a vortex of deception and self-deception. The tragedy is that the West became sucked into it too.

* * *

When it came to WMD, Saddam was attempting to juggle two conflicting objectives. On the one hand, he wanted potential rivals within his country and from the region to think of him as the wrong guy to tangle with. He often reminded his advisers that Iraq lived in a dangerous neighbourhood where even the perception of vulnerability drew predators; chemical and nuclear weapons were the equivalent of a BEWARE THE DOG sticker on Iraq's front door. On the other hand, he knew that as long as the West believed he had WMD, he would endure crippling sanctions and face the threat of American military action. So he allowed in the UN inspectors while signalling to his neighbours that he wasn't *really* doing as the Americans wished. But of course, foreign leaders noticed him make the same hints and boasts, which strengthened their suspicion that Saddam was hiding something.

Saddam Hussein was far from stupid or hot-headed. He was a talented reader of other people's intentions and emotions; as Kevin Woods points out, he had to be in order to survive for so long as head of a country riven by tribal, familial and sectarian rivalries, and constantly threatened by external enemies.[21] Saddam's ability to read other people, however, deteriorated precipitously the further his interlocutors were from home. By necessity, he was a pronounced Cynic (rather than a Truster), and not nearly as good as he thought at divining the motivations of foreign leaders, especially those outside of the Middle East. Like the participants in Ellen Langer's card game, he too readily allowed his confidence in an area of competence to flow into one of incompetence.

By the time Saddam realised that the Americans were serious about invading, it was too late. As 2002 drew to a close, he accepted that UN inspectors should be given full access and ordered his officers to remove all traces of previous WMD programmes. When the Americans tapped into this frantic clearing-up activity, they viewed it through the prism of a decade of deceit and assumed it was an effort to hide an ongoing programme. When they arrived in Iraq and turned up nothing, they were amazed. (So were Iraqi officials, who had assumed that if Bush didn't find WMD, he would plant them.)

Perhaps part of the reason that Western intelligence agencies were fooled is that they picked up on the genuine beliefs of many in Saddam's government that the programme persisted. Woods asked Iraq's head of research into WMD what he thought was a straightforward question: did he ever think it possible there was a secret supply of WMD he didn't know about? To Woods's surprise, the man nodded. He explained that the regime was too compartmentalised and secretive for any one person – apart from Saddam, perhaps – to know everything. But the main reason he thought that Iraq might possess WMD was because '*Your* president said it was so.' He and other senior Iraqi officials couldn't fathom that America would bring itself to the brink of war unless it had very good reasons to believe in the existence of Iraq's illegal weapons. So they came to believe it themselves. After all, the CIA wouldn't get something like this wrong.

Saddam had constructed a hall of mirrors into which all parties were drawn, and within which each saw only what they wanted to see. In the year leading up to war, Saddam loudly declared that he had no WMD, and that he would never back down in the face of American threats. In a collective and calamitous failure of mind-reading, Western leaders and diplomats assumed that the first was a lie and the second a bluff. But, for once, Saddam was telling the truth. As Woods says, Saddam may have been deluded, but 'so too was the United States in thinking he was *not* deluded.'

Keeping Politicians Honest

One of the underrated virtues of a liberal democracy is that it militates against delusion in its leaders. Democratic leaders are subject to critical oppositions, and to a free press which helps keep their feet on the ground and punctures information bubbles. Dictators, who have no such checks and hear only good things about themselves, are much more likely to cross the frontier that separates a healthy margin of self-deception from dangerous delusion. Of course, democratic administrations are capable of collective acts of self-deception too; some argue that this is what the US and UK governments succumbed to during the run-up to the Iraq war. But the chance of this happening in free societies is lower than in authoritarian regimes. Perhaps the greater problem for mature democracies is that their electorates and media have developed a distorted ideal of honesty. By striving to eradicate all forms of deception from our public life, we may have only ended up fooling ourselves.

For most of the twentieth century, the relationship between the press and its ruling classes was governed by a discreet decorum. It was accepted that politicians had private lives that might contrast with their public image, which was understood as a kind of benign deceit. Then, partly because of political scandals like Watergate and partly because of our growing thirst for and access to information, a culture of radical honesty developed. We demanded, quite rightly, to know more about the activities of our elected rulers; more dubiously, we started to insist that a politician's public mask was ripped off so that we might see the 'real' person underneath and ensure that their every thought and action was consistent, and seen to be consistent. The end result isn't, as one might have hoped, a better class of political rulers and a healthier polity; we are more dissatisfied with our politicians than ever before, and more likely than ever to think of them as deceitful.

Keeping our politicians honest seems to have become confused with demanding honest politicians. Throughout this book I've tried to show that deceitfulness is a natural part of being human, and that facile distinctions between 'honest' people and 'liars' merely obscure subtler truths about our conduct in different environments. The mistake we make too often is in viewing honesty solely as a *trait* — something that individuals have or don't have — rather than as a *state*: something that people adapt to under conducive conditions. Thus we routinely denounce all politicians as exceptionally dishonest, but it takes only a moment's thought to realise how unlikely it is that, by coincidence or otherwise, only sociopathic liars get elected to public office.

If we want a more honest politics, we will have to create

conditions that steer our politicians towards honesty. First, we need to be more honest about ourselves. As we've seen, most of us like to think of ourselves as a little more unselfish, virtuous and honest than we actually are. This is as true of us as voters as it is of us as colleagues or friends; polls find time and again that people are willing to pay more taxes to improve public services, yet people usually vote for the party that will lower their tax bill. Politicians understand that we are inveterate self-deceivers. They deliberately appeal to the instincts that voters don't admit to, as well as those to which they do – and we hate them for it. It's a society-wide example of what Freud called 'displacement activity'. We unload uncertainties about our own probity on to a group that everyone feels comfortable in pillorying.

Second, we need to get used to accepting unsettling political truths. At the moment, it's as if we don't actually want our politicians to be honest. We get uncomfortable or angry when they change their minds, or confess that some problems are insoluble, or exhibit anything other than a pretence of superhuman command. Neither do we like it when they say anything that isn't expected. Sometimes, when presidential candidates or British cabinet ministers find themselves in hot water over an unscripted remark, it's because the remark is stupid or offensive; more often, it's because it's true. In fact, the very definition of a gaffe, according to the American journalist Michael Kinsley, is an occurrence of a politician telling the truth in public. Like the children in School B, our politicians have learned that they will get flayed whatever they say — so they may as well lie, or at least avoid giving you an honest answer. Perhaps we don't need to give our politicians a moral education so much as a better set of choices.

Lies We Live By: Part One

The Medicine of Deceit

The last two decades have seen the emergence of an innovative new treatment for heart disease. Laser surgery has been carried out across the world on thousands of patients suffering from severe angina and related conditions. The NHS doesn't offer it, and even in America, where it originated, it is considered a treatment of last resort. But the doctors who practise laser heart surgery eulogise it, telling stories of patients who have gained relief from what seemed to be incurable suffering.

Dr William O'Neill, of William Beaumont Hospital in Michigan, told a reporter from the Associated Press that 'in twenty years of medicine, I have never seen anything that gives as much symptomatic benefit for patients.' One of O'Neill's patients was Frank Warren, an auto-worker in his forties. Warren had suffered from heart problems for years. He always felt short of energy, and the slightest exercise brought on a burning sensation. Sometimes the pain came when he was resting. Over the years he had had eight operations; none of them helped. After undergoing laser surgery, however, he experienced immediate results: 'I felt a warmth in my face. My colour seemed to change.' One year later, Warren finished a marathon in a very respectable four hours, twenty-nine minutes.

When somebody suffers from angina it's because their arteries are clogged, stymieing the flow of blood and therefore oxygen to the heart. As a result they get short of breath very quickly, find it hard to exercise, suffer from debilitating pain, and live with the constant risk of a fatal heart attack. In a routine coronary bypass, the surgeon takes healthy arteries from elsewhere in the patient's body and weaves them into the heart, so that blood can be diverted around the blocked vessels.

During laser treatment, an incision is made in the side of the chest between two ribs. The outer layer of the heart (the pericardium) is pulled back to expose the heart muscle itself (the myocardium). But instead of grafting on a new artery, the surgeon pierces the heart muscle. She takes aim at the patient's heart with a laser gun, which is attached to an expensive, impressive-looking machine. A dot of red light tells her where the laser will hit. She pulls the trigger (actually, a foot-pedal), fires the laser, and blasts a tiny, pinhead-sized hole in the myocardium. This is repeated twenty or more times. Drilling holes in the heart might seem like an odd thing to do when you're trying to save somebody's life, but the idea is that by opening up new channels the surgeon creates the equivalent of a new artery, allowing blood to flow to the heart's oxygen-starved flesh.

Surgeons who practise laser surgery don't have to rely on their own experiences to support their confidence in it. By the late 1990s a number of large-scale trials had been carried out involving patients with serious heart conditions (the term often used is 'end-stage' conditions). The results were remarkable, with success rates in the range of seventy-five to ninety per cent, comparing very favourably with more established heart surgery procedures.

There is only one problem with this wonder treatment: no-one quite knows how it works. The theory behind it is plausible, and the results are undeniable. But the blood-lines close up within hours of being opened, and there is no evidence that the blood flow to the heart muscle actually increases.

Dr Martin Leon, a professor of medicine at Columbia University in New York, is one of the world's leading cardiologists. He knew that laser heart surgery had performed well in tests versus other treatments. But it hadn't, he noted, been tested against *no treatment at all*. In 2005, Leon oversaw a study of three hundred patients, in their fifties and sixties, with heart conditions. They were very sick: most had previously undergone heart surgery at least once, and all were suffering from continuing problems. The patients were divided into three groups: high-dose (twenty to twenty-five laser punctures), low-dose (ten to fifteen), and a mock procedure that merely *simulated* laser treatment; the patients were shown the machine and had its workings explained. Then they were heavily sedated, blindfolded, and played music to create an effect of 'sensory isolation'. When they awoke, those who had had the fictional surgery were told it had gone well.

Twelve months later, and most of the patients who had undergone actual laser surgery were in much better shape. They revelled in a rediscovered capacity for physical exercise. They reported that their heart pains had receded and that they were feeling healthier and fitter than they had done in years. A battery of objective tests showed they weren't making this up. But the strange thing was that patients in the third group – the sham group – were also rejuvenated. Despite not having had any surgery, or any physical treatment at all, they too felt years younger and full of beans, and the frequency of their angina pains declined. In fact, in terms of the effects on patients, there was no significant difference between all three treatments.

It would appear that you can enjoy the amazing benefits of laser heart surgery without once coming into contact with a laser.

* * *

Placebo is Latin for 'I will please'. The words *Placebo Domino* (I will please the Lord) are in Psalm 116 in the Latin translation of the Bible that was used throughout the Middle Ages, and the phrase formed part of the Catholic Vespers for the dead. Perhaps because priests charged fees for performing the rites in which these prayers were sung, the word came to be used pejoratively, to mean an insincere consolation, or an act of sycophancy.[22] The seventeenth-century philosopher Francis Bacon used it in the course of issuing a warning to rulers not to express their own opinions too openly when taking advice, lest their subordinates tell them only what they think they want to hear: a king's advisers might 'sing him a song of placebo'. The first known use of placebo in a medical context occurs in 1785: the second edition of George Motherby's *New Medical Dictionary* defines it as 'a commonplace medicine or method'. Already there is a hint of disparagement, and it soon became a byword for treatments that, rather than being based on sound scientific principles, were dispensed merely to please patients.

Modern physicians know that they can relieve the symptoms of an anxious patient by offering a fake treatment. But most feel uncomfortable about curing with lies. Not only is it seen as morally dubious, but some still regard it as close to nonsensical, in scientific terms. Today's medical establishment was founded on a hard-won separation between science and superstition, a distinction closely related to that between physical and mental phenomena, which the so-called placebo effect seems to resist. In the words of Edzard Ernst, a professor of medicine at Exeter University, placebo effects are the 'ghosts that haunt the house of scientific objectivity'. As a consequence, they have been dismissed as illusory, unreal and unworthy of study. It wasn't until the second half of the twentieth century that the healing power of deception began to be taken seriously, following a discovery made by a doctor in the frenzy of battle.

Henry Beecher's Epiphany

On 22 January 1944, British and American troops swarmed ashore a fifteen-mile stretch of Italian beach near the old resort town of Anzio. In a perfectly executed operation that took the Axis powers by surprise, the Allies established a beachhead from which they prepared to break out and advance. Within a week, however, German troops surrounded them in large numbers and began the task of excising what Adolf Hitler called the 'Anzio abscess'. The next four months saw some of the most savage fighting of World War II. Nearly five thousand Allied troops were killed, and eighteen thousand wounded.

Henry Beecher was among those who landed in Italy that day. Beecher wasn't a soldier. He was a doctor and a Harvard professor of medicine who volunteered to join his country's war effort. He specialised in the science of pain relief. In a makeshift hospital on the beach he tended to wounded American soldiers awaiting evacuation to the safety of Allied territory. Medical supplies were limited, however, and on days when casualties were particularly heavy, the demand for painkillers would outstrip supply. One day, a soldier with particularly horrific injuries arrived just as the morphine ran out. Beecher worried that without it the operation required would be so unbearably painful it might induce cardiovascular shock. But he could see no other option. In desperation, one of the nurses injected the soldier with diluted salt water, allowing him to think it was an anaesthetic.

What Beecher observed next changed his view of medicine forever. The patient, who had been in agony, settled down immediately following his injection, reacting in exactly the same way Beecher had observed previous patients respond to morphine. During the operation his patient seemed to feel very little pain, and displayed no symptoms of full-blown shock. Beecher was amazed. The nurse's benign deception had worked as effectively as one of the most powerful painkillers in the medical arsenal. In the following months, as the battle raged on, Beecher and his team repeated the trick whenever morphine supplies were exhausted. It worked again and again.

Beecher returned home convinced that what a patient *believed* about his treatment could profoundly affect his physical reaction to it. Back at Harvard, he gathered his colleagues and proposed a rigorous investigation of the phenomenon. The papers that Beecher and his colleagues went on to publish, which were based on reviews of clinical drug trials, contended that placebo effects were far more widespread than had been acknowledged. Beecher forced the medical world to confront what it had long tacitly recognised but hadn't, until then, attended to: the real benefits of imaginary medications.

If people's bodies responded to treatments that existed only in their minds then it followed that there was probably an imaginary component to the effects of genuine medical interventions. In a 1955 paper entitled 'The Powerful Placebo', Beecher argued that clinical trials of new drugs were incomplete and inaccurate unless they took the placebo effect into account. Even with drugs that worked, patients improved partly because of the therapeutic effect of the very act of taking a pill from a clinician. To test a new drug, it was therefore necessary to subtract the improvements in health due to placebo effects from the actual effects of the medication. Beecher proposed trialling every new medicine on two groups of patients: one which received the drug, and one which received what they thought was a drug, but was in fact inert – a sugar pill or similar.

Beecher's work was the catalyst for a fundamental change in clinical practice in America and across the developed world. Now, to win government approval, a new medication has to beat a placebo in two authenticated trials. What's more, the trials must be double-blind. Since the placebo effect seems to be affected by what people believe about the drug, neither doctors nor patients are meant to be able to discriminate between the placebo pill and the real pill. The double-blind clinical trial represents an attempt to strip out the effects of deception and self-deception from the actual effects of a treatment.

Beecher showed that placebo drugs had objectively

measurable physiological effects, sometimes matching or exceeding those of powerful drugs. Even so, there remained a sense within the medical profession that such effects were an aberration from the norm, and somehow illegitimate. Explanations were sought in the personalities of the individual patients. Medical researchers, confident as ever in their own vice-like grip on reality, speculated that 'placebo reactors' were unusually suggestible people – delusional, neurotic, or simply not that bright. A 1954 paper in the *Lancet* remarked that the placebo effect was useful in treating only 'unintelligent or inadequate patients'. But no substantial evidence has ever been found to support the idea that certain individuals are more prone to placebo effects than others.

In the 1980s, advances in brain science started providing hard, 'biochemical' explanations for the power of placebos. A psychiatrist called Robert Ader administered saccharin-flavoured drinking water to rats, and at the same injected them with a chemical that suppressed their immune system and made them ill. When a group of the same mice were fed the same flavoured water but without the injections, they reacted the same way. The drink, because originally associated with the injections, now triggered the same illness as the poison. Ader had created a placebo with undeniable physiological effects (strictly speaking he had created a 'nocebo' – an inert drug or otherwise benign event that triggers illness. Nocebo means 'I shall harm').

Later studies confirmed the strange ability of placebos

to create real physical changes in the human body. Fabrizio Benedetti, a neuroscientist at the University of Turin, has been experimenting with placebo treatments for nearly twenty years, and observed them alleviate physical pain, digestive illnesses, depression, and even Parkinson's disease (by telling a Parkinson's sufferer, falsely, that a surgically implanted electronic module in their brain had been switched to 'on', he found he could relieve their symptoms, albeit only temporarily). He has closely mapped the biochemical responses of his patients' bodies to their different beliefs about the treatment. According to Benedetti, placebos act as a catalyst for the body's own internal healthcare system. If you hear a fire alarm and see smoke, your adrenalin shoots up and your heart rate increases, preparing you for a quick escape. Similarly, when the act of taking a placebo sends a signal to the brain that it's time to start getting better, the body's healing chemicals go to work.

The placebo effect has its limits. There's no evidence to suggest it can stop the growth of cancerous tumours, for instance. It seems to work particularly well for conditions involving physical pain, or those related to higher-level mental functions, like depression. In those cases, if we expect to feel better, we are more likely to get better, even if this expectation is based on a lie. The pharmaceutical industry now treats placebo effects as significant, and the research of Benedetti and others has gone some way towards establishing that placebo effects involve real physiological actions. Nonetheless, such effects are for the most part still studied through the lens of biology, because this is the sole context in which medical science traditionally thinks about human bodies. But perhaps placebo effects ought to be taken as a hint to broaden the scope of modern medicine. If a lie heals it's because it has meaning – and meaning is made between people, not inside them.

The Seeds of a New Science: Franklin vs Mesmer

On 22 May 1784, a group of the most eminent thinkers in France gathered in the elegant gardens of the American ambassador's residence at Passy, just north of Paris. The distinguished gentlemen were there to witness a spectacle that the uninformed visitor might have taken for a bizarre initiation rite or obscure theatrical performance. A twelve-year-old boy wearing a blindfold was being guided from tree to tree by an older man. Each time they stopped by a tree, the boy would embrace it for two minutes. At the first tree, he began to sweat, cough, and foam at the mouth. At the second, he complained of dizziness. At the third, his symptoms worsened, and by the time he touched the fourth he collapsed, moaning, to the ground. The man picked the boy up and laid him out on the lawn in front of the spectators. The boy contorted into a series of strange shapes, before he abruptly rose to his feet, dusted himself down, and declared himself cured.

The gentlemen did not applaud. Perhaps one or two of them nodded gravely, or wrote a note. Among them was the ambassador himself. Benjamin Franklin, we may assume, was experiencing a somewhat weary satisfaction in being proved right again.

This scene wasn't a rite, it was a test; although the man whose ideas were being tested wasn't present. The discoverer of 'animal magnetism' would have nothing to do with any investigation of his methods.

Other than being immortalised in the word 'mesmerise', if Franz Anton Mesmer is remembered at all today it's as a quack, a fraud and a showman. But Mesmer, German by birth, regarded himself as an enlightened man at the vanguard of science. As a young physician at Vienna University he became fascinated by the medical implications of Newton's discovery of gravity and set out to find whether human bodies were in harmony with celestial bodies. Mesmer experimented with passing magnets over and around his patients' bodies. His (mostly female) subjects reported strong sensations of energy rippling across them as he did so; some succumbed to violent convulsions, and afterwards felt much invigorated.

Mesmer then discovered he could derive the same effects by simply waving his hands over the patient's body. This was the apple falling from the tree. He concluded that he had discovered a form of magnetism that was exerted by all living bodies upon one another through the medium of an invisible fluid that flowed from the stars, surrounding and penetrating everyone. Sickness resulted when its flow through the body was blocked by an obstacle; health was restored when the fluid was set free. Since the universe tended towards harmony anyway, the physician's role was merely to assist and augment natural healing. It was an art which only Mesmer and select disciples were qualified to practise. Mesmer, who was sceptical of the established church, had done nothing less than reframe the religious art of exorcism for a more secular, scientific age — and made himself a priest.

A man of few words, Mesmer cut a commanding figure; tall with piercing eyes and a broad, blank screen of a forehead. His colleagues in Vienna were hostile to his radical ideas, and so in 1778, aged 44, he moved to Paris, the centre of Europe's intellectual ferment. With the help of his wife's money, he rented a grand apartment on Place Vendome, laid down heavy, sound-muffling carpets, and filled the main room with various exotic *objets*. The room's centrepiece was an impressive-looking, if bizarre, apparatus: a ten-foot tub made of oak, filled with bottles of 'magnetised water'. The tub had holes in the lid, out of which protruded jointed iron rods. When everything was in place, the mysterious doctor from Vienna announced that he was open for business.

Mesmer favoured communal healing sessions. They soon became the hottest ticket in town. With the curtains drawn, Mesmer's fashionably attired patients sat cross-legged in concentric circles around the tub. Holding hands in the dim light, and bound to one another by a rope cord, they formed a 'chain' through which the fluid could flow, like electricity through a circuit. Ethereal, other-worldly music floated in from the next room. When the last whispering died away, Mesmer entered. Dressed in a lilac taffeta robe, he moved slowly amongst his patients, gently prodding them with an iron wand. Now and then he might sit directly opposite a patient, foot against foot, knee against knee, place his hand on their head or shoulder, and stare directly into their eyes. His subjects sighed, shrieked, fell into trances or collapsed, writhing, on the floor, at which point an assistant would carry them to a special, mattress-lined 'crisis room' to restore their composure. When Mesmer's patients walked out, blinking, into the light of a Parisian afternoon, they declared themselves miraculously cured of ailments ranging from ennui to asthma to gout and epilepsy.

Mesmer had arrived in Paris in the year of Voltaire's death, when the city's chattering classes, already bored with the dry old Enlightenment strictures of reason and scepticism, were falling in love with a new enchantment: popular science – and barely-examined pseudo-science. The world was full of mysterious, wonderful forces: Newton's gravity, Franklin's electricity, Lavoisier's oxygen, the gases of the Montgolfiers that – did you see? – could transport men through the air. Who was to say that Mesmer's invisible fluid was less real than these or the countless other substances (ether, miasma, phlogiston) said to be permeating the world?

In these hothouse conditions Mesmerism quickly become a sensation, and Mesmer one of the most talked-about men in Europe. He grew wealthy from a steady stream of rich patients, and by franchising his methods to secret societies. Mesmer's practice was discussed in journals, portrayed in salacious cartoons, parodied on stage, sponsored by Queen Marie Antoinette, and hotly argued over in academies, cafes and salons. There were more pamphlets produced on Mesmerism than on politics during this period, even as the French state creaked and revolution brewed. Mesmer's followers regarded him as the man who had solved the problem of human suffering. His critics denounced him as a charlatan, and a dangerous seducer who preyed on the women he stroked and excited.

Mesmer's popularity was a source of anxiety to conventional doctors and scientists, whose credibility and livelihoods were at stake. In 1784 the king agreed, after considerable lobbying, that it was time to draw a line separating science from superstition, truth from lies. He formed a Royal Commission to establish once and for all whether Mesmer's treatments worked through the action of animal magnetism, or simply because people were deceived into *thinking* that they worked. The commissioners included Antoine Lavoisier, now regarded as the father of modern chemistry, the astronomer Jean-Sylvain Bailly, and Dr Joseph-Ignace Guillotin, a professor of anatomy who gave his name to the device that would eventually slice off the heads of Lavoisier and Bailly. Even in this august company, the commission's most prestigious member was Franklin.

Given that this was a purely domestic affair it might seem odd that the king should request the involvement of the American ambassador, especially one whose primary job was squeezing loans out of his government in order to underwrite an experiment in republicanism. But Franklin held a special place in the hearts of the French. Back home, he was an admired but distant figure, whose affection for England and France made him suspect in the eyes of some. In France, however, he was revered. Monsieur Franklin was lionised as the man who tamed lightning and founded America. He was esteemed for his devotion to liberty and free-thinking, and adored for his exuberant, lavishly dispensed charm. His image was found everywhere, in paintings and prints, on snuff boxes, rings and coins. Placing Franklin on the commission was a shrewd move on the king's part: if anyone could convince the public that this investigation wasn't a cynical exercise in the humiliation of an over-popular foreign celebrity, it was the ultimate foreign celebrity himself.

Franklin had met the man whose methods he'd been charged with investigating. Oddly enough, their paths had crossed due to a kind of musical placebo: the armonica, a glass-based instrument, known for its healing qualities. It was an instrument that Franklin had invented and Mesmer loved.[23] The German had one in his mansion in Vienna and liked to play it for guests, including his friend Leopold Mozart and Leopold's son, Wolfgang Amadeus, who later composed several pieces for the instrument. Mesmer took it to Paris and in 1779 he invited Franklin and Madame Brillon, a mutual friend, to his home to hear him play. At least, that was the pretext. Mesmer was still angling for the approval of the Establishment at that time, and he spent the evening attempting to engage Franklin in a discussion of his magnetic fluid. Franklin took great interest in his host's armonica-playing.

By the time the Royal Commission was formed, Mesmer had given up his search for official approval, and he refused to cooperate with it. He knew that the Establishment cronies gathered in Franklin's garden would label him a fraud: that was what their instincts for self-preservation compelled them to do. As far as he was concerned, what mattered was that his methods *worked*. Hundreds of satisfied patients would testify to that. 'It is to the public I appeal,' he said, cannily framing the contest as one between the honest masses and a corrupt elite. The commissioners, serious men, weren't asking whether Mesmerism worked, however, but *why*. When Mesmer's patients collapsed on to his thick-pile carpets, what were they falling for?

In deference to Franklin's age (seventy-eight) and his physical discomfort with travelling (he had a painful kidney stone), much of the commission's work was carried out at Passy. In Mesmer's place, Doctor Charles Deslon agreed to act as the advocate for Mesmerism. Deslon, a former court physician, was the only convert to Mesmerism from the medical establishment, and had been expelled from the faculty of medicine for his heresy. He was eager to prove that Mesmerism was legitimate; Mesmer denounced and disowned his former disciple for his cooperation.

After spending a few weeks listening to Deslon lecture on the theory of Mesmerism, the commissioners underwent mesmerising themselves, to little effect (Franklin reported only boredom). They then embarked on a series of elegant experiments. In one, they told a female subject falsely that she was being mesmerised by Deslon, behind a door in the next room. This was enough to send her into a violent crisis. Another woman, previously very responsive to mesmeric treatment, was blindfolded and ministered to by Deslon without her knowledge, yet reported no effects at all. Five cups of water were held before another of Deslon's patients; the fourth produced convulsions, yet she calmly swallowed the fifth, the only one to have been mesmerised. Then there was the experiment with which we opened this story. Deslon 'magnetised' an apricot tree in Franklin's garden by passing his wand across it. Deslon was then invited to choose the subject of the test – he deemed the sickly boy especially sensitive to animal magnetism. The boy went into a crisis before reaching the magnetised tree. With these experiments the commissioners had designed the first application of placebo-controlled blind testing in the history of modern medical science.

The commission's report, published in September 1784, is a masterpiece of the clear thinking for which Franklin and his colleagues were renowned. It carefully explains how the investigation looked for evidence of the existence of Mesmer's magnetic fluid but found none. The effects were real — there was no suggestion that the sickly boy or any of the other subjects were faking their crises or their recoveries — but it was necessary to look elsewhere for causes:

> Thus forced to give up on our search for physical proof, we had to investigate mental circumstances, operating now no longer as physicists but as philosophers . . . Whereas magnetism appears nonexistent to us, we were struck by the power of two of our most astonishing faculties: imitation and imagination. Here are the seeds of a new science, that of the influence of the spiritual over the physical.

Mesmerism remained popular in France for a few years more, though after his humiliation by the Establishment Mesmer himself left Paris for England and Italy, hoping for a new start that never came. He died in relative obscurity in 1815, by the shores of Lake Constance in Germany, not far from where he was born. The chimes of an armonica sang him to his rest. Deslon died in August 1786, while being mesmerised.

* * *

The authors of the Mesmerism report found that the cures by animal magnetism were in fact produced by social and mental causes ('imitation and imagination'). Crucially, they were careful not to dismiss such effects as irrelevant or unworthy of study. The 'new science' they proposed implied something like a fusion of what today we call social sciences – psychology, anthropology, sociology – with biological medicine.

For two centuries, the medical profession failed to culti-vate the seeds sown by Franklin and Lavoisier. In its struggle to distance itself from superstition, magic and quackery, it built a wall between science and everything intangible. As a result, the 'influence of the spiritual over the physical' became something of a taboo question, regarded by physicians and researchers alike as beneath or behind them. Doctors saw themselves as scientists of the physical world whose object of study happened to be the human body, a machine of nature that operated according to reliable laws. (This is also, of course, how Mesmer saw things.) As the medical historian David Morris puts it, if you conceive of the body as a machine, then believing in the power of lies to erase pain is 'as irrational as filling the gas tank of a car with tea'.

Only in recent years has it begun to be accepted that sickness and health aren't just biological affairs. 'Imitation' is increasingly viewed as playing a significant role in the health of individuals and populations. Mesmer's treatment worked more powerfully when his patient was surrounded by other patients sharing the same experience, and there's now plenty of evidence to show that our behaviours and health are strongly influenced by those around us, including large-scale studies that track the spread of conditions like heart disease and obesity through social networks.

Our own health is bound up with our relationships to other people, particularly those who seek to cure us. Much depends on the signals the physician sends, consciously or unconsciously, about his confidence in the treatment; in the phrase of the medical anthropologist Daniel Moerman, the physician's demeanour seems to 'activate the medication'. Medical researchers who carried out a historical review of the literature on the treatment of angina found that drugs that worked in the 1940s and 1950s dramatically decreased in effectiveness in the 1960s. This change was hard to explain in biochemical terms: the drugs hadn't changed, and nor had the human body. The authors of the study concluded that it hinged on the rise of the double-blind trial, which revealed to the medical profession that some of the drugs they had been using worked no better than placebos. In other words, patients who received the medication from doctors who truly believed that it was powerful were much more likely to get better than those who received it from doctors who had their doubts.[24]

It's not just the doctor himself who affects our confidence or inspires our imaginations, it's everything that surrounds him; the cultural symbols of health and healing. The psychologist Irving Kirsch enrolled students on the pretext of trialling a new anaesthetic cream to which he gave the impressive-sounding name of Trivaricane. The students were shown the bottle. On the label were the words *approved for research purposes only*. The experimenter — introduced as a 'behavioural medicine researcher' — wore a white coat and snapped on a pair of surgical gloves, explaining that she wanted to be sure she wasn't over-exposed to the Trivaricane. After administering the sham cream and giving it a minute or two to 'work', a mechanical gadget was used to apply a sharp force to the student's fingers, one finger at a time. The students were asked to rate the pain on each finger and reported feeling much less pain on the finger that had been 'treated'. A British study of headache pills showed that an unbranded, real pill worked better than an unbranded sham pill, but worse than a placebo pill that came in the packaging of a famous brand of headache remedies. The real branded pill worked best of all.

When a person receives a genuine medical treatment and makes a recovery, three things are going on at once. First, the surgical procedure, or the physiologically active pharmaceuticals of the drug, act on the body. Second, the body's superb self-healing system gets to work, its actions enhanced by the patient's expectations of recovery, which are catalysed by the treatment. Third, the patient's belief in the person treating them, or the symbols associated with the treatment, affect their expectations and thus their physiological state. The term placebo effect is used to cover the last two, which of course can take place without the first, but it might be better named the 'belief effect' — after all, a placebo pill does nothing, by definition. Placebo is just a word for the healing that happens because somebody believes that the treatment they've received will make them better. If you don't believe in a lie, it won't make you better.

* * *

Franklin's scepticism about Mesmerism was evident in a letter he sent, shortly before joining the commission, in reply to a sick man who had asked him whether, in his opinion, it would be worthwhile taking a trip to Paris to see Dr Mesmer. Typically of Franklin, it is written in plain language but is dense with insight:

> There being so many disorders which cure themselves and such a disposition in mankind to deceive themselves and one another on these occasions . . . one cannot but fear that the expectation of great advantage from the new method of treating diseases will prove a delusion.
>
> That delusion may, however, in some cases, be of use while it lasts. There are in every great city a number of persons who are never in health, because they are fond of medications, and by always taking them, hurt their constitutions. If these people can be persuaded to

forbear their drugs in expectation of being cured by only the physician's finger or an iron rod pointing at them, they may possibly find good effects tho' they mistake the cause.

Franklin hints here at the usefulness of medical lies — they help people feel better without creating dependence on potentially damaging physical treatments. But is it ever acceptable to deceive patients? Many doctors persuade themselves that it is. According to Anne Helm of the Oregon Health Sciences University, between thirty-five and forty-five per cent of all medical prescriptions are placebos. A 2003 study of eight hundred Danish clinicians found that almost half prescribed a placebo at least ten times a year. These aren't 'pure' placebos; doctors prescribe medications with small active elements in them, though not something that's going to act on the ailment in question.

Although it's commonplace, placebo-prescribing is a controversial practice within the medical community. After all, the healing power of doctors, and indeed, the very possibility of placebo effects, relies in part on the trust that patients place in them. As the philosopher Sisella Bok puts it, 'to permit a widespread practice of deception . . . is to set the stage for abuses and growing mistrust.' Other parties to the process are forced to become accomplices to the deception; an article in the *Journal of the American Pharmaceutical Association* provides a script for the pharmacist faced with a prescription that is clearly a placebo: 'Generally, a larger dose is used for most patients, but your doctor believes that you'll benefit from this dose.'

Of course, doctors aren't deceiving for the sake of it; they are usually doing so for the good of their patients, and anyway, identifying what does or doesn't constitute deception in this context is not straightforward. If a doctor prescribes a pill to a patient, knowing that the pill itself will have no effect on their condition but hoping that the act of administering it will encourage the patient's recovery, is he deceiving? He's certainly not being entirely honest. If he were, he would say something like, 'The pill I'm giving you has no active ingredient that will cure your symptoms, but all you really need is something to believe in, and this will do.' But if he said this, he would quite obviously be undermining the very effect that might lead to the patient feeling better. On the other hand, he doesn't have to engage in outright deception either. Walter Brown, professor of clinical psychiatry at Brown University, suggests that sometimes doctors should be able to tell patients that although the pill they are dispensing contains no active drug, 'Many people with your condition have found that it helps.'

What definitely *would* constitute deception is if the doctor invented a false 'scientific' story to explain how the treatment works. This is what upsets scientists about the alternative medicine industry, which seems to borrow, deceitfully, from the language of biomedical science to enhance its own authority. The homeopathic establishment, with its talk of molecule clustering and nanobubbles, dresses up its treatments in the language of pharmacology. What sceptics find infuriating about homeopathy is that it manages to have it both ways, presenting itself as an alternative to traditional medicine while at the same time relying on its vocabulary for a specious authority.

Homeopathic treatments can work, however, even if most evidence suggests they work purely through the belief effect, and from the therapeutic experience of an encounter with a sympathetic practitioner. Given this, even the sceptic might argue it would be wasteful and destructive to ban them from our pharmacy shelves, or indeed from the NHS. Indeed, it might be dangerous for conventional doctors to shun alternative cures entirely. If some patients see conventional medicine and 'complementary' medicine as a competition between science and caring (or between technology and tradition), then they may refuse conventional treatments that offer their only hope of a cure.

Rather than defending their turf, perhaps evidence-based physicians ought to focus their efforts on expanding it. Already, doctors increasingly accept that the wider, intangible aspects of well-being are important; that a physician who stares at his computer screen while you tell him about your symptoms is less likely to cure his patient than one who looks like he cares; that the best way for a person to stay healthy in old age is to stay socially active – and that these are scientific truths as much as folk wisdoms. But there is a long way to go before our doctors become 'scientists of the spirit' as well as the body.

Scientifically grounded medicine is a vastly welcome but very late development in the human story. For most of our history we've been blundering from one mistaken idea about how the body works to another. Metaphor, ritual and symbol were all we had for combating disease, whether we knew it or not.[25] If people responded positively to the touch of the shaman, the apothecary's elixir, or even harmful treatments like bloodletting – and one of the reasons such treatments persisted is that they often did work – it was at least partly because they believed in them, or in the physician dispensing them.

Lavoisier and Franklin were avid readers of Montaigne, and their report was influenced by an essay of his entitled 'The Power of the Imagination' (1574), in which he argued that medicine was based on deceit. Physicians, said Montaigne, exploit the credulity of their patients with 'false promises' and 'fraudulent concoctions'; if their cures work it is mainly because of the patient's lively imagination. He described a woman who was convinced that she had swallowed a pin in a piece of bread and was ill as a result. Her doctors didn't believe her but had no success in relieving her symptoms, until one day they gave her an emetic and secretly placed a needle in her vomit. She was cured. (The metaphor of exorcism or excision, in which something malign – a spirit, a tumour, a gallstone – is removed from the body by the healer, is one of the most enduring and powerful tropes of medicine. A 2009 study found that patients undergoing surgery to correct painful spinal tears reported greater improvement when, after the operation, they were shown fragments of the removed disc.)

Although nobody quite knows why it is that beliefs – regardless of whether they're true – are so central to our physical well-being, the behavioural scientist Dylan Evans has proposed an intriguing explanation. Noting that we are the only animal to practise medicine (chimps take care of each other when injured, but primatologists have never observed one chimp giving medical assistance to another), he suggests that it began as a way of stimulating positive beliefs about recovery:

> By the time the human lineage began to diverge from that of the chimpanzees, some five million years ago, the capacity for immune conditioning was well established. At some point our ancestors discovered they could activate it deliberately. They found quite by chance that they could train their immune systems to respond to certain stimuli in ways that felt quite beneficial. These stimuli – dabbing leaves on each other's wounds, perhaps, or giving each other special herbs when sick – were the origins of medicine.

Early humans who had access to the power of the belief effect — activated through culture — would have secured an advantage over those who did not. In other words, the very survival and reproduction of our species has relied on our ability to deceive ourselves and others into thinking that we are going to get better even when there is no objective reason why we should. Small wonder, then, that lies continue to exert such a far-reaching effect on our health and happiness.

Lies We Live By: Part Two

The power of stories to shape our lives

We tell ourselves stories in order to live.

Joan Didion

In 2002, the research director of the pharmaceuticals giant Merck announced that his company's aim was 'to dominate the central nervous system'. According to Steve Silberman of *Wired* magazine, the key to this grandiose ambition was the development of a powerful new anti-depressant, codenamed MK-869, which would enable Merck to take on competitors like Pfizer and GlaxoSmithKline who had created some of the best-selling and most famous anti-depressants. In early tests, MK-869 had performed brilliantly: those taking it reported pronounced and lasting improvements in their sense of well-being. But when it was tested against a placebo pill MK-869 suddenly looked less impressive. The volunteers in the group taking the placebo felt much happier too, and to a degree comparable to those who had taken the real thing. In trial after trial, Merck couldn't prove that MK-869 worked better than a sugar pill. In the evocative phrase used by the industry to describe a drug that fails in testing, MK-869 crossed 'the futility boundary', and was abandoned.

It was far from the only one to do so. In the first decade of the twenty-first century, the failure rate of new drugs in trials against placebos was higher than it had been since such testing became standard. Expensively produced, highly effective anti-depressants consistently failed to prove themselves against placebos — as did new wonder treatments for schizophrenia, Crohn's disease, and Parkinson's disease. It wasn't just new drugs that were crossing the futility boundary. Drugs that had been around for decades, including some of the industry's greatest hits, like Prozac, have faltered in recent tests against placebos. If they were to undergo testing by the regulatory authorities now, they might not pass. These medications aren't any weaker than they used to be, and nor are new drugs becoming pharmacologically less sophisticated — quite the opposite. But in the competition to dominate our central nervous systems, the expensively developed drugs produced by the pharmaceutical companies are facing a seemingly much improved, terrifyingly effective competitor: the sugar pill. If they want to keep charging high prices for their drugs, they will need to find out why this is.

The answer probably doesn't lie in the laboratory. We can get closer to it by way of wine-drinking, the ailments of war veterans and the marketing of breakfast cereals.

*

For over seventy years the cereal brand Shreddies has been a fixture of the supermarket shelves and kitchen cupboards of Britain, Canada and New Zealand. Anyone who has grown up in those countries will instantly recognise these squares of waffled whole wheat. Shreddies is owned by Post Cereals, which is part of the global food company Kraft. For marketers, a brand like Shreddies is both a blessing and a problem. On the one hand, it is so well-known and so entrenched in the repertoires of shoppers that its sales can be relied upon to provide a steady stream of revenue. On the other, familiarity breeds passivity; consumers barely notice brands they know well and are easily distracted by more novel and exciting alternatives. The challenge for a brand manager, therefore, is to do what the Russian school of formalist criticism described as the task of literature: to defamiliarise the familiar. Or in this case, to make Shreddies seem new again.

This is hard – there are only so many things you can say about a square of wheat, and over the preceding decades pretty much all of them had been said. But this was the problem presented to the Toronto office of ad agency Ogilvy and Mather in 2006, when the Shreddies client asked the agency to come up with a new poster and TV campaign to give its venerable brand a jolt of excitement. It would be the first time for several years that serious money had been spent on advertising Shreddies, and the brief went to all of the agency's senior creative teams, who were asked to work on ideas for a TV and poster campaign, and to make it their first priority. At the same time, another, somewhat less high-profile brief landed on the desk of a twenty-six-year-old copywriting intern called Hunter Somerville. He was asked to come up with a concept for the back of the Shreddies box — something new and fun to catch the eye of shoppers. He faced the same problem as his more senior colleagues, albeit in a miniature form: to say something about Shreddies that was neither a cliche nor a lie.

After a career as an improvisational comedian, Somerville had come to advertising on the basis that it couldn't be that difficult to pen an advertising script that was funnier than most of those he saw on TV. As a consumer, one of the things that annoyed Somerville about ads was the way they constantly made up phony reasons to say 'new' when it was patently clear they had nothing new to say at all. 'Now with added X' or 'Now with all X removed'; it all seemed fraudulent, and a little desperate. Now that he was on the other side, Somerville at least understood where the desperation came from. When deadline day arrived he only had one idea, and it was so absurd, so deeply silly, that he feared he might be marched out of the building the moment he shared it. 'I just thought it was funny,' he told me. Somerville's idea was to show a picture of a Shreddie rotated by forty-five degrees so that it balanced on its tip. This, the copy announced, was a 'new' type of Shreddie — the 'Diamond Shreddie'.

Later that day, the creative directors of the agency

reviewed ideas for the new campaign and didn't see anything that excited them. When Somerville presented his idea to them, there was a moment's silence. Then his bosses began shaking with laughter. Diamond Shreddies was the funniest thing they'd seen all day. 'It was almost embarrassing, how much they laughed,' Somerville said later. He was asked to write TV scripts along the same lines, followed by posters, and a website. The more the creative directors saw how the idea might play out, the more they liked it. When they took it to Post's director of marketing, she loved it too.

Somerville's silly idea became the basis of a major advertising campaign, the premise of which was that Shreddies were launching an exciting new format – an 'angular upgrade', devised by a team of 'cereal scientists', that would revolutionise breakfast-time. Packs of Diamond Shreddies – with an outsized and upended Shreddie on the front – appeared on supermarket shelves and billboard poster sites. Mimicking the conventions of product launches, the agency conducted focus groups on the new format and filmed them. Two plates were presented to the group, each with several rows of Shreddies laid out on them. On one plate, the Shreddies were turned at an angle. The focus group moderator asked participants to sample one Square Shreddie and one Diamond Shreddie each. Consumers generally preferred the Diamond Shreddie: 'It had more flavour,' said one man; 'It was crunchier,' said another.

The campaign was tongue-in-cheek, though plenty of

consumers took it seriously, writing emails to Post expressing either approval or disgust at the brand's new manifestation. Others took the joke and ran with it; one man auctioned what he claimed to be 'the last square Shreddie' on eBay and sold it for thirty-six dollars.[26] More than ten thousand people voted online for their favourite shape. In business terms the campaign proved a stunning success: after years of steady but unspectacular growth, sales of Shreddies soared. Hunter Somerville was delighted that so many people responded so positively, though he wasn't particularly surprised. 'Sometimes I believe the diamonds taste better myself,' he laughed.

Rory Sutherland, a British ad executive and spokesperson for the industry, argues that the story of Diamond Shreddies is merely an extreme illustration of the way all modern branding works: as a form of placebo. Whether it's sneakers or soft drinks, products in most categories haven't changed fundamentally in years and aren't likely to any time soon – and often there's little to choose between competing offers. The job of advertising, says Sutherland, isn't just to communicate information but to create 'symbolic value', for which consumers are willing to pay. If you believe that wearing this brand of trainers will make you a better basketball player, then you'll pay a higher price for them.

You may just play better basketball as a result. Economists at the Massachusetts Institute of Technology approached students entering the university's gym and offered to sell them a bottle of SoBe Adrenalin Rush, an 'energy drink' that promised to impart 'superior functionality.' Some of the students were sold the drink at full price; others bought it at a discount. After they had exercised the students were asked if they felt better or worse than they usually did after working out. Those who drank the SoBe said they felt a little less fatigued than normal. That was plausible enough — the drink contained a shot of caffeine — but more interesting was that those who paid full price for the drink reported less fatigue than those given the discount. Striking as it was, this result was based on self-assessment, so the researchers designed a more objective test, this time of SoBe's claim to provide 'energy for the mind'. Once again, half the participants were sold the drink at full price, and the others got a discount. They were then set a series of word puzzles. The people who paid the discounted price solved about thirty per cent fewer puzzles than those who paid full price. They were convinced that their drink was less potent, and this belief made them a little stupider.

Advertisers are often accused of selling lies to the public, but advertising can be deceptive without being dishonest. It's true that, for example, no deodorant really has the power to turn adolescent boys into girl magnets. But the truth status of most advertising is like that of fiction; consumers are openly invited to suspend disbelief. Both the advertiser and the advertised-to generally understand that a little deception (or self-deception) is good for us.

The person who prefers the taste of Heinz Baked Beans to other brands but fails a blind taste test isn't necessarily being duped; the brand is a perfectly legitimate component of her pleasure in the food, and if the pleasure of using an Apple MacBook or driving a BMW is bound up with the associations we have with those brands, it seems reasonable for the brand-owners to charge more for the enhanced experience.

To think otherwise is to adopt a rather narrow view of the satisfactions people gain from shopping. It's often assumed that people buy things solely to gain material satisfaction. But they are also paying, knowingly and willingly, to be deceived, in a mentally and emotionally stimulating way. In *The Romantic Ethic and the Spirit of Modern Consumerism*, the sociologist Colin Campbell proposes that consumption is not so much about mere acquisition as it is about the languorous pleasures of imagining. For Campbell, the modern consumer is a self-deceiving 'dream artist', with 'the ability to create an illusion which is known to be false but felt to be true'; an illusion that is woven around the object of desire.

In her short story *The New Dress*, Virginia Woolf describes a young woman trying on a dress for the first time:

> Suffused with light, she sprang into existence. Rid of cares and wrinkles, what she had dreamed of herself was there − a beautiful woman. Just for a second . . . there

looked at her, framed in the scrolloping mahogany, a grey-white, mysteriously charming girl, the core of herself, the soul of herself; and it was not vanity only, not only self-love that made her think it good, tender, and true.

The dress allows Woolf's protagonist to dream up — to try on — a new version of herself. When she first wears the dress to a party, however, the dream vanishes. Tortured by the conviction that everyone thinks she looks ridiculous, she is 'woken wide awake to reality'. Campbell argues that the woman in Woolf's story enacts the modern consumer's oscillation between willed self-deception and disillusion. The reality of a product is never quite as good as the dream — but then if it was, there would be no reason to dream again. The product itself is merely an excuse to experience the pleasures of anticipation, longing and pretending. We pay for the reflection, not just the dress; a reflection that advertising helps to create.

Apart from anything else, says Rory Sutherland, enriching the symbolic value of the brand via advertising is a more environmentally responsible way of improving a product than using more or better materials. Meaning is not a finite resource.

Thinking about such mutually satisfactory deceptions can make us uncomfortable because we tend to imagine there's a realm of pure, spontaneous, authentic experience, over which those wily advertisers draw a veil of deceit (it's that serpent in the garden again). But our physical and aesthetic sensations are inextricable from the meanings we attach to things. The practice of wine-buying tells us something about the relationship between our experience and our beliefs. The fortunes of individual wines, and indeed entire wineries, turn on the decisions of experts who award ratings and dish out medals in competitions, a system built on the premise that a given wine has something like an objectively measurable and consistent quality. The work of Robert Hodgson, published in the *Journal of Wine Economics*, places a large question mark over this assumption.

Hodgson is a retired professor of statistics who runs a small winery in Humboldt County, California, and got interested in the question of why a wine of his might win a gold in one competition and come nowhere in another. So he did something nobody had done before: he performed a large-scale quantitative analysis of the judgements of wine experts, running his own blind taste tests with judges from the California State Fair Wine Competition, and analysing the data from hundreds of wine competitions. He found that judges often gave the same wine very different scores, and that gold medals seemed to be spread around at random, rather than following the same wines consistently.

Hodgson's findings would come as no surprise to Frederic Brochet, a cognitive psychologist at the University of Bordeaux who, several years before, had served fifty-seven

French wine experts from two bottles, one with a Grand Cru label, the other with the label of a cheap table wine. The experts greatly preferred the Grand Cru and explained why with great eloquence – though both bottles contained the same wine. According to Brochet, the lesson of his experiment is that the brain is incapable of sending us objective reports on the world; what we experience is always a mixture of the raw data coming in and our expectations, which 'can be much more powerful in determining how you taste a wine than the actual physical qualities of the wine itself'. These expectations are, of course, inherited from others. Brochet's subjects were wine critics; if they'd been from a culture where the name Grand Cru meant nothing, the wine would have tasted differently.

The same goes for that frequent accompaniment to wine, cheese. The psychologist Edmund Rolls presented twelve subjects with an ambiguous, cheesy-smelling odour that was labelled either 'cheddar cheese' or 'body odour'. People rated the smell as much more pleasant when it was labelled cheese. In fMRI scans, the brain regions involved in interpreting smells and connecting them to feelings were activated more strongly by the positive label. The food scientist Harold McGee has pointed out that the pungent smell of certain cheeses, like Vieux Boulogne, is the smell of decay – something we are hard-wired to find disgusting (and thus to avoid for our own good). That some people, in certain countries – especially France, of course – find such smells appetising is testament to the extent that our senses are in thrall to the beliefs we inherit from the culture in which we live.

One of our beliefs is that more expensive wine tastes better. Researchers at the California Institute of Technology and Stanford organised a wine-tasting for members of the Stanford Wine Club, serving them five different cabernet sauvignons that were only distinguishable by price. What the subjects didn't know was that there were only three wines – so sometimes they'd be tasting the same wine with a different price label. They consistently reported that the same wine tasted better when the label said it was more expensive. Similar experiments have been carried out before, but in this one the subjects sipped wine while lying supine inside an fMRI machine (the wine was pumped through tubes into the subjects' mouths). When subjects thought they were drinking more expensive wines, the scans revealed more activity in the brain region that determines whether or not we find an experience pleasurable. Higher prices primed them for pleasure, and so pleasure is what they experienced.

When we take a sip of Grand Cru (if we're lucky enough to do so), we're drinking a belief first and a liquid second. The same goes for when we go and see a well-reviewed film or look at a painting we're told is by Picasso. Of course, if the film is really bad or the painting is truly appalling, we might notice, and adjust our response accordingly. But our beliefs (preconceptions, assumptions, expectations and desires) determine our responses much more than we like to think. What's more, we don't even originate these beliefs; they are stories that come to us through the cultural ether — Picasso is a great artist, expensive wines taste better — and are written by other people, living and dead. Our conviction that we can escape these shared preconceptions and experience the world purely as individuals is just another of the stories we tell ourselves.

Pain Stories

During his stint in the combat zone, the potency of deception wasn't the only thing by which Henry Beecher was amazed. Men bearing the most terrible injuries seemed to feel far less pain than he would have expected. Given that Beecher wanted to preserve his limited supplies of morphine for those most in need, he started to ask his patients if they wanted a painkiller injection before giving it to them, being careful to phrase the question so that they could accept it without embarrassment. 'Are you in pain?' he would ask. If the answer was yes, he would then say, 'Could you do with some help for it?' Time and again came the answer — from men with fractured bones, burnt skin, and stomachs ruptured by shrapnel — 'No Doc, I'm OK.' Keen to further his research even in battle, Beecher kept a tally of their responses. Three-quarters of the badly wounded men said they felt no need for a painkiller, long after the effects of their last morphine injection had worn off.

In a paper published after the war, Beecher presented his puzzling findings and speculated on their cause. He compared the situation of these injured soldiers to the kind of case he was used to dealing with as a hospital anaesthetist back in Boston. A man who crashed his automobile on the highway might suffer exactly the same wounds as one of the soldiers at Anzio, yet his pain would be far more intense. Perhaps, thought Beecher, this had something to do with how each man regarded the significance of his injury. Almost as soon as the car accident happens, a civilian begins to think about a future that has been radically transformed, and not for the better: possibly permanent physical damage; insurance claims; time off work leading to financial problems; the strain that all this will put on his wife and family. By contrast, when a soldier in a war zone is hit by a bullet, he is suddenly released from a dangerous and terrifying environment. He knows that he will be taken to the safety of the hospital and allowed to recuperate at his own pace, and, thinking further ahead, he envisages himself returning home, acclaimed as a war hero. 'His troubles are over,' wrote Beecher, 'or at least he thinks they are.' The civilian's accident represents a calamity and the beginning of uncertainty; the soldier's injury is a dignifying liberation from chaos.

There is no sensation more physical, visceral or immediate than pain; it requires no language skills or education to know the feeling of being slapped, or burned, or struck by a speeding lump of lead. Yet Beecher was suggesting that the pain we feel is deeply affected by the meaning we attach to it. The soldier and the civilian can suffer identical injuries, and their experience of it — their *physical* experience — depends on how they see the injury fitting into the story of their lives. The empirical truth or falsity of the story is less important than its potency — the power of the idea of a war hero, for example, or a crippled husband.

For years after World War II, America's hospitals were dealing with its human cost. Wards, surgeries and beds were occupied by veterans lucky enough to have survived the war, but struggling to cope with the long-term injuries it bequeathed them. In the 1950s these patients were joined by men who had been injured fighting in Korea. All of them were attempting to put their lives back together while dogged by persistent, sometimes unbearable pain. While resting, or waiting to see the doctor, patients at Knightsbridge Veterans Hospital in the Bronx and, later, Mount Zion hospital in San Francisco, would find themselves approached by a slight, pale, softly spoken man with large, soulful eyes and a thick Russian accent, asking whether they would be prepared to take part in an interview about their condition. Although he worked for the hospital, the man explained, he wasn't a doctor. He was an anthropologist.

Mark Zborowski was born in Ukraine in 1908. When he was a young boy his family moved to Poland to escape the Russian Revolution. As a student, Zborowski joined the Communist Party, to the dismay of his parents. In 1928 he left Poland, possibly to avoid imprisonment for radical activities, and travelled to France, where he studied anthropology at the University of Grenoble and worked as a waiter. In 1933 he moved to Paris and became deeply involved in anti-Soviet Trotskyite politics, working for a group led by Trotsky's son Lev Sedov which agitated to undermine Stalin's regime. Quiet, unassuming and a tireless worker, Zborowski became Sedov's most trusted lieutenant.

In 1941, as Europe was torn apart by war, Zborowski moved to the United States, his path smoothed by wealthy New Yorkers sympathetic to Trotsky. One of them introduced Zborowski to the most prestigious cultural anthropologist of the day, Margaret Mead. Impressed by his first-hand knowledge of the culture of European Jewry, Mead offered him a post as her research assistant, a position from which he was able to launch a successful academic career.[27] In the mid-1960s, with Mead's support, he was appointed staff anthropologist at Mount Zion hospital, where he resumed work on a topic he had begun investigating in New York: the ways in which people from different backgrounds cope with pain. He later published his research in the form of a book, called *People In Pain*.

For the purposes of his study Zborowski classified his

patients in four groups: Irish, Italian, Jewish and Old American, or what we'd now call WASP (White Anglo-Saxon Protestants). He was interested in how ex-soldiers coped with their pain, and whether or not their coping strategies reflected their cultural heritage. He expected a high degree of homogeneity in their responses to the pain itself: after all, they had all suffered injuries fighting for the same army, most of them in the same war, and it would seem a truism that a heart attack experienced by an Italian Catholic feels the same as one suffered by a Polish Jew. But as he carried out his interviews with patients and spoke to the hospital's doctors and nurses, he found that something surprising: 'People responded to their pain not only as individuals,' he later wrote, 'but also as Italians, Jews, Negroes, or Nordics.'

The Italians and Jews were often grouped together in the minds of the hospital's staff, because they were regarded as highly emotional, and as having a 'lower pain threshold' (though Zborowski pointed out that previous research demonstrated such variations in pain thresholds were a myth). They were more likely to express their pain with theatrical gestures, florid language and loud cries, both at moments of peak intensity (when a nurse removed a bandage, for example) and in conversations with the doctor about their condition. Jews and Italians wanted and needed to talk about their pain, to describe the sensation of it but also its effect on their families and careers. They were demonstrative, unembarrassed to shed tears.

Zborowski found significant differences between the two groups, however. The Italian patients were mainly concerned with the immediate sensation of pain as it was experienced in the moment, while the Jews were more focused on its *meaning*. Italians expressed concerns about how their pain itself would affect their immediate situation (their job and family life); Jews were much more likely to talk, not about the pain itself so much as what it signified for their underlying condition, and for their future – they practised a hermeneutics of pain.

The two groups also had different attitudes to treatment. Italian patients would call out for relief when in pain, but once an analgesic had been administered they would forget their suffering immediately and display 'a happy and joyful disposition'. Jewish patients were more reluctant to accept medication. They would express concern about side-effects and worry that the drug might be habit-forming, and that though it alleviated their symptoms it would not treat the underlying cause. Sometimes they would only pretend to take the pill, hiding it underneath the pillow. Even when they did take it, they remained anxious and downcast, waiting balefully for the pain to return. Whereas the Italians were sublimely confident in the ability of their doctors to banish their pain, Jewish patients worried that a doctor's recourse to painkilling drugs meant he wasn't skilful enough to cure the illness itself, and they frequently sought second and third opinions from specialists.

The biggest contrast to the Jewish and Italian responses

to pain was provided by WASPS, who were determinedly unemotional in their responses. They would refer to their pain in a way that minimised its impact. It's just cramp, they would say, a sore muscle or a backache. They avoided all discussion of it whenever possible. They feared being seen as over-dramatic, and often made remarks to the effect that complaining 'won't help anybody'. When pressed, they might quietly admit that the pain sometimes became unbearable, even that it drove them to tears. But they would never cry in the presence of others, and so they sought out solitude. In Zborowski's clinical but heartbreaking words, 'Withdrawal from society seems to be a frequent reaction to strong pain.'

Unlike the Jews or Italians, the WASPs much preferred the impersonality of hospital treatment to home treatment. When with the doctor, they assumed the role of a detached observer of their own body, providing an objective description of their state so as to facilitate the correct diagnosis and treatment. Emotionalism was seen as a hindrance in a situation requiring knowledge and skill. WASPs talked about their bodies as if they were cars that needed to be checked periodically and, when out of order, taken to a specialist to be fixed. Their faith in doctors was formed from a respect for scientific knowledge. They were optimists – though their suffering continued, it would only be a matter of time before medical science found the answer for it.

The Irish, like the WASPs, preferred to suffer quietly, but their conception of pain was not without drama. When

Zborowski asked Irish patients what they did to relieve their pain, they said things like:

— *Well, what can you do? Have to take it.*
— *Just have to take it, that's all.*
— *I don't mind taking it. I can take it if I had to.*

For the Irish, pain had to be 'taken' as a fighter must learn to take a punch; it was an opponent, worthy of respect. It would batter them, but it would never take them down. To absorb pain wasn't passive suffering but a character-forming action in itself, one that bred courage and heroic endurance. 'Taking it' was a refusal to surrender, a redemptive act of overcoming. Zborowski contrasted this approach to that of Jewish patients. Here's how one Jewish interviewee described his experience:

Well, I tell you what I think was pain — and to me I think it's a lot of pain. Do you know what a gall bladder attack is? Well, for eight months I took it. I rolled on the floor from this wall to that wall, chewing the carpet. For eight months! Now do you think that's pain?

Although this patient refers to 'taking' pain, he means something very different from the Irish patients quoted above. Here, the pain is more like a demon or a ferocious animal at the throat of the patient. He doesn't ignore his pain, or manfully soak it up; he wrestles with it, trying to throw it off. There is no morally ennobling contest of wills, just a desperate struggle to escape. In a commentary on Zborowski's study, the writer David Morris points out that a prominent tradition within Judaism regards pain as evil, without any of the redemptive powers assigned to it in Christianity.

Zborowski's study is rarely cited by scholars these days, in part because any assignation of characteristics to ethnic groups can be seen as racist. There is justification for such wariness, but it needn't obscure the truth that our bodies are not just biological machines; they are embedded in social and cultural worlds. The physiology of pain, wrote Zborowski, must be looked at 'not only in laboratories and clinics but also in the complex maze of society'.

* * *

Days after the Royal Commission's report on Mesmerism was published, Benjamin Franklin (a pronounced sceptic about religion) wrote a letter to his twenty-four-year-old grandson, Temple:

[The report] makes a great deal of talk. Everybody agrees that it is well-written; but many wonder at the force of imagination describ'd in it, as occasioning convulsions, etc, and some fear that consequences may be drawn from it by infidels to weaken our faith in some of the miracles of the New Testament. Some think it will put an end to mesmerism. But there is a wonderful deal of credulity in the world, and deceptions as absurd have supported themselves for ages.

Franklin might have been intrigued by a 1993 study that collected information on the deaths of twenty-eight thousand Chinese-Americans, together with a control group of nearly half a million white Americans.

In Chinese tradition, the five elements of wood, metal, fire, water and earth are thought to shape the relationship between the body and the natural environment, and each year is assigned to one of them. The researchers found that Chinese-Americans were significantly more likely to die earlier than normal if they had a combination of disease with a birth-year which Chinese astrology and medicine consider ill-fated. For example, those born in earth years are deemed more susceptible to diseases involving lumps or tumours, and Chinese-Americans born in those years who died from cancer did so, on average, nearly four years earlier than those who were born in other years and who suffered from the same condition. Chinese medicine considers the lung to be an organ of metal, and Chinese-Americans who were born in metal years and who suffered from lung disease died, on average, five years earlier than lung cancer patients born in other years. The same was true of a range of other conditions. In all cases, the same did not apply to the control group. What's more, within the Chinese-American group, the intensity of the effect was correlated with 'strength and commitment to traditional Chinese culture'. The more people believed in the story, the more likely they were to succumb to the death foretold by it.

People literally live and die by stories. Numerous other studies have found that religious belief is strongly associated with living longer. Even when you grasp the power of the belief effect, it's still hard to comprehend that metaphors and symbols permeate the flesh as well as the spirit: that they can multiply blood cells, generate protein and disable nerve receptors. But an ability to create and respond to the lies we tell each other seems to be part and parcel of being a creature endowed with imagination, language and culture. Deception is essential to our well-being and, in some form or other, to all of our endeavours. Perhaps there is such a thing as Mesmer's invisible fluid, surrounding and sustaining all of us.

* * *

As the medical anthropologist Daniel Moerman has documented, one of the important determinants of a drug's efficacy is the colour of the pill it comes in. When people suffering the symptoms of depression are given the same drug in different colours, they are most likely to get better when the pill is yellow. Sleeping pills, by contrast, tend to be more effective when they're blue. This last is true of every country it's been tested in, except Italy, where there is a puzzling difference between the genders. For women, blue sleeping pills are highly effective. For men, they're much *less* likely to work than pills of other colours. Although it hasn't been proven, Moerman's explanation is that blue has a particular meaning for Italian men: it's the colour of all Italian sports teams, including the national football team; instead of making them feel sleepy, blue makes Italian men think *Forza Azzuri*!

Other studies have shown that green pills are better at reducing anxiety, and white pills are best for soothing ulcers. Patients who take four sugar pills a day clear their gastric ulcers faster than those who take two sugar pills a day. Large pills work better than medium-sized pills, and very small pills work best of all. Placebos that patients believe to be expensive work better than those they think cost less. Fake surgery involving impressive-looking, excitingly-named machines works extremely well indeed.

Understanding that pills are not just pharmaceutical capsules, but symbols embedded in a shifting universe of stories helps to explain the mystery of the strengthening placebo effect. During the 1980s and 1990s the global pharmaceutical companies did very well out of the massive popularity of new mood-enhancing drugs. Taking a pill to make you feel happier went from being a science fiction fantasy to an unremarkable fact of life. At the same time, and aided by the loosening of advertising restrictions, the drug companies got much better at marketing their pills. The most powerful brands became instantly recognisable symbols of psychological uplift. As a result of the industry's success at marketing itself, volunteers taking part in twenty-first century trials are more willing to believe that the pill they are taking will make them feel happier — and so, for increasing numbers, that is what happens. The ingredients of a placebo pill exert no effect; that hasn't changed. What has changed is the cultural meaning of the act of taking a pill.

The Murderer at the Door

Is there any such thing as a white lie?

Perfection is one thing, and obligation another.

Henry Garnet, *Treatise on Equivocation*

The Hiding Place, by Corrie ten Boom, is a gripping account of life in a Dutch town under Nazi occupation. The ten Boom family of Haarlem were devout Christians, active in the local community, whose home had for years been known as an open house for those in need. When the Germans invaded in 1942 Corrie was living with her sister Betsie, her eighty-four-year-old father Casper and various other family members. One day a woman with a suitcase knocked on the door. Anxiously, she told Corrie's father that she was a Jew whose husband had been arrested and whose son had gone into hiding. She had just been visited by hostile German soldiers issuing threats, and did not want to return home for fear of worse. She had heard that the Boom family was friendly to Jews and wondered if she might take refuge in their home. Corrie's father welcomed her in. Within weeks, the family was harbouring a group of Jewish refugees in the cellar of their home, accessible only via a concealed trapdoor. From then on, their home became known as a safe house for Jews and members of the Dutch resistance.

One evening, two years later, there was another knock on the front door. This was the visit everyone in the house had been dreading. The SS had been tipped off about the Boom family's illicit hospitality by a neighbour, and now they were demanding to know if there were Jews hiding in the house.

Versions of this scenario have been a recurring theme in the debates over lying for hundreds of years. It appears in various guises but is usually called 'the murderer at the door', and often takes the form of a simple question: is it right to lie to the murderer who asks you to tell them the whereabouts of your friend? It's an important dilemma, not because people are constantly being confronted with it, but because it frames a fundamental question about the morality of lying in the most stark and dramatic terms possible. Is a lie an inherently bad thing – or is it what you do with it that counts?

Corrie had no hesitation; she lied. The SS searched the house anyway, though they didn't find what, or who, they were looking for. Two Jewish men, two Jewish women and two members of the Dutch underground remained undiscovered, hidden behind a false wall in Corrie's bedroom. Corrie was arrested that day, and she and her family were imprisoned. Corrie and Betsie were sent to concentration camps. Betsie died in captivity, as did Casper. It is estimated that 800 Jews were saved by the actions of Corrie's family and their friends

The Hiding Place also contains an example of somebody taking a very different attitude to telling lies. Corrie's younger sister Nollie, a pious girl, rarely without her Bible, and known for her rigid honesty. Nollie believed strongly that the Bible condemned lying, and that God brooked no exceptions. One day, previous to the incident described above, Nollie was in the house when members of the SS charged in. She was in the living room with a refugee called Annaliese, whose blonde hair and flawlessly forged papers meant that the German authorities hadn't discovered she was Jewish. The SS pointed at Annaliese and asked Nollie, 'Is she a Jew?' Nollie, unable to break with her principles, said yes. Both girls were arrested, and Annaliese was taken to an old theatre in Amsterdam where Jews were held before being transported to the concentration camps.[28]

* * *

The Bible isn't as clear on the subject of lying as Nollie believed. It's often assumed that the Ten Commandments include an injunction not to lie. This isn't quite so. The closest to one is the ninth commandment (the eighth for Catholics and Lutherans): 'Thou shalt not bear false witness against thy neighbour.' This is clearly a prohibition of perjury, but it doesn't expressly forbid any form of lying (the commandment's wider, metaphorical resonance is a question of interpretation). The New Testament isn't much help either. Jesus doesn't explicitly address the question of whether or not it's ever right to lie, which perhaps suggests it wasn't a very important issue to him or his first followers.

The Bible's ambiguity meant that during the first few hundred years of Christianity its major thinkers were vague and contradictory on the question of lying. Some noted that the scriptures contain episodes that appear to endorse deception: God deceives Abraham into thinking he must kill his son Isaac, as a means of testing his faith; Jacob, in collusion with his mother Rebekah, deceives his father into thinking that he is Esau, his brother; in the book of Exodus, the Egyptian midwives lie to the Pharoah, with God's approval, in order to save the Hebrew children. In the New Testament, Jesus appears to two disciples on the road to Emmaus, following his death and resurrection, and pretends to be someone else. Some Christian scholars interpreted such instances as evidence that the Bible considered lying to be legitimate when it was in the service of a righteous cause.

This changed in the fifth century, when Augustine entered the debate. In two magisterial surveys of the subject, *On Lying* and *Against Lying*, Christianity's greatest philosopher transformed the church's thinking on the matter, and exerted a profound influence on future generations, including our own; it's not much of an exaggeration to say that Augustine invented the modern concept of lying. He laid down two fundamental precepts: first, he defined a lie, with greater clarity than ever before, as a 'false statement made with the intention to deceive'. This is the imperfect but workable definition that most discussions of lying still use as a starting point. Second, he unequivocally pronounced lying as morally wrong, regardless of context and without exception.

Augustine argued that God had given speech to men so that they could make their thoughts known to each other. Using it to deceive is therefore a sin, because this is the opposite of what God intended. He also identified lying as a threat to the authority of the church. If Christians allowed for the possibility of a white lie (the 'helpful lie') then the whole edifice of Christian belief and practice risked corruption and, ultimately, collapse, because 'whenever someone finds something difficult to practise or hard to believe, he will follow this same dangerous precedent and explain it as the idea or practice of a lying author.' He concluded that *every* lie must be defined as a sin, even a lie told to preserve someone's life. To the person asked to betray the whereabouts of an innocent person to a murderer, Augustine's advice was to answer 'I know where he is but will never disclose it,' regardless of consequences.

Even Augustine didn't argue, though, that all lies are sins of equal gravity. He put together a hierarchy of lies, depending on how difficult it was to pardon them. Here's the list, with the least forgivable at the top:

1. Lies in teaching religion
2. Lies which hurt someone and help nobody
3. Lies which hurt someone but benefit someone else
4. Lies told for the pleasure of deceiving someone
5. Lies told to please others in conversation
6. Lies which hurt nobody and benefit someone
7. Lies which hurt nobody and benefit someone by keeping open the possibility of their repentance
8. Lies which hurt nobody and protect a person from physical defilement.

The next major treatise on the subject was written by the Italian scholar Thomas Aquinas in the thirteenth century. Aquinas accepted Augustine's basic framework — that lying involved intent to deceive and that it was always sinful — but added further distinctions and qualifications. Aquinas didn't mind a joke: lies told in jest were not mortal sins in his book. Nor did he consider unpardonable the kind of helpful lie that Augustine railed against. Only malicious lies — 'lies told to do harm' — were impossible to forgive.

For the first fifteen hundred years of Christianity's existence, the morality of lying was largely a matter of rarefied debate amongst scholars. After Martin Luther made his incendiary declaration at Wittenberg, and the church split asunder, lying became a question of survival.

If ever there was an Age of Deceit, it was in Europe at the turn of the seventeenth century. Relatively tolerant attitudes to religious diversity had given way to wide-spread persecution, inquisitions, and thought control. Thousands of religious leaders – Catholics, Protestants and Jews – were forced to choose between staying true to their faith, and exile or death; many chose to pretend to be something, or someone, they were not. At the same time, governments were extending control over their subjects (the murderer at the door was often a civil servant), and the practice of politics was beginning in earnest. Royal courts were growing in size and sophistication, drawing more and more ambitious, career-minded young men towards the luminous centre of power. Ordinary people became used to the idea of politicians (or courtiers, in those days) as ruthless liars who would say anything to advance their own interests.

England in particular was seized by what the literary critic Lionel Trilling termed 'cultural paranoia'. Its writers and thinkers were simultaneously gripped and appalled by the phenomenon of deceit. Francis Bacon, a reader of Machiavelli, analysed the art of self-concealment, concluding that it was best 'to have openness in fame and opinion; secrecy in habit; dissimulation in seasonable use; and a power to feign, if there be no remedy'. Shakespeare's Hamlet, revolted by the courtly fashion for dissembling, says, 'Nay, I know not "seems", and I have that within which passes show.' The plays of Shakespeare are peopled with brilliant liars, elaborate disguises and ingenious forms of deception, as are those of Marlowe, Chapman and

Webster. All of these dramatists took as one of their primary themes the difference between what *seems* and what is, between what a character says and what he or she thinks.

Their audiences were deeply invested in such questions; it wasn't only priests who faced terrible choices between truth and deceit. Many commoners were forced either to besmirch their deepest beliefs, or to live a lie. Even when only outward conformity was required, an inner hell might be created; in the 1550s Richard Wever of Bristol, a Protestant, drowned himself in a mill-race rather than pollute himself by appearing at Catholic mass. Those unwilling to take such drastic action resorted to various forms of deception, either by attending and then secretly not participating in services, or by sending a proxy to sit in their place with the aim of deceiving the congregation into thinking they had attended.

In royal courts and religious colleges across Europe, learned men were reading and constructing sophisticated defences of dishonesty. The doctrinal rationalisation of deceit was, in the phrase of the historian Perez Zagorin, like 'a submerged continent' in the political, religious and intellectual life of the era. To deceive in order to survive or advance was one thing; to deceive while remaining true to God might be allowable. Casuistry, a method of moral reasoning that took each case as it came rather than relying on unbending rules, grew popular among Jesuit scholars in particular.

Casuists searched for loopholes in Augustine's condemnation of lying. As early as the thirteenth century, Raymund of Pennafort had pondered the question of what to tell the murderer at the door. He proposed that a man might deceive the murderer whose intended victim he has given refuge to by saying *non est hic*, which can mean *either* 'he is not here' or 'he is not eating here'. This technique — employing double meanings of words to tell the literal truth while concealing a deeper meaning — became known as 'verbal equivocation'. The casuist St Alfonso de Liguori suggested it was permissible to reply 'I say no' to a question to which one knew the answer was yes, simply because the speaker doesn't in fact say 'no'.[29] As priests and commoners across Europe opened doors to find potential murderers interrogating them, casuists pushed the boundaries of equivocation ever further. Eventually they took the momentous step of arguing that a false statement can be made true by the addition of a 'mental reservation'. That's to say, you can say something you know to be false if you add words, *in your head*, that make it true.

The most influential advocate of what became known as 'the doctrine of mental reservation' was the Spanish theologian Dr Navarrus, who wrote that there are some truths 'expressed partly in speech and partly in the mind'. According to Navarrus, the Christian's overriding moral duty is to tell the truth to God; 'reserving' some of that truth from the ears of human hearers is moral if it serves the greater good. For example, the user of mental reservation could reply 'I know not' aloud to a human interlocutor but silently add 'to tell *you*', and still be telling the truth. The doctrine's adherents claimed that Christ himself practised it: he told his disciples that he did not know the Day of Judgement, even though his omniscience meant that he must have known.

In 1606, the English Catholic priest John Ward was asked by his Protestant captors whether he was a priest and whether he had ever been across the seas – that's to say, studied Catholicism in France or Italy. He replied no to both questions. In fact, both were true. Later, when presented with evidence that his answers were false, he claimed not to have lied, explaining that he had mentally added *of Apollo* after his first answer, and reserved *Indian* before 'seas' in his second answer.[30] By the time Ward was tried, the doctrine of mental reservation was already notorious in England, following the trials of two priests called Robert Southwell and Henry Garnet.

* * *

In 1586, when he was twenty-five, Southwell journeyed to England from France in the company of his older friend Garnet, on a clandestine mission that he knew might result in his death. He was returning to his native country after an absence of ten years. The youngest of eight children, Southwell was raised in a family of Catholic gentry in the Norfolk town of Horsham St Faith. He had been sent to France when he was fifteen to study at a Catholic college in Douai in the north of the country. After attending schools in Paris, and in Tournai in Belgium, he was admitted to the Jesuit college in Rome. He became familiar with the arguments of the casuists and with the doctrine of mental reservation. A gifted student, who also wrote exquisite poetry (Ben Jonson remarked that he would happily destroy most of his own poems in exchange for Southwell's *The Burning Babe*), he was ordained to the priesthood in 1584 and within two years had embarked on his mission to England.

As Catholic missionaries, Southwell and Garnet faced mortal danger. Several of their predecessors had been executed and Queen Elizabeth, worried about the threats from Spain and from Rome, viewed every Catholic as a potential traitor. She passed a law stating that any English subject ordained abroad as a priest who remained in England longer than forty days would be put to death, and any person who aided them likewise. Missionaries were forced to do their work disguised as laymen; to assume false names; to take up pretend occupations. They took refuge in Catholic households brave enough to risk harbouring them and willing to construct hiding places in the event of a search. They needed to be ready for dangerous questions at any moment, and to prepare a mental and verbal strategy in the event that they were arrested.

Southwell evaded capture for six years. He was finally caught when betrayed to the authorities by a young woman called Anne Bellamy, the daughter of a family in whose home he had often secretly lodged. In prison he was brutally tortured, as his captors sought to elicit information about his friends and contacts. Apart from admitting that he was a Jesuit priest, Southwell told his interrogators nothing, not even the colour of a horse he was riding on a certain day. In 1595, after three years of imprisonment, he was tried for treason. Anne Bellamy testified that Southwell told her it was acceptable to lie when questioned by the authorities — that if asked whether or not there was a priest in the house she could swear in the negative as long as she added the mental reservation 'not with the intention to tell you'.

At the trial, the attorney-general Sir Edward Coke seized on this testimony, and accused Southwell of corrupting the morals of the girl with wicked Jesuit doctrine. Southwell, an eloquent defendant, did not deny Anne's evidence; rather, he argued that the practice of mental reservation was true to the word of God. He posed his own 'murderer at the door' question to Coke. What would you do, he asked, if the French king were to invade England, forcing the queen to flee for her life, and you alone knew of her whereabouts? If questioned, would you not deny knowledge of where she was, even under oath, using a mental reservation? Coke's reply is not recorded, but the chief justice of the court was unpersuaded: 'If this doctrine should be allowed, it would supplant all justice, for we are men, and no Gods, and can judge but according to men's outward actions and speeches, not according to their secrete and inward intentions.'

Southwell was declared guilty by the jury and on 20 February 1595 he was sent to be executed at Tyburn. Having been dragged through the streets on a sled, he was allowed to address the people at some length from the scaffold, and did so movingly. He confessed that he was a Jesuit priest, and prayed for the salvation of queen and country. Hung from the noose, he attempted a sign of the cross before expiring. His lifeless body was disembowelled and quartered, the severed head displayed to the crowd. No one gave the traditional shout of 'Traitor!'

Henry Garnet remained at large until he was arrested in connection with the Gunpowder plot (or the Powder Treason as it was known at the time). Garnet wasn't directly involved in this Catholic conspiracy to assassinate James I and members of Parliament, but it was thought he had foreknowledge of it, and the government was determined to make an example of him. Their investigators came across a treatise Garnet had composed in 1598, arguing for the legitimacy of equivocation and mental reservation. It was dedicated to his friend Southwell and intended as a defence of his actions. Sir Edward Coke, prosecuting once again, was delighted with this find and made it a centrepiece of the trial.[31] He labelled Garnet a 'Doctor of Dissimulation and Destruction'. Coke declared that God had joined heart and tongue in marriage, equivocation being the 'bastard offspring' of 'speech conceived in adultery'. Garnet was found guilty of treason. On the scaffold in St Paul's churchyard, he was mockingly bidden by an official to make a full confession and not equivocate. Garnet replied, 'It is no time now to equivocate.'

* * *

Until the trials of Southwell and Garnet, most people in England had been unaware of the doctrine of mental reservation; laymen had no reason to know of obscure internal debates within the Catholic church. But after their exposure to it via these sensational and widely reported trials they reacted with revulsion and anger. Politicians and Protestants wasted no time in denouncing the doctrine as a prime example of un-English, Jesuitical immorality. To the ordinary man and woman, mental reservation was no more than downright lying dressed up in fancy clothes, all the more hypocritical for claiming not to be what it plainly was. This wasn't even honest lying.

During the seventeenth century the controversy continued to do significant harm to the reputation of the Catholic church. Pope Innocent XI sought to mitigate what had become a public relations disaster by condemning the doctrine in 1679. This may have saved the church further bad publicity but it didn't solve the fundamental question of what to do when faced with a choice of lying or self-incrimination.[32] As a result, the doctrine of mental reservation survived within the Catholic church long after the Pope's interdiction. Indeed, it lives on today.

In 2009, a report on the widespread allegations of clerical child abuse in Ireland was published by a commission established by the Irish government. In it, the report describes, in a tone of some bemusement, the commissioners' discovery of mental reservation, 'a concept developed and much discussed over the centuries, which permits a church man knowingly to convey a misleading impression to another person without being guilty of lying.' An example is given:

John calls to the parish priest to make a complaint about the behaviour of one of his curates. The parish priest sees him coming but does not want to see him because he considers John to be a troublemaker. He sends another of his curates to answer the door. John asks the curate if the parish priest is in. The curate replies that he is not. This is clearly untrue, but in the Church's view it is not a lie because, when the curate told John that the parish priest was not in, he mentally reserved the words '*to you*'.

Cardinal Desmond Connell, himself under investigation, had explained the concept to the commission:

Well, the general teaching about mental reservation is that you are not permitted to tell a lie. On the other hand, you may be put in a position where you have to answer, and there may be circumstances in which you can use an ambiguous expression, realising that the person who you are talking to will accept an untrue version of whatever it may be – permitting that to happen, not willing that it happened, that would be lying. It really

is a matter of trying to deal with extraordinarily difficult matters that may arise in social relations where people
may ask questions that you simply cannot answer.
Everybody knows that this kind of thing is liable to
happen. So mental reservation is, in a sense, a way of
answering without lying.

During their investigations the commission discovered
that priests were using the old tools of equivocation and
reservation to evade inquiries. Marie Collins, who was
abused by a Dublin priest, testified that when the Dublin
archdiocese said in a 1997 press statement that it had
co-operated with the police over her complaint of abuse
she was upset because she had good reason to know this
wasn't true. When a priest made inquiries on her behalf
he was told by the archdiocese 'we never said we co-
operated *fully*'.

Cardinal Connell felt compelled to emphasise that he
did not lie to the media about the use of diocesan funds
for the compensation of clerical child sexual abuse victims.
According to the report, this is how the Cardinal explained
away his misleading statements to the press:

. . . that diocesan funds ARE [report's emphasis] not used
for such a purpose; that he had not said that diocesan
funds WERE not used for such a purpose. By using the
present tense he had not excluded the possibility that
diocesan funds had been used for such purpose in the

past . . . Cardinal Connell considered that there was an enormous difference between the two.

One can imagine Augustine shaking his head in sorrow and fury at this. The trouble with exceptions, he might say, is that once you allow for any at all, other people get to choose which ones are permissible and why.

* * *

If Augustine wrote the moral rulebook for lying, Immanuel Kant translated it for a secular age — an age in which an idea of a universal human morality took the place of a God-given one, and the rights of the individual became the anchor point for discussions of right and wrong. Kant was the philosophers' Robinson Crusoe, constructing sturdy moral dwellings out of earthly materials, hacking out paths through the ethical jungle of modern life. When it came to lying, Kant essentially agreed with Augustine: it was wrong, always and everywhere, with no exceptions.

The bedrock of Kant's argument was the dignity of the individual. We have to tell the truth to the man who wants to kill our friend because every person — even a murderer — has a right to the truth. (Kant didn't get into the question of whether, if our friend survived, he'd want to be friends with us any more.) Deny someone truth, and you deny their humanity, a quality even the worst of us must be accorded. Not only that, but the liar besmirches his own humanity:

The greatest violation of a human being's duty to himself regarded merely as a moral being (the humanity in his own person) is the contrary of truthfulness, lying . . . For the dishonour that accompanies a lie also accompanies a liar like a shadow. By an external lie a human being makes himself an object of contempt in the eyes of others; by an internal lie he does what is still worse: he makes himself contemptible in his own eyes and violates the dignity in his own person. By a lie a human being throws away and, as it were, annihilates his dignity as a human being.

Kant's ideas on lying formed part of his first contribution to moral philosophy, *Groundwork of the Metaphysics of Morals*. It was published in 1785, when he was sixty-one. The treatise was well-received by his contemporaries, who regarded Kant with respect verging on awe; he had already established himself as the most important living philosopher. Not everyone accepted the book's arguments, however. In 1796 a young writer in Paris was bold enough to question them in public.

Benjamin Constant was a Swiss-born nobleman, the descendant of Huguenots who had fled France in the sixteenth century to avoid oppression. Born in 1767, he was a man of the world, educated in Germany, France and Scotland, and one of the first self-consciously liberal thinkers, arguing passionately for the rule of law, the rights of man, and the abolition of slavery. He was dashing and handsome, a gambler and a womaniser who frequently fought duels with cuckolded husbands and was usually juggling the romantic attentions of more than one lady at a time. The great love of his life, however, was Madame De Staël, the brilliant writer, socialite and *grande dame* of European society. The two pursued a tempestuous, intellectually vibrant affair for ten years. After meeting Constant in Switzerland, Mme De Staël took her young lover to Paris in 1795 and introduced him to salon society. He threw himself into the city's intellectual and political life.

Constant published an article that posed the 'murderer at the door' question to Kant. For Constant, this was not just a hypothetical question. Paris was still reeling from the Reign of Terror that followed the French Revolution, which saw thousands of men lose their lives on an arbitrary basis. Although the city was peaceful by the time of Constant's arrival, most households were familiar with the fear of a murderer coming to visit; many had been encouraged to give up their friends to those who would harm them. Living in what Professor Stephen Holmes, a biographer of Constant, describes as an 'hysterical environment', Constant was acutely aware of why a man might lie to protect himself, his family or friends (he may or may not also have been thinking about his rather complicated love life).

For Constant, says Holmes, 'the idea that one could just pronounce all lying to be immoral seemed absurd'. In

Constant's own words, 'The moral principle stating that it is a duty to tell the truth would make any society impossible if that principle were taken singly and unconditionally.' Constant accepted that sometimes lying is necessary, and he also knew that a man might be put to death on the basis of a lie. But to focus on the morality of lying as if it existed in a vacuum was dangerous. Unsurprisingly, Constant felt strongly that all moral arguments needed to be grounded in reality. He was living in a city that was recovering from a period in which abstract principles were taken to extremes; the result had been a murderous terror. Lying was a fact of life; the real imperative was to strengthen society's *institutions* — the rule of law, parliament — thus ensuring that people weren't thrown into jail or relieved of their heads on the basis of malicious untruths.

Kant replied to Constant in 1797, in an essay called 'On the Supposed Right to Lie From Philanthropy'. He stuck rigidly to his position, arguing that it is always wrong to lie, even when the murderer is at your door and asking after your friend. Kant was contemptuous of the idea that there should or could be exceptions to the universal moral law of truth-telling. Exceptions are self-defeating: if everybody agrees it's okay to lie to murderers, then murderers won't believe a word anyone says. You've got to hold the line, and preserve the sacredness of truth. Some principles are more important than your friend's life.

* * *

Two hundred years after this debate, Professor Kang Lee became intrigued by Western attitudes to lying. A Canadian citizen, Lee has lived in Toronto for over twenty years, though he was raised in China and retains an outsider's perspective on the mores of his adoptive culture. Lee was struck by the vigour with which people in the West denounced deceit. The media screamed 'liar' at politicians. Preachers fulminated against deceit from the pulpit. Teachers lectured students and parents warned children against lying. Yet it seemed plain to Lee that every member of those groups, and indeed everyone else, lied as a matter of course, and even endorsed a category of lies known as white lies that seemed to expand and contract according to no obvious logic.[33] What, he wondered, was at the root of this strange example of collective hypocrisy?

Lee had grown up with a rather different attitude to lying. 'In China and in the East generally,' he says, 'it's just much more accepted that there are all sorts of situations in which lying is appropriate.' There is no self-torturing debate over this, he says; legitimate lying is just an unremarkable fact of life. Telling the truth can also be considered wrong — especially if it involves trumpeting one's achievements. This last insight helped Lee to form a hypothesis: that the Western prohibition on lying was based on its elevation of the individual; whereas the Chinese attitude to lying was formed around its reverence for the coherence and harmony of the group.

In 2001 and again in 2007, Lee carried out experiments

on the attitudes to lying among children from China and Canada. The North American children had been raised in a society that places great emphasis on individual achievement, self-esteem and ambition, and on individual rights and freedoms: the culture of Descartes, Crusoe, Thomas Jefferson and Michael Jordan. The Chinese children, by contrast, had been raised in a culture that celebrated the superiority of *Da Wo* (the big me – the collective) over *Xiao Wo* (the small me – the self), an outlook that drew not just on communist ideology but on a deep well of religious and cultural tradition.

In Lee's first study, Chinese (and Taiwanese) children, and Canadian children, all aged between seven and eleven, were read four brief stories. Two stories involved a child carrying out a good deed, while the other two showed a child carrying out a bad deed. When the story character is questioned by a teacher, he answers with either a truthful or an untruthful statement. Sometimes the child is shown lying about his bad deed; other times he's shown lying about his good deed. After hearing the stories, the children were asked if what the character told the teacher was a lie, and then they were asked whether what the character had done was good or bad. All the children, regardless of nationality, demonstrated a basic understanding of what it means to tell a lie, and all the children judged lying about the bad deed as wrong. But when the children were asked to evaluate the story in which the child carried out a good deed and lied about it, a significant difference opened up between the two groups.

The Canadian children were overwhelmingly likely to judge the child's lie as a bad thing, simply because it was a lie; that was enough to condemn it in their eyes. The Chinese children were much more likely to deem the child's lie about his good deed as a morally positive act. When they were asked to explain, they commented that the character 'did not seek praise . . . is not bragging' and is telling a 'well-intentioned lie'. They also gave a relatively negative assessment of the character who tells the truth about his good deed, criticising him for seeking praise. The Canadians, raised in a culture of self-confidence and self-esteem, rated this character's truth-telling positively.

Lee believes this 'modesty effect' derives from Confucianism, which encourages self-effacement in the name of the greater good (as do Buddhism and Taoism). In that philosophy, the good life depends on the health of our key social relations, starting with the family and extending outwards. One of the *Analects of Confucius* makes it clear that honesty is never a matter for the individual alone:

The Governor of She declared to Confucius: 'Among my people, there is a man of unbending integrity: when his father stole a sheep, he denounced him.' Confucius replied, 'Among my people, men of integrity do things differently: a father covers up for his son, and a son covers up for his father – and there is integrity in what they do.'

According to the scholar Daniel Bell, the key questions with which Confucianism is concerned are about the roles we occupy and the obligations we have in those roles. When it comes to the moral evaluation of a lie, concern for an abstract idea of truth or for individual rights are less important than the effect of the lie on those to whom we're obliged – that's to say on the harmony and integrity of the group. This is rather different from Kant's starting point.

Lee had included Taiwanese children so that he could check for the effects of communist ideology. Communism emphasises the collective over the individual, but it is a relatively recent import, grafted on to a Confucian culture. Chinese children in Taiwan have grown up in a capitalist society with superficially different values. But unlike in China, where Confucianism was officially abandoned following the Cultural Revolution, Confucian ideas and values are openly followed and deeply entrenched in Taiwanese society. The evaluations of the Taiwanese children were broadly the same as those of the Chinese; indeed they showed an even bigger contrast with the Canadian children. This indicated to Lee that values of modesty and self-effacement were not derived from the recent political past, but from the deep structures of Chinese culture, transmitted via many generations of parents and teachers.

In a second study, Lee presented Canadian and Chinese children with four different scenarios, based on events with which they would be familiar. In each one, the child protagonist of the story faces a dilemma over whether to tell the truth that helps a friend but harms the group, or harms a friend and helps the group. For instance:

> Here is Susan. Susan's class had to choose some of their classmates to represent the class in a spelling competition at their school. Susan's friend Mike couldn't spell very well, but he really wanted to be in the competition, so he asked Susan to pick him. Susan thought to herself 'If I pick Mike, our class will not do as well at the spelling competition, but Mike is my friend, and if I don't pick him, he will be very upset.' When Susan's teacher asked her who she was going to pick . . .

Children were then asked, 'If you were Susan, what would you do?' In another example, Kelly's friend Jimmy, the best runner in the class, tells her, on school track and field day, that he doesn't feel like running today, and that he's off to the library to read a book. He asks her not to tell anyone. But Kelly knows that if Jimmy isn't on the team then her class don't stand a chance of winning. When the teacher asks Kelly if she knows where Jimmy is, should she tell the truth to help her class or lie to help her friend?

As with Lee's earlier study, the way that the children reacted to these questions was influenced by the culture in which they'd been raised. A Canadian child would be more likely to tell the teacher he was picking Mike because he was good at spelling and that he didn't have a clue where

Jimmy had gone. A Chinese child would be more likely to leave Mike out of the spelling team and have Jimmy dragooned into the track and field team. The divergence grew more pronounced as the children grew older, which Lee takes as evidence of the children becoming more attuned to the norms of their respective cultures.

* * *

Nobody has yet discovered a culture in which all lying is acceptable, or in which no lying is allowed. Some types of lie are always regarded as acceptable, others as reprehensible. Where cultures differ is over what constitutes *acceptable* lying. It's here that cross-cultural misunderstandings can occur. In 1960, anthropologists who spent time with the islanders of Manam in Papua New Guinea noted that European visitors tended to think of the Manam as liars who said one thing and did another, whilst the islanders thought the same of their white visitors. As the researchers put it, 'The difficulty is that the situations which call for a conventional hypocrisy among Manam islanders are not those which call for precisely the same technique in any one kind of European.' Both sides thought they were lying appropriately, neither understood the other's lying etiquette.

In 1991 the British anthropologist Frederick Bailey noted that when he first carried out research in India he was puzzled and annoyed by the number of times polite young Indians responded to his requests for assistance by assuring him that they would 'do the necessary', without, it later turned out, having had any intention of doing anything of the kind. Eventually he came to see that their idea of what constituted an acceptable lie was different from his own. Janet Suskind, who studied the Sharanahua people of Peru, reported that the meat of wild animals was highly valued as food, and people liked to display generosity with it. It was also scarce, however, and more often than not there wasn't enough to share. Direct refusals were perceived as insulting, but it was not an insult to be called a liar. People openly lied about their supplies of meat – indeed such lying was considered 'an essential social grace'. For the Sharanahua, lying solved a conflict between the small amount of game and their social obligations. White lies are the sticking plaster we put over everyday social problems. This suggests a fruitful line of anthropological enquiry: if you want a shortcut to understanding the tensions within a particular social system, find out what kinds of lies it deems legitimate.

The economist Timur Kuran argues that minor private deceptions can have larger public implications. Most of us have, at some point, perhaps in the back of a cab or around the office canteen table, found ourselves faced with a choice between pretending to agree to a political state-ment in which we don't believe or risking an unpleasant argument or, worse, inviting social ostracism. In Kuran's terms, we all have to deal with conflicts between our 'expressive utility' – our desire to be truthful – and our 'reputational utility' – our standing in the community. We often choose to do so by lying.

If everyone was completely honest about their beliefs all the time millions more arguments and fights would start and society would splinter. But a seemingly harmless lie can have ramifications beyond your own conscience. The lie you tell to maintain your reputation might have a knock-on effect if it reaffirms the belief of others in the room — who may privately think the same thing as you — that the 'correct' social behaviour is to say otherwise. An accumulation of these small lies can lead to large public lies, enabling the perpetuation of outmoded traditions or social practices long after people cease believing in them. Kuran uses communism in Eastern Europe as an example of when the majority thought differently than their public personas led others to believe; as soon as the regimes started to crumble, public support for them abruptly collapsed. 'Not a few men who cherish lofty and noble ideas hide them under a bushel for fear of being called different,' said Martin Luther King.

The human capacity for deception was born from the need of our ancestors to navigate relationships with others in the African savannah. To put it mildly, things haven't got any simpler since then. Our intensely social nature is at once the best reason to tell the truth and the reason we can't do without lying.

Lying resists moral rule-making and rule-following because, of all the sins, it's the one we need most in order to get along with each other. At every turn, life undermines any strict adherence to truth-telling because life, if it's any good at least, involves other people, and as Henry Garnet suggested, our obligations to other people will inevitably come into conflict with our desire to be perfectly truthful. Kant argued that lying was always wrong because it fatally undermined our relationships with others. That is surely true, and Browne's Law reminds us that truth-telling is the only possible default in a functioning society. But it's also true that those same relationships require us to lie from time to time. A theologian or a philosopher of metaphysics can propose universal moral imperatives; the rest of us want to maintain good relations with our mother-in-law – or save a friend from harm.

Even Kant may not have been quite as unyielding on the subject as he claimed. In the *Metaphysics of Morals*, the same writer who would – in theory – give his friend away to a murderer rather than lie, ponders more quotidian questions, like whether it's acceptable to write 'your obedient servant' at the close of a letter, or what to say to an author who asks you whether you like his work, when the true answer is no. One might choose to laugh off such questions with a quip, muses Kant, but 'who always has his wits about him?' Never has the great man sounded more human. 'The slightest hesitation,' he writes, 'is already a mortification for the author. May one flatter him, then?' In these frowning, shrugging sentences we can hear Kant struggling with the moral muddiness of everyday life, and coming close to an admission that equivocation has its uses.

Afterword: How to be Honest

Three Principles of Living Honestly

1. Share the Work

Realising how central lies are to our existence forces us to think harder about what being honest really means. Honesty is not effortless, but something at which we have to work.

Kant famously expressed his awe at 'the starry sky above us, and the moral law within'. Darwin and his successors, however, have portrayed the human species as being in possession of a rather erratic internal moral compass. Although we are by no means a purely selfish animal, we are what the contemporary philosopher Peter Railton terms 'us-ish': naturally inclined to look after our own kith and kin first. We are also, as we've seen, wrapped in useful illusions. Our brains aren't designed to seek the truth, about either ourselves or the world around us. The anthropologist Robin Fox put it to me like this: 'The brain's business is not to give us an accurate or objective view of the world, but to give us a useful view — one we can act on.' Its primary job is to help the packet of tissue, bone and muscle in which it's encased to survive and thrive; reporting on reality is an important but secondary consideration. So is telling the truth to others.

That's not to say Kant's admiration was misplaced. We have somehow managed to straighten the crooked timber of our own nature; to overcome our natural partiality and bias and get closer to the truth. How? By acting in concert. First, we've developed social norms of truth-telling; an understanding, expressed in written or unwritten ethical codes, that telling the truth is usually preferable to lying. Second, we've developed habits of shared enquiry; the procedures of logic and rigorous scientific procedure of the kind bequeathed to us by Voltaire, Bacon, Lavoisier and Franklin. Third, we've evolved institutions of law, democracy and the right to free expression, so that every claim to truth is challenged, every partial viewpoint opposed or contrasted with another.

None of these is a perfect guard against dishonesty or corruption, of course — far from it — and they don't change our fundamental nature. But that was Benjamin Constant's point: man is a flawed creature, but it's his social obligations rather than abstract moral rules that keep him honest, which is why we must engage in a constant struggle to maintain and improve the institutions of an enlightened, liberal society. It's also why we should take care to design and sustain social environments — at school, at work — that reward truth-telling more often than not. Honesty is something we do together.

2. Distrust Your Own Certainty

The idea of trusting yourself runs deep in modern culture, we're all taught to follow our hearts and believe in our instincts. But our instincts can be misleading. The research of Timothy Wilson, for instance, suggests that we can't even predict our own behaviour very well – that our friends, or even informed strangers, have a much clearer idea of how we're going to act than we do. Yes, we have privileged access to our own thoughts and motivations, but often this results in a case of too much information. Unable to see the behavioural wood for the mental trees, we make flaky predictions about what we're going to do, based on flawed analyses of our own characters. We over-estimate the likelihood that we'll stick to a diet or an exercise regime, and under-estimate our propensity to fall for entirely unsuitable partners. We profess to motivations and intentions that don't exist and deny the existence of real ones.

An important and under-estimated facet of being honest with yourself, then, is not trusting your own sense of certainty. Most of us have been in situations where even if we know we don't have all the facts to hand, we *just know* we're right about something. We have a natural tendency to think that the more passionately convinced we are of something, the more likely it is that we're correct. But this just isn't so. The neurologist Robert Burton argues that the correlation we discern between the strength of a conviction and the likelihood of it being right is a self-deceiving illusion spun by the brain — what he calls the 'feeling of knowing'. The warm rush of certainty we experience when arriving at a definite point of view or reiterating a long-held belief is not to be trusted. It's something we are biologically programmed to feel but the programme, although intended to help us come to a decision — to act — has little to do with whether or not we're actually right.

The feeling of knowing can lead us astray in all sorts of ways, because it encourages us to shut our minds off to discussion or contradictory opinion, thus allowing in-built, irrational biases and prejudices to rule our mental roost.[34] (Our over-confidence about being able to tell whether someone is lying to us being just one example.) We have to be on our guard against the many ruses of the self-deceptive mind. 'The first principle is that you must not fool yourself, and you are the easiest person to fool,' said the physicist Richard Feynman.

Of course, it's nigh on impossible to live without certainty — it's probably best to be certain that stepping in front of a moving car will kill you, that you will need to eat again at some point, or that *Seinfeld* is the best sitcom ever made. As much as is reasonable, however, we might experiment with replacing the words *I know* with *I believe*, even if that means we admit to not being so certain about whether God exists or if man-made climate-change is real. The economist Tyler Cowen has remarked that whereas most people seem to work with a model of nearly a hundred per cent probability that their political beliefs are correct, it would be more sensible to work with something like a sixty per cent probability. Such an internal admission of fallibility is easier said than done – try it now, with whatever you consider your core beliefs, and you'll see what I mean. But the world might be a better place if we all listened a little less to our feeling of knowing and a little more to each other.

3. Accept a Necessary Margin of Illusion

Between Vancouver Island and the Pacific coast of North America is a slender strip of water, home to fjord-like inlets, sounds, and hundreds of densely forested, rocky, almost impenetrable islands. For thousands of years a fishing people known as the Kwakiutl populated this archipelago, as well as the northern part of Vancouver Island and the adjoining mainland. The Kwakiutl were famed for their beautiful art and pottery and for idiosyncratic customs like the potlatch, in which the chiefs of different bands competed to give away the most wealth. They were also known for their shamans: healers who could cure people of sickness by communicating with the spirits. In 1887 the anthropologist Franz Boas made a primitive recording of a Kwakiutl shaman singing a healing song. The shaman's name was Quesalid (pronounced *Kesalid*). After recording his voice, Boas transcribed Quesalid's account of how, many years before, he became a shaman.

In his youth, Quesalid was an angry young man. Shamans in Native American tribes were something like a cross between priests, doctors and rock stars; highly respected, even feared, and paid highly for their services. Almost alone amongst his family and friends Quesalid was resentful of the shamans, their riches and their prestige; in his eyes they were frauds who preyed on the needy, the vulnerable and the foolish. So he concocted a plan to expose them. First, he would win their trust so that they would share their secrets with him. Then he would tell the world, and break their power for ever.

He started hanging around with the local shamans until, eventually, one of them offered him an apprenticeship. Sure enough, Quesalid's first lessons were an education in deception: he was taught how to simulate fainting and nervous fits (sometimes shamans would appear to be in a battle with the spirits) and about the practice of 'dreamers': spies employed by the shamans to eavesdrop on private conversations around the village and report back to them, so that later they could seem to intuit the symptoms and origin of the patient's condition.

He even learnt the greatest secret of all — the truth behind the signature move of Kwakiutl shamans. When a member of the tribe fell sick the shaman would be called for a consultation and, if he deemed it worthwhile, an elaborate ritual would be enacted. At a fire-lit ceremony filled with music, singing and chanting, the shaman would lean over the body of the sick person, place his mouth to the affected part — the patient's chest, for example — and appear to suck out a physical manifestation of the evil spirit. Now Quesalid learned how it worked: the shaman hides a little tuft of eagle down in his mouth and bites his tongue to make it bleed. He bends over the patient. As the drums beat faster and the music comes to a crescendo, he lifts up his head and spits out the blood-soaked tuft.

Quesalid's worst suspicions were confirmed: the highest magic of the shamans was nothing more than a sleight-of-hand, a shabby deceit. He resolved to publicise his findings. But then something unexpected happened. His apprenticeship amongst the shamans had become common knowledge, and one day he was summoned by the family of a sick boy who had dreamed of Quesalid as his healer. It was known that when this happened, whoever the ailing person had dreamed of would be most likely to cure them. The family, who lived on a nearby island, were desperate for help; Quesalid could hardly say no. As night fell, men from the boy's village came in their canoes to collect him. Having already secreted some eagle down under his upper lip, Quesalid set off to perform his first healing ceremony.

Once ashore, he was welcomed into the house of the boy's grandfather. In the middle of the house was a fire, surrounded by men, women and children from the village.

Music was being played. At the rear of the house was the boy, who seemed weak, his breath short. As Quesalid knelt down beside him, the boy opened his eyes and, pointing to his lower ribs, whispered, 'Welcome. Have mercy on me that I may live.' The apprentice shaman placed his mouth to the boy's body, biting on his own tongue as he did so. After a few seconds he lifted his head and spat the bloody down into the palm of his hand. The musicians played loud and fast as he danced around the fire, singing a sacred song and holding out the boy's disease for everyone to see. Then he buried it in the hot ashes of the fire. The boy sat up. He was better already.

Here is the American anthropologist Alfred Kroeber, writing in 1952:

Next, there is the old question of deception. Probably most shamans or medicine men, the world over, help along with sleight-of-hand in curing and especially in exhibitions of power. This sleight-of-hand is sometimes deliberate; in many cases awareness is perhaps not deeper than the foreconscious. The attitude, whether there has been repression or not, seems to be as towards a pious fraud. Field ethnographers seem quite generally convinced that even shamans who know that they are frauds nevertheless also believe in their powers, and especially in those of other shamans: they consult them when they themselves or their children are ill.

Afterword: How to be Honest

Without willing it, Quesalid had gone from posing as a shaman's apprentice to *being* a shaman, and from being an enemy of deceit to the perpetrator of an illusion. Although his story takes place in a society far removed from our own it raises questions that all of us, at some level, are engaged in every day.

The playwright Alan Bennett remarked that 'be yourself' is a 'baffling injunction'. Perhaps what it really means, he said, is 'pretend to be yourself'. The sociologist Erving Goffman pointed out that the line between stage acting and real life is alarmingly fine. Of course, it takes skill and training to become a good actor, but that needn't obscure the fact that most people, given a script and a simple set of directions, can convey some sense of realness to an audience. This is because, says Goffman, 'life itself is a dramatically enacted thing'. Ordinary social intercourse consists of improvisation around a repetoire of ready-made lines, expressions and gestures that we draw upon to make our 'performance' convincing. (It's not insignificant that the word 'person' derives from the Latin word for a mask worn by an actor.) In Goffman's view, we're all actors who have half-forgotten that we're acting. Most of the time we play a double game, aware that others are performing for us and yet believing in the performance at the same time. In *Penny Lane*, The Beatles sing about a series of characters – the banker, the fireman, the barber – who make up the life of the street. A young nurse selling poppies from a tray gets the feeling that she is in a play. 'She is anyway,' sings Paul McCartney.

A character in Henrik Ibsen's *The Wild Duck* remarks, 'Deprive a man of his life-lie and you rob him of his happiness.' Ibsen believed that many of us find reality so unpleasant that we wear a mask of idealism — a mask which is also a shield — and create an alternative life for ourselves. It's a theme that runs through much modern drama and literature, and, particularly in the American tradition, it comes tied up with a bleak vision of bourgeois life. Think of Arthur Miller's salesman, John Cheever's swimmer, the constantly yearning and shrinking characters of Richard Yates or, in film, the slow self-destruction of Lester Burnham in *American Beauty*. In these stories the life-lie is portrayed as a dishonest flight from truth; a mask which it's the artist's job to remove. But perhaps this is competitive jealousy on the part of the artist. There is another way of looking at our capacity for deception and self-deception: as an expression of our defiantly creative nature — our refusal to accept that the world as it is, is all there is. The protagonist of Eugene O'Neil's *The Iceman Cometh* declares 'the lie of a pipe dream is what gives life to the whole misbegotten mad lot of us, drunk or sober'. Hannah Arendt, the political philosopher, remarked that 'our ability to lie — but not necessarily our ability to tell the truth — belongs among the few obvious, demonstrable data that confirm human freedom.'

Afterword: How to be Honest

Our need to keep in touch with reality exists in tension with an equally strong need to make up stories that aren't true — and to believe in them. Without the former, we couldn't get on for long with our environment or with each other. Without the latter, we wouldn't have the imaginative reach that has driven all human progress. Perhaps we should accept our need for both and wear our masks with equanimity, while not letting ourselves forget they are masks. In the words of Wallace Stevens, 'The final belief is to believe in a fiction which you know to be a fiction.'

After curing his first patient, Quesalid was acclaimed as a great shaman. The only person who didn't believe that Quesalid had performed something magical was Quesalid. But success had shaken his cynicism. As word of his triumph spread, he accepted invitations to practise his technique at the healing ceremony of neighbouring tribes, and found that he could cure patients thought to be beyond hope. In the years that followed he grew famous and wealthy by practising the art he once dismissed as a sham. Although Quesalid told Boas that he was still a sceptic, he took great pride in his work.

Notes

1   While this is inherently true of language *per se*, it may be that there are some languages in which it is harder to lie than in others. The language of the Matses, an Amazonian tribe, has a structure that obliges its speakers to specify exactly how they know what they're saying is true. Instead of saying 'An animal passed here,' the Matses speaker must specify whether he saw the animal passing, or saw its footprints and made an inference, or made an educated guess, or heard it from somebody else. If somebody makes a statement without backing it up like this, it's considered a lie. According to the linguist Guy Deutscher, if you ask a Matses man how many wives he has, unless he can actually see his wives at that very moment he'll answer in the past tense and say something like 'There were two last time I checked.' After all, he can't be absolutely certain that one of them hasn't died or run off with another man since he last saw them, even if this was only five minutes ago – so to report it as a fact would be deceitful.

2   Talwar relates that the creativity of the lies told by children

337

in this test is impressive, ranging from 'That's great, my dad really needs a bar of soap.' To 'I collect soap.'

3 This awful story ended with more violence. After his arrest, Weddell was released on bail. He travelled to his mother-in-law's house, shot her, then turned the gun on himself.

4 Larson brought back Margaret Taylor for another session the day after her first, ostensibly to find out whether the questioner was affecting the subject and hence the reliability of the test. He asked her to lie to him, and then he asked her out. Within a year they were married.

5. The polygraph was also adopted by organisations wishing to screen for homosexuality. The Royal Canadian Mounted Police experimented with a device that monitored the diameter of a subject's pupil while he was shown pictures of naked men. Faced with inconclusive results, the Mounties designed a fluid-filled tube that fastened around the subject's penis, registering any tumescence whilst he viewed lurid images of men, women and children. The penile plethysmograph is used in the assessment of sex offenders to this day.

6. By contrast, the police questioning of Omar Ballard was brief, casual, and completely lacking in the high-pressure techniques applied to the Norfolk Four. Unlike their confessions, Ballard's testimony matched the known facts of the crime and contained verifiable details that had not been publicly disclosed.

7. Michelle's parents, who watched the tapes of the confessions, continue to believe that the men convicted of the

crime are guilty, and expressed fury at the conditional pardons.

8. By publicly casting doubt on the phenomenon of recovered memories, Loftus became a pilloried and even hated figure among its almost cult-like devotees. She received death threats, and for a while armed guards were required to accompany her at speaking events.

9. Three-quarters of a million dollars was spent investigating the Ingram case. Police flew night helicopter patrols, searching for the fires of a satanic cult meeting in progress; all they found were a few terrified students drinking from kegs of beer. Doctors examined the Ingram daughters for evidence of physical violence or sexual abuse, and identified none. A forensic archaeologist, Dr Mark Papworth, was called in to search for the bones of dead babies, with the help of maps that the daughters had helped the police to draw up, identifying the supposed burial spots. After much digging he found nothing except the toe bone of an elk. Papworth later recounted telling one of the detectives that there was 'No evidence. None at all. Zero.' The detective replied, 'If you were the Devil would you leave any evidence?'

10. The cognitive scientist Mark Changizi explains why this works better for Fitzgerald than keeping his eye on the ball. It takes a tenth of a second between the time the light from the ball strikes his eye to the time his brain perceives it. When the ball and the person are moving fast, a tenth of a second is a long time; if Fitzgerald's brain is

working with a perception of what the world is like when light hits his eye, the ball will fly past him. So he closes his eyes and takes a highly educated *guess* on what the world will look like in a tenth of a second's time.

11. If you lost this 'sixth sense' you would become painfully aware of its importance. The clinical neurologist Jonathan Cole has written about a patient who suffered nerve damage from a viral illness at age nineteen, and lost all proprioception. He became entirely reliant on his *conscious* attention for working out what his body was doing. Unless he watched his arm or leg to keep it still, it moved uncontrollably. After a Herculean effort to train his body he was able to stand, and eventually resume something like a normal life. He learned to walk, to dress himself, even to drive, by applying fierce attention to his own body. But if the lights went out, he collapsed to the floor.

12. In *Ethics*, published posthumously in 1677, the Dutch philosopher Baruch Spinoza wrote that 'Men believe themselves to be free, simply because they are conscious of their actions, and unconscious of the causes whereby those actions are determined.'

13. When the researcher holds up the alternative cards (photographs) in this experiment he is actually holding two in each hand, with the opposite choice of each card tucked behind it. The two cards at the front have a black back. When the participant chooses a card, from say, the researcher's left hand, the researcher lays both cards in that hand face-down, and slides the one on top – the oppo-

site of the one chosen — across the table. The participant doesn't see that his actual choice remains face-down on the table, because its black back blends with the black tabletop.

14. This is a slight simplification. A few people seem to have language facility in the right brain. But *where* it resides isn't so important. What matters is that specific brain systems handle specific tasks.

15. 'How does it feel,' wonders the neuroscientist Christof Koch, 'to be the mute hemisphere, permanently encased in one skull in the company of a dominant sibling that does all of the talking?'

16. Marion's husband was not a believer. He went to bed as usual that night, and slept soundly.

17. For the purposes of publication, Festinger changed the place in question to a town in Michigan. He also invented the names for the people involved; those are the ones used here.

18. There is some evidence to suggest that men are more prone to positive illusions than women, who are more likely to have some negative illusions about themselves — to regard themselves as slightly less skilled and competent than they really are. But it's hard to tell whether this is a function of gender or of power: women in dominant power relations are more likely to have positive illusions; men in subordinate positions are more prone to negative illusions.

19. Woods had commanded an Apache helicopter company in the first Gulf War. During the course of his 2003 interviews he realised that one of the men he was about to

meet, a senior member of Iraq's Republican guard, had been the commander of an armoured tank brigade that Woods and his company had destroyed in the open desert of northern Kuwait. After a couple of sessions with this man Woods told him about their previous encounter. The Iraqi calmly recounted the horror of the incident from the other side of the gun sight.

20. According to the Iraq Survey Group (a separate fact-finding mission organised by US intelligence services), Saddam knew his subordinates had a tendency to lie, but his earlier efforts to check their claims through personal tours of inspection of military facilities decreased as he became more and more reclusive. He was deeply shaken by the 1998 joint US and UK bombing operation 'Operation Desert Fox', during which one of his palaces was reduced to rubble. Following this, he retreated even further into a small, closed and secretive world.

21. Nobody rated Saddam's people skills more highly than Saddam, who would often boast of his ability to see the hidden hearts of those around him. On one of the tapes that Woods listened to, Saddam declares to his assembled generals and ministers that 'I know which one of you will betray me before you know.'

22. Psalm 116 describes the psalmist's gratitude to God for saving him from physical danger and spiritual despair. In the English (King James) translation verse 11 reads: 'I was greatly afflicted: I said in my haste, All men are liars.'

23. Back in 1761, when he was in London, Franklin had

attended a performance of music produced by stroking the rims of glasses filled with liquid to various levels. Charmed, he resolved to design a glass-based instrument that would be easier to play. His invention consisted of a row of glass bowls of different sizes, fitted on a wooden axle that was rotated by the action of a foot-pedal. The performer spins the bowls with his foot and touches the rims of the glasses with his moistened fingers. The result is an ethereal, mystical music; notes seem to float in from nowhere, like ghosts, and linger in the air. By 1762 the armonica (Franklin derived its name from the Italian word for harmony) was being commercially produced and was soon taken seriously by composers and musicians (its fans included Beethoven and Goethe). Franklin himself loved to play it and wasn't above encouraging the popular belief that it had healing qualities. Princess Izabella Czartoryska of Poland describes in a diary how she was ill with 'melancholia' when she met the great American, so ill that she was already writing her testament and farewell letters. Franklin – an epic flirt – took her hands, gazed into her eyes, and murmured *'Pauvre jeune femme'*, before playing the armonica for her. *'Madame,'* he declared after finishing, 'you are cured.' Sure enough, she immediately felt like her old self again.

24. In his 1911 play *The Doctor's Dilemma,* George Bernard Shaw presents a doctor who is incompetent in every scientific sense, and yet effective nonetheless. Dr Sir Ralph Bloomfield-Bonington ('B.B.') is described as 'healing by

the mere incompatibility of disease or anxiety with his welcome presence. Even broken bones, it is said, have been known to unite at the sound of his voice.' The ideal physician, of course, has both skill-sets.

25. David Morris points out that cultural beliefs have sometimes evolved to create illness as well as to relieve it, as a means of heading off greater dangers. Apaches, from ancient times until the twentieth century, suffered from certain maladies unique to their people. Merely crossing the path left by a snake was enough to bring on horrible facial sores (which the shaman would then have to treat). Any contact with a bear – even touching bear fur – could bring on physical deformities. These conditions seem to have developed as the strongest possible signal to keep away from potentially fatal encounters.

26. The vendor described his Shreddie as 'not in mint condition – one corner is chipped'.

27. Zborowski was not the man Mead thought he was. His most significant professional experience was not in anthropology, but spying. All the time he worked for Sedov he was actually feeding information about the Trotskyites to Stalin's secret police, the GPU (Stalin was said to take a special interest in his reports). Several of Zborowski's anti-Stalinist friends died sudden, violent and mysterious deaths, including Sedov himself, whom Zborowski then replaced as leader of the group. His GPU handlers then tried to persuade him to go to Trotksy's hideout in Mexico (the cable urged him to 'get to the OLD MAN'), but Zborowski

contrived to remain in Paris, where he was studying anthropology at the Sorbonne. When Zborowski moved to the United States he continued to spy for the GPU, this time on the activities of his American Trotskyite friends. His spying was revealed to a Senate committee in 1955 by the defector Alexander Orlov. Brought before the committee, Zborowski admitted to spying but said he ceased doing so after 1937. Later evidence proved this to be false, and in 1963 he was sentenced to five years in prison, of which he served two before being released. He lied to Margaret Mead, who remained a loyal friend to the end, telling her the Soviets forced him to work for them by threatening his relatives. His academic career was largely unhindered. He rose to become Director of the Pain Institute at Mount Zion hospital, where he remained until retirement. Mark Zborowski died in 1990 in San Francisco, aged 82.

28. Luckily, she escaped six days later after being freed by resistance fighters.

29. Students of Bill Clinton's impeachment trial may find this style of argument familiar.

30. One useful, possibly unintentional side-effect of this doctrine might have been to make the deceit more convincing. Actors are sometimes trained in a similar technique.

31. Following Garnet's trial, Shakespeare gave a line to the Porter in *Macbeth* that audiences would have recognised as a reference to Garnet, Southwell, and Jesuit casuistry: 'Here's an equivocator, that could swear in both the scales against either scale, who committed treason enough for

God's sake, yet could not equivocate to heaven.' Indeed, as the critic Frank Kermode pointed out, verbal equivocation is one of the play's themes. The witches employ linguistic trickery to lead on Macbeth, such as their promise that none of woman born may harm him. Only when it is too late does Macbeth 'begin/to doubt th' equivocation of the fiend/That lies like truth'.

32. Protestants faced the same dilemma, and some reached similar conclusions as the Jesuit casuists. William Tyndale declared that 'to lie also, and to dissemble, is not always sin.'

33. Lee was particularly struck by a piece of research from Italy showing that children agreed that all lying was wrong, *unless* the lie in question was endorsed by a priest.

34. Burton intended his book to act as a counterweight to the slew of popular psychology books urging us to trust in our intuitions, a trend started by Malcolm Gladwell's *Blink*, which suggested that 'instant cognition' is often wiser than years of study or the sifting of evidence. Burton's point is not that we should disregard our intuitions about people or situations when we're trying to work out what we think – such feelings can indeed provide very significant data, rooted as they often are in sophisticated unconscious processes. But the more certain we feel, the more we should question ourselves, interrogate other possibilities, and listen to contradictory opinions. Always blink twice.

Further Reading

Introduction and Chapter One: The Lying Animal

Robert Feldman's book *Liar: The Truth About Lying* summarises his research on the topic and is a good survey of the role of lies in everyday life. Bella DePaulo's work in this area is essential, and a guide to it can be found at her website, www.belladepaulo.com. It was Byrne and Whiten's theory of Machiavellian Intelligence that first made me think about a book on lying, and when researching a piece for *The Times* science supplement, *Eureka*, I was lucky enough hear about the development of this theory from Richard Byrne himself. He pointed me in the direction of Nicholas Humphrey's seminal paper 'The Social Function of Intellect'. Robin Dunbar's theory about the importance of social groups to brain size can be found in his book *Grooming, Gossip and the Evolution of Language* amongst other places. The anecdotes about primate deceit are drawn from Byrne and Whiten's *Machiavellian Intelligence* and from Frans de Waal's work, including *Our Inner Ape*, a successor to *Chimpanzee Politics*. I found the stories about Barnum and Jerry Andrus in a piece by Errol Morris for the *New York Times*, entitled 'Seven Lies About Lying'. George Steiner's thoughts on the importance of lying to human development can be found in his book *After Babel*. Bernard Knox writes about the contrast between Odysseus and Achilles in the introduction to Robert Fagles's translation of *The Odyssey* (I thank Stephen Brown for the pointer).

Chapter Two: First Lies

Vasudevi Reddy's book *How Infants Know Minds* explores the mental and social development of very young children and their burgeoning skills of fakery and deception. Victoria Talwar and Kang Lee have probably done the most and the best work on the topic of children and lying, and their lucidly written papers are well worth reading. I'm grateful to Victoria Talwar for sharing with me her paper on punitive environments and for taking me through her fieldwork in West Africa. Simon Baron-Cohen's essay 'I Cannot Tell a Lie – What people with autism can tell us about honesty' can be found online, at the website of the periodical *In Character*. I was alerted to Sir Thomas Browne's take on lying while reading the very stimulating *A Pack of Lies: Towards A Sociology of Lying*, by J.A. Barnes. Readers interesting in learning more about Browne, a fascinating figure who had much to say about the nature of truth (and many other things), might start with *The World Proposed*, a collection of essays about him and his work, edited by Reid Barbour and Claire Preston.

Further Reading

Chapter Three: Confabulators

William Hirstein's book *Brain Fiction* is a good overview of the significance of confabulation and its links to self-deception and storytelling. Will Self was generous enough to spend time discussing with me the nature of his creative process as part of my research for a previous book that never saw the light of day; I'm glad to be able to use some of his illuminating insights here (it was he who put me on to David Hume's thoughts on the nature of imaginative creation). The story of Jonathan Aitken's fictional car chase is drawn from *The Liar*, by Luke Harding, David Leigh and David Pallister, a compelling account of the court case as seen from the *Guardian*'s side. My description of Marlon Brando's acting class is based on the journalist Jod Kaftan's account of his relationship with the great man, first published in *Rolling Stone*, though I heard it in an episode of National Public Radio's *This American Life* to which Kaftan contributed. I first read about Charles Limb's experiment with jazz musicians on the superb psychology blog *Mind Hacks*, the point of embarkation for many a journey. I'm indebted to Jonah Lehrer's various reflections on the mental processes behind creativity, including his excellent piece on it for *Seed* magazine. I read about the experiment on high-creativity versus high-IQ students in Robert Sternberg's comprehensive survey of the field, the *Handbook of Creativity*. I spoke to Adrian Raine about his research on the psychopathic brain when researching a piece about his work for *Eureka*.

Chapter Four: Tells and Leakages

Along with many other people I first read about the work of Paul Ekman in Malcolm Gladwell's essay for the *New Yorker*, 'The Naked Face'. Ekman's own books, including *Telling Lies* and *Why Kids Lie* offer highly readable introductions to his work on facial expressions and deception. I'm grateful to Robert Hunter for discussing with me the theory and practice of lie detection and its relevance to legal process, and for the concept of 'the demeanour assumption'. I came across the research on rape investigations at *Deception Blog* (http://deception.crime psychblog.com), a wonderful trove of links to contemporary deception research, the discovery of which helped convince me that there was a book to be written on this subject (I thank its anonymous compiler). I became interested in the Charles Ingram case after reading an article by Jon Ronson for the *Guardian* in which he reconsiders his earlier assessment of Ingram's guilt after reading James Plaskett's meticulous dissection of the prosecution case, available online. The analysis of the Iranian election was published in the *Washington Post* shortly after the election had taken place. Its statistical reasoning has subsequently been questioned; those wishing to follow the debate may start here: http://bit.ly/fqGQ3T. I offer it here as a vivid example of a very interesting new discipline.

Further Reading

Chapter Five: The Dream of a Truth Machine

My account of the polygraph's invention and development relies heavily on Ken Alder's exhaustively researched social history, *The Lie Detectors*. I also referred to the very readable report on the polygraph produced by National Academy of Sciences, available free online, as is the Pentagon's 2001 *Annual Report on the Polygraph*. Tim Weiner, David Johnston and Neil Lewis write about Aldrich Ames's encounters with the polygraph in their book *Betrayal*. I first came across Ames's letter to Steven Aftergood on the wonderful *Letters of Note* blog. I am grateful to Ruben Gur, Daniel Langleben and Jane Campbell Moriarty for sharing with me their expertise on the new forms of lie detection technology; any views expressed here are very much my own. Ian Herbert's excellent discussion of the power of false confessions in court cases led me to the Bill Bosko case and to the research of Saul Kassin. Elizabeth Loftus's papers are all well-written, colourful and worth reading in the original, as are her books. William Saletan has written a very good survey of Loftus's career for *Slate* magazine. My account of the Paul Ingram case relies largely on the work of Lawrence Wright, whose reports on the case originally appeared in the *New Yorker* before being published in the form of a book, *Remembering Satan*. I also referred to a detailed account of the case written by Ethan Watters for *Mother Jones* magazine.

Chapter Six: I Me Lie

My account of how the brain creates its version of reality owes a very significant debt to Chris Frith's excellent, accessible overview of the subject, *Making Up The Mind*, and to a conversation I had with him after reading it. I found the phrase that I borrow from David Eagleman in the transcript of a conversation he had with Robert Krulwich for NPR, available online. Reed Albergotti wrote about the mystery of Larry Fitzgerald's 'blind' catching for the *Wall Street Journal*. The experiment involving love on a precarious bridge, and the patient who suffered from a lack of proprioception, are both described in Timothy Wilson's *Strangers to Ourselves*, a powerful argument for the importance of unconscious processes to our behaviour and moods. Petter Johansson was kind enough to spend time with me discussing his research (as well as explaining exactly how that sleight-of-hand worked). Michael Gazzaniga writes compellingly about his work with split-brain patients in his book *The Social Brain*, among other places, and Daniel Dennett has been the primary exponent of the implications of Gazzaniga's work for our ideas about consciousness. I first came across Arthur Schopenhauer's description of the novelistic mind in John Gray's book *Straw Dogs*. In *Opening Skinner's Box* Lauren Slater offers fresh insight into the significance of Leon Festinger's fieldwork with the Lake City cultists. I've been fascinated by the story of Sabbatai Zevi ever since reading about it in Paul Johnson's *A History of the Jews*. The definitive book on the Zevi phenomenon is by the historian Gershom

Scholem. I also found Matt Goldish's account of the Sabbatean movement helpful.

Chapter Seven: I Am Nice and In Control

Shelley Taylor is the most lucid exponent of her own research, and I have based my account of her work on her book *Positive Illusions: Creative Self-Deception and the Healthy Mind*. I first heard about Caroline Starek's research on self-deception and championship swimming while listening to an episode of the NPR programme 'RadioLab', an early influence on my thinking; I'm grateful to the RadioLab team for this and for generally being such an splendidly fertile source of stimulation and inspiration — anyone who hasn't checked out their podcasts should do so at the earliest opportunity. Virginia Postrel's short but incisive article 'In Praise of Irrational Exuberance' (available online) pointed me to the passage I quote from Adam Smith, and to Colin Campbell's take on consumerism. My version of Pizarro's rout of Atahualpa's army is based on the first-hand accounts quoted in Jared Diamond's *Guns, Germs and Steel*, and I borrowed the idea of juxtaposing that episode to Custer's Last Stand from Dominic Johnson — indeed, much of this chapter was inspired by Johnson's eye-opening exploration of the role of over-confidence in warfare, in his book *Overconfidence and War*. My conversation with Kevin Woods about his work on the Iraq Perspectives Project was one of the most fascinating I had in the course of researching this book, and his report is essential reading if you're interested in the background to the war (as is the Duelfer Report).

Chapter Eight: Lies We Live By: Part One

The literature on placebo effects is wide. Dylan Evans's book *Placebo* is a good place to start. I found Michael Brooks's cogent and perceptive overview of the topic in *Thirteen Things That Don't Make Sense* to be very helpful. Anne Harrington's books offer rich historical context. Daniel Moerman's *Meaning, Medicine and the 'Placebo Effect'* contains the most penetrating arguments about this phenomenon, placing it in a wider context of culture and meaning, and questioning the capacity of medical science as currently constituted to fully explain it. My account of Henry Beecher's discovery is drawn from a combination of these sources and Beecher's own published papers. Robert Darnton's *Mesmerism and the End of the Enlightenment in France* offers a lively account of Mesmer's rise and fall. Other places to read about this extraordinary episode include Claude-Anne Lopez's lively essay and Stacey Schiff's masterly account of Franklin's years in Paris.

Chapter Nine: Lies We Live By: Part Two

My interest in this subject was sparked by Steve Silberman's excellent report for *Wired*, available online. I heard about the Diamond Shreddies case study when watching the video of Rory Sutherland's talk at TED Global 2009, and the campaign's originator Hunter Somerville was kind enough to tell me the story from his side. I was inspired to explore the research into wine tasting after reading Jonah Lehrer's discussion of it in his book *The Decisive Moment*. I came across Mark Zborowski's anthropological investigation of the nature of pain in Daniel Moerman's book, and read about Zborowski's extraordinary life in Steven Zipperstein's essay for the *Jewish Review of Books*.

Chapter Ten: The Murderer at the Door

I relied on multiple sources for my brief history of the Christian church's relationship with lying, including and especially Johann Somerville's essay 'The New Art of Lying', in Leites's *Conscience and Casuistry in Early Modern Europe*, and Perez Zagorin's overview of lying and religion in the early modern period, *Ways of Lying*. Christopher Devlin's biography of Robert Southwell covers his dangerous expedition to England, and Antonia Fraser's history of the Gunpowder Plot has more on the capture and trial of Henry Garnet. Anyone wanting to explore the life and thoughts of Benjamin Constant should pick up *The Cambridge Companion to Constant*, which includes an essay by Stephen Holmes, who was kind enough to share his knowledge of the debate between Constant and Kant with me in conversation, and who, in so doing, helped me join some of the dots in my thinking. I found the example of the Manam islanders, and summaries of Frederick Bailey and Janet Suskind's findings, in J.A. Barnes's *A Pack of Lies*.

BORN LIARS

Afterword: How to be Honest

The story of Quesalid, although first published by Franz Boas, became better known when it was retold in an essay by Claude Levi-Strauss called 'The Sorcerer And His Magic'. Erving Goffman's thoughts on the theatrical nature of real life can be found in his classic work, *The Presentation of Self in Everyday Life*. The Wallace Stevens quote is from *Adagia*, the poet's collection of aphorisms. The full quote is as follows: 'The final belief is to believe in a fiction, which you know to be a fiction, there being nothing else. The exquisite truth is to know that it is a fiction and that you believe it willingly.'

Bibliography

United States Department of Defense, *Annual Polygraph Report to Congress*, 2001.

The Polygraph and Lie Detection, National Academy of Sciences, National Academies Press, 2003.

'Comprehensive Report of the Special Advisor to the Director of Central Intelligence on Iraq's WMD', 30 September 2004 ('Duelfer Report')

'Iraq Perspectives Project', Joint Center for Operational Analysis at United States Department of Defense, March 2006.

Addley, Esther, 'I Could Not Stop Crying', *Guardian*, 21 October 2006 (on the Orkney Child Abuse case)

Albergotti, Reed, 'The NFL's Most Exciting Receiver', *Wall Street Journal*, 16 January 2009.

Alder, Ken, *The Lie Detectors: The History of an American Obsession*, Free Press, 2007.

Amanzio, Martina et al., 'A systematic review of adverse events in placebo groups of anti-migraine clinical trials', *Pain* (146 (3), December 2009.

Anderson, Cameron, and Brion, Sebastian, 'Overconfidence and

357

the Attainment Status in Groups', Working Paper Series, Institute for Research on Labor and Employment, UC Berkeley, April 2010.

Arendt, Hannah, 'Lying in Politics: Reflections on the Pentagon Papers', *New York Review of Books*, November 1971.

Ariely, Dan, *Predictably Irrational*, Harper, 2008.

Balcetis, Emily, and Dunning, David (2009), 'Wishful Seeing: More desired objects are seen as closer', *Psychological Science* 21 (1), 147–52.

Barnes, J.A., *Pack Of Lies*, Cambridge University Press, 1994.

Baron-Cohen, Simon: 'I Cannot Tell a Lie – What people with autism can tell us about honesty', *In Character*, Spring 2007.

Baron-Cohen, Simon, *Mindblindness: An Essay on Autism and Theory of Mind*, MIT Press, 1995.

Bateson, P.P.G. and Hinde, R.A. (eds), *Growing Points in Ethology*, Cambridge University Press, 1976.

Beber, Bernd, and Scacco, Alexandra, 'The Devil is in the digits', *Washington Post*, 20 June 2009.

Beecher, H.K., 'The Powerful Placebo', *Journal of the American Medical Association* 159 (17), 24 December 1955, 1602–6.

Beecher, H.K., 'Pain In Men Wounded In Battle', *Annals of Surgery* 123 (1), January 1946, 96–205.

Bell, Daniel, 'On Confucius', *Five Books*: http://fivebooks.com/interviews/daniel-bell-on-confucius

Bennett, Brian, 'The Disturbing Case of the Norfolk Four', *Time*, 11 November 2008.

Benson, H., and McCallie, D.P. (1979), 'Angina pectoris and the placebo effect', *New England Journal of Medicine* 300.

Bibliography

Boas, Franz, *The Religion of the Kwakiutl Indians*, Columbia University Press, 1930.

Bogen, Joseph E., 'The neurosurgeon's interest in the Corpus Callosum, in A History of Neurosurgery', *American Association of Neurological Surgeons*, 1997.

Bollingmo, Guri C. et al., 'Credibility of the emotional witness: a study of ratings by police investigators', *Psychology, Crime and Law* 14 (1), January 2008.

Bond, C.F., and DePaulo, B.M. (2006), 'Accuracy of deception judgments', *Personality and Social Psychology Review* 10, 214–34.

Broks, Paul, *Into the Silent Land*, Atlantic Books, 2003.

Brooks, Michael, *Thirteen Things That Don't Make Sense*, Profile, 2009.

Bruner, Jerome S. and Goodman, Cecile C. (1947), 'Value and need as organizing factors in perception', *Journal of Abnormal and Social Psychology* 42, 33–44.

Buunk, B.P., 'Perceived superiority of one's own relationship and perceived prevalence of happy and unhappy relationships', *British Journal of Social Psychology* 40 (4), December 2001, 565–74.

Byrne, R., and Corp, N. (2004), 'Neocortex size predicts deception rate in primates', *Proc. Roy. Soc.* London: B. 271, 1693–9.

Byrne, R., and Whiten, A., (eds), *Machiavellian Intelligence*, Clarendon Press, 1988.

Byrne, R., and Whiten, A. (eds) *Machiavellian Intelligence II: Extensions and Evaluations*, Cambridge University Press, 1997.

Campbell, Colin, *The Romantic Ethic and the Spirit of Modern Consumerism*, Blackwell, 1987.

Campbell Moriarty, Jane (2008), 'Visions of Deception: Neuroimages and the search for truth', *Akron Law Review* 42 (3). 739–61.

Carter, Nancy L., and Weber, J. Mark, 'Not Pollyannas: Higher generalized trust predicts lie detection ability' (2010), *Social Psychological and Personality Science*, 1 (3), 274–9.

Chance, Zoe, and Norton, Micheal I., '"I read *Playboy* for the articles": Justifying and rationalizing questionable preferences', Harvard Business School Working Paper, No. 10-018, September 2009.

Changizi, Mark, 'Wide receivers who catch with their eyes closed explained': http://www.scientificblogging.com

Cleckley, Hervey, *The Mask of Sanity*, Plume, 1982.

Cohen, Ed, 'The placebo disavowed', *Yale Journal for Humanities in Medicine*, 2002.

Cross, K. Patricia, 'Not can, but will college teaching be improved?' (2006), *New Directions for Higher Education* 1977 (17), 1–15.

Damasio, Antonio et al., 'Amnesia following basal forebrain lesions', *Archives of Neurology* 42, 263–71.

Damasio, Antonio, *Descartes' Error: Emotion, Reason and the Human Brain*, Quill, 1995.

Darnton, Robert, *Mesmerism and the End of the Enlightenment in France*, Harvard University Press, 1968.

Darwin, Charles (1877), 'A Biographical Sketch of an Infant', *Mind* 2, 285–94.

Bibliography

Darwin, Charles, *The Expression of the Emotions In Man and Animals*, Penguin Classics, 2009.

De Araujo, Ivan E., Rolls, Edmund T., Velazco, Maria Ines, Margot, Christian,

and Cayeux, Isabelle, 'Cognitive modulation of olfactory processing', *Neuron* 46 (4), 19 May 2005, 671.

Defoe, Daniel, *Robinson Crusoe*, Penguin Classics, 2007.

Dennett, Daniel, *Brainstorms*, MIT Press, 1978.

DePaulo, B.M., Kashy, D.A., Kirkendol, S.E., Wyer, M.M., and Epstein, J.A. (1996), 'Lying in everyday life', *Journal of Personality and Social Psychology* 70, 979–95.

Deutscher, Guy, *Through The Language Glass: How Words Colour Your World*, William Heinemann, 2010.

Devlin, Christopher, *The Life of Robert Southwell, Poet and Martyr*, Farrar, Straus and Cudahy, 1956.

De Waal, Frans, *Chimpanzee Politics*, Johns Hopkins University Press, 2000.

De Waal, Frans, *Our Inner Ape*, Riverhead Books, 2005.

Diamond, Jared, *Guns, Germs and Steel: A Short History of Everybody For The Last 13,000 Years*, Vintage, 1998.

Dickie, John, *Cosa Nostra: A History of the Italian Mafia*, Hodder & Stoughton, 2004.

Dror, I., and Charlton, D., 'Why experts make errors', *Journal of Forensic Identification* 56 (4), 600–16.

Dunbar, Robin, *Grooming, Gossip and the Evolution of Language*, Harvard University Press, 2004.

Ekman, Paul, *Telling Lies: Clues to Deceit in the Marketplace, Politics, and Marriages*, W.W. Norton & Co., 1985.

Ekman, Paul, *Why Kids Lie*, Penguin, 1989.

Ekman, P. (ed.), *Darwin and Facial Expression: A Century of Research in Review*, Malor Books, 2006.

Ekman, P., and Friesen, W.V. (1969), 'Nonverbal leakage and clues to deception', *Psychiatry* 32, 88–106.

Ernst, Edzard, 'Towards a scientific understanding of placebo effects', in David Peters (ed.), *Understanding the Placebo Effect in Contemporary Medicine*, Churchill Livingstone, 2001.

Evans, Dylan, *Placebo: The Belief Effect*, HarperCollins, 2003.

Feinberg, Todd, *Altered Egos*, Oxford University Press, 2001.

Feldman, Robert, *Liar: The Truth About Lying*, Virgin, 2010.

Fenton-O'Creevy, M., Nicholson, N, Soane, E., and Willman, P. (2003), 'Trading on illusions: Unrealistic perceptions of control and trading performance', *Journal of Occupational and Organisational Psychology* 76, 53–68.

Festinger, Leon, Riecken, Henry, and Schacter, Stanley, *When Prophecy Fails*, Harper Torchbooks, 1964.

Fraser, Antonia, *The Gunpowder Plot: Terror and Faith in 1605*, Phoenix, 2002.

Freud, Sigmund, 'Creative Writers and Day-Dreaming' (1908), in Person et al. 1995.

Frith, Chris, *Making up the Mind: How the Brain Creates our Mental World*, Blackwell, 2007.

Fotopoulou, A., 'False selves in neuropsychological rehabilitation: The challenge of confabulation', *Neuropsychological Rehabilitation*, May 2008.

Fotopoulou, Aikaterina, Solms, Mark, and Turnbull, Oliver

(2004), 'Wishful reality distortions in confabulation: a case report', in *Neuropsychologia* 47, 727–44.

Fotopoulou, A. et al. (2007), 'Self-enhancing confabulation: Revisiting the motivational hypothesis', *Neurocase*, 13, 6–15.

Gallo, David A., and Finger, Stanley (2000), 'The Power of a Musical Instrument: Franklin, the Mozarts, Mesmer and the glass armonica', *History of Psychology* 3 (4), 326–43.

Gazzaniga, Michael, *The Social Brain*, Basic Books, 1985.

Gilovich, Thomas et al. (1998), 'The Illusion of Transparency: Biased assessments of others' ability to read one's emotional states', *Journal of Personality and Social Psychology* 75 (2), 332–46.

Gladwell, Malcolm, 'The Naked Face', *New Yorker*, 5 August 2002.

Goffman, Erving, *The Presentation of Self In Everyday Life*, Penguin, 1990.

Goldish, Matt, *The Sabbatean Prophets*, Harvard University Press, 2004.

Gopnik, Alison, unpublished essay, cited in Simon Baron-Cohen, *Mindblindness: An Essay on Autism and Theory of Mind*, MIT Press, 1995.

Gray, John, *Straw Dogs*, Granta, 2002.

Haggard, Patrick, and Libet, Benjamin W., 'Conscious intention and brain activity', *Journal of Consciousness Studies* 8 (11), November 2001, 47–63.

Haigh, Christopher, *English Reformations: Politics, Religion and Society Under The Tudors*, Clarendon Press, 1993.

Haney, Daniel Q., 'Not everyone agrees laser holes ease chest pain', *Los Angeles Times*, 19 March 2001.

Hansen, Mark, 'True Lies', *ABA Journal*, October 2009.

Harding, Luke, Leigh, David, and Pallister, David, *The Liar: Fall of Jonathan Aitken*, Penguin Books, 1997.

Harrington, Anne, *The Cure Within: A History of Mind–Body Medicine*. W.W. Norton & Co., 2008.

Harrington, Anne (ed.), *The Placebo Effect: An Interdisciplinary Exploration*, Harvard University Press, 1997.

Hasel, L., and Kassin, S., 'On the presumption of evidentiary independence: Can confessions corrupt eyewitness identifications?' *Psychological Science* 3 (2), 2009.

Helm, Anne, 'Truth-telling, placebos and deception', *Aviation, Space and Environmental Medicine*, January 1985.

Herbert, Ian, 'The psychology and power of false confessions', *Association for Psychological Science*, December 2009.

Hirstein, William, *Brain Fiction: Self-Deception and the Riddle of Confabulation*, MIT Press, 2005.

Holmes, Stephen, 'The liberty to denounce: Ancient and modern', in Rosenblatt 2009.

Homer, *The Odyssey*, trans. Robert Fagles, Penguin, 1997.

Hróbjartsson, Asbjørn (2003), 'The use of placebo interventions in medical practice – A national questionnaire survey of Danish clinicians', *Evaluation and the Health Professions* 26, 153.

Humphrey, N.K., 'The social function of intellect', in P.P.G. Bateson and R.A. Hinde (eds), *Growing Points in Ethology*, Cambridge University Press, 1976.

Bibliography

Hunter, Robert, 'A question of guilt', *Legal Week*, 10 December 2009.

Hyman, Ira E., and Billings, James F. (1998), 'Individual differences and the creation of false childhood memories', *Memory* 6 (1), 1–20.

Ibsen, Henrik, *The Wild Duck*, ed. Stephen Mulrine, Nick Hern Books, 2006.

Jackman, Tom, and Kumar, Anita, '3 of "Norfolk 4" conditionally pardoned in rape, killing', *Washington Post*, 7 August 2009.

Jervis, Robert, *Perception and Misperception in International Politics*, Princeton University Press, 1976.

Johnson, Dominic, *Overconfidence and War*, Harvard University Press, 2004.

Johnson, Paul, *A History of the Jews*, Phoenix, 1987.

Kaftan, Jod, 'The Oddfather', *Rolling Stone* 894, 25 April 2002.

Kittsteiner, H.D., 'Kant and Casuistry', in Leites 1988.

Kant, Immanuel, *Groundwork of the Metaphysics of Morals*, edited by Mary Gregor, trans. Christine M. Korsgaard, Cambridge University Press, 1998.

Kant, Immanuel, *The Metaphysics of Morals*, edited by Mary Gregor, trans. Christine M. Korsgaard, Cambridge University Press, 1996.

Kaptchuk, T.J., Kerr, C.E., and Zanger, A., 'Placebo controls, exorcisms, and the devil', *The Lancet* 374 (9697), 10 October 2009, 1234–5.

Kaptchuk, T.J. et al., 'Components of placebo effect: randomised controlled trial in patients with irritable bowel syndrome',

British Medical Journal, 336 (7651), 3 May 2008, 999–1003.

Kermode, Frank, *Shakespeare's Language*, Penguin, 2000.

Kirsch, Irving, and Montgomery, Guy, 'Mechanisms of placebo pain reduction: An empirical investigation', *Psychological Science* 7 (3), 174–6.

Koch, Christof, *The Quest For Consciousness: A Neurobiological Approach*, Roberts & Company, 2004.

Kuran, Timur, *Private Truths, Public Lies: The Social Consequences of Preference Falsification*, Harvard University Press, 1997.

Kroeber, A.L, *The Nature of Culture*, University of Chicago Press, 1952.

Krulwich, Robert, 'The Secret Advantage of Being Short', Vermont Public Radio, 18 May 2009 (transcript http://bit.ly/h4Lgca).

Kuhn, G., and Land, M.F. (2006). 'There's more to magic than meets the eye', *Current Biology*, 16(22), R950–R951.

Landy, David, *Culture, Disease and Healing*, Collier Macmillan, 1977.

Larkin, Philip, *Collected Poems*, Faber and Faber, 2003.

Lee, Kang, and Talwar, Victoria, 'Little liars: Origins of verbal deception in children', in S. Itakura and K. Fujita (eds), *Origins of the Social Mind*, Springer, 2006.

Lee, Kang, and Talwar, Victoria, *Punitive Environment Produces Better Young Liars: A Natural Experiment*, Unpublished, 2010.

Lehrer, Jonah, 'Creation on command', *Seed*, May 2009.

Lehrer, Jonah, *The Decisive Moment: How the Brain Makes Up its Mind*, Canongate, 2009.

Bibliography

Leites, Edmund (ed.), *Conscience and Casuistry in Early Modern Europe*, Cambridge University Press, 1988.

Leslie, Ian, 'Arrested development', *The Times* (*Eureka*), 4 February 2010.

Leslie, Ian, 'The honest truth about man's ability to lie', *The Times* (*Eureka*), 5 November 2009.

Levi-Strauss, Claude, *The Sorcerer and His Magic, in Structural Anthropology*, Penguin Books, 1977.

Lewis, Michael, and Saarni, Carolyn, *Lying and Deception in Everyday Life*, The Guilford Press, 1993.

Leys, Simon, *The Analects of Confucius*, W.W. Norton & Co., 1998.

Libet, B., Gleason, C.A., Wright, E.W., and Pearl, D.K. (1983), 'Time of conscious intention to act in relation to onset of cerebral activity (readiness potential): The unconscious initiation of a freely voluntary act', *Brain* 102, 623–42.

Lichtenberg, Pechtan, and Nitzan, Uriel (1983), 'Questionnaire survey on use of placebo', *British Medical Journal*, 329, 944.

Lifton, Robert Jay, *The Nazi Doctors: Medical Killing and the Psychology of Genocide*, Basic Books, 2000.

Loftus, Elizabeth F., and Pickrell, Jacqueline E., 'The formation of false memories', *Psychiatric Annals* 25, December 1995, 720–5.

Loftus, Elizabeth et al., 'Pluto behaving badly: False beliefs and their consequences', *American Journal of Psychology* 121 (4), Winter 2008, 643–60.

Loftus, E.F., and Palmer, J.C. (1974), 'Reconstruction of automobile destruction: An example of the interaction between language and memory', *Journal of Verbal Learning and Verbal Behaviour* 13, 585–9.

Lopez, Claude-Anne (1993), 'Franklin and Mesmer: An encounter', *Yale Journal of Biology and Medicine* 66, 325–31.

Machiavelli, Niccolo, *The Prince*, trans. George Bull, Penguin Classics, 2003.

McCullough, Michael E. et al., 'Religious involvement and mortality: a meta-analytic review', *Health Psychology*, 19 (3), May 2000.

McGarry, Patsy, 'Church "lied without lying"', *Irish Times*, 26 November 2009:

http://www.irishtimes.com/newspaper/breaking/2009/1126/breaking86.html

Mitchell, Robert W., and Thompson, Nicholas S. (eds), *Deception: Perspectives on Human and Non-human Deceit*, State University of New York Press, 1986.

Montaigne, Michel De, *The Essays (A Selection)*, trans. and ed. M.A. Screech, Penguin Classics, 2004.

Morgan, Edmund S., *Benjamin Franklin*, Yale University Press, 2002.

Mezulis, A.H., Abramson, L.Y., Hyde, J.S., and Hankin, B.L., 'Is there a universal positivity bias in attributions?', *Psychology Bulletin*, 130(5), September 2004, 711–47.

Moerman, Daniel, *Meaning, Medicine, and the 'Placebo Effect'*, Cambridge University Press, 2002.

Morris, David B., *The Culture of Pain*, University of California Press, 1993.

Bibliography

Morris, David B., 'Placebo, pain and belief: A biocultural model', in Harrington 1997.

Morris, Errol, 'Seven lies about lying', Parts 1 & 2, *New York Times*, 5/6 August 2009.

Muller, S. et al., 'How do world-class cricket batsmen anticipate a bowler's intention?' *Quarterly Journal of Experimental Psychology*, 59 (12), December 2006, 2162–86.

Norton, M.I., and Ariely, D. (2008), 'Self-deception: How we come to believe we are better than we truly are', cited in Zoe Chance and Micheal I. Norton, '"I read *Playboy* for the articles": Justifying and rationalizing questionable preferences', Harvard Business School Working Paper, No. 10-018, September 2009.

Nye, John V.C. (1991), 'Lucky fools and cautious businessmen: On entrepreneurship and the measurement of entrepreneurial failure', in Joel Mokyr (ed.), 'The Vital One: Essays in honour of Jonathan R.T. Hughes', *Research in Economic History* 6, 131–52.

Ofshe, Richard, and Watters, Ethan, *Making Monsters: False Memories, Psychotherapy, and Sexual Hysteria*, University of California Press, 1994.

Olsson, John, *Wordcrime: Solving Crime Through Forensic Linguistics*, Continuum IPG, 2009.

Onishi, Kristine H. et al. (2005), 'Do 15-month-old infants understand false beliefs?' *Science* 308, 255.

Perner, Josef, *Understanding the Representational Mind*, MIT Press, 1991.

Person, Ethel et al., *On Freud's 'Creative Writers and Daydreaming'*, IPA Publications, 1995.

Pessoa, Ferdinand, *The Book of Disquiet*, trans. Margaret Jull Costa, Serpent's Tail, 2010.

Phillips, D.P., Ruth, T.E., and Wagner, L.M., 'Psychology and Survival', *Lancet* 342 (8880), 6 November 1993, 1142–5.

Plaskett, James, *The Millionaire Three*: http://www.the millionairethree.com/

Plassman, Hilke, O'Doherty, John, Siv Baba, and Rangel, Antonio (2007), 'Marketing actions can modulate neural representations of experienced pleasantness', *Proceedings of the National Academy of Sciences*, 105, 1050–4.

Porter, Stephen et al., 'Negotiating false memories: Interviewer and rememberer characteristics relate to memory distortion', *Psychological Science*, 11 (6), November 2000, 507–10.

Postrel, Virginia, 'In praise of irrational exuberance', *Big Questions Online*, 28 October 2010.

Proffitt, D.R., Creem, S.H., and Zosh, W.D., 'Seeing mountains in molehills: Geographical slant perception', *Psychological Science* 12 (5), September 2001, 418–23.

Pronin, Emily, 'How we see ourselves and how we see others', *Science* 320, 30 May 2008.

Pronin, Emily, Lin, Daniel Y., and Ross, Lee, 'The bias blind spot: Perceptions of bias in self versus others', *Personality and Social Psychology Bulletin* 28 (3), March 2002, 369–81.

Railton, Peter, 'Moral camouflage or moral monkeys?', *New York Times*, 18 July 2010.

Raine, Adrian, Yang, Yaling et al., 'Localisation of increased prefrontal white matter in pathological liars', *Br J Psychiatry* 190, February 2007, 174–5.

Raine, Adrian, Yang, Yaling et al., 'Prefrontal white matter in pathological liars', *Br J Psychiatry* 187, October 2005, 320–5.

Reddy, Vasudevi, *How Infants Know Minds*, Harvard University Press, 2008.

Ronson, Jon, 'Are the Millionaire Three innocent?', *Guardian*, 17 July 2006.

Rosenblatt, Helena (ed.), *The Cambridge Companion to Constant*, Cambridge University Press, 2009.

Roth, Philip, *American Pastoral*, Vintage, 2005.

Saletan, William, 'The Memory Doctor', *Slate*, 4 June 2010.

Salmon, Felix, 'Helen Thomas, Christopher Hitchens, and being wrong', Reuters, 7 June 2007.

Sartre, Jean-Paul, *The Wall*, W.W. Norton & Co., 1969.

Schopenhauer, Arthur, *The World as Will and Representation*, cited in Gray 2002.

Schauer, Frederick, 'Can bad science be good evidence: Lie detection, neuroscience, and the mistaken conflation of legal and scientific norms', *Cornell Law Review*, August 2010.

Scholem, Gershom, *Sabbatai Zevi: The Mystical Messiah*, Routledge & Kegan Paul, 1973.

Shiv, Baba, Carmon, Ziv, and Ariely, Dan (2005), 'Placebo effects of marketing actions: Consumers may get what they pay for,' *Journal of Marketing Research* 42 (4), 383–93.

Silberman, Steve, 'Placebos are getting more effective', *Wired*, 24 August 2009.

Simons, D.J., and Levin, D.T. (1998), 'Failure to detect changes to people in a real-world interaction', *Psychonomic Bulletin and Review*, 5 (4), 644–9.

Slater, Lauren, *Opening Skinner's Box*, Bloomsbury, 2005.

Smith, Adam, *The Theory of Moral Sentiments*, Cambridge University Press, 2002.

Somerville, Johann, 'The new art of lying', in Leites 1988.

Snyder, M.L., Kleck, R.E., Strenta, A., and Mentzer, S.J. (1979), 'Avoidance of the handicapped: An attributional ambiguity analysis', *Journal of Personality and Social Psychology* 37, 2297–306.

Starek, Joanna, and Keating, Caroline (1991), 'Self-deception and its relationship to success in competition', *Basic and Applied Social Psychology* 12 (2), 145–55.

Sternberg, Robert J., and O'Hara, Linda, 'Creativity and intelligence', in Sternberg 1999.

Sternberg, Robert J. (ed.), *Handbook of Creativity*, Cambridge University Press, 1999.

Stevens, Wallace, *Opus Posthumous: Poems, Plays, Prose*, ed. Milton J. Bates, Vintage, 2002.

Stouthamer-Loeber, Magda, 'Adults' perception of verbal misrepresentation of reality in four-year-olds'. Unpublished, University of Pittsburgh, cited in Perner 1991.

Sutherland, Rory, 'Life lessons from an adman', TED Talks July 2009: http://www.ted.com/talks/rory_sutherland_life_lessons_from_an_ad_man.html

Svenson, Ola, 'Are we all less risky and more skillful than our fellow drivers?', *Acta Psychologica* 47 (2), February 1981, 143–8.

Bibliography

Tait, M.J. et al., 'Improved outcome after lumbar microdiscectomy in patients shown their excised disc fragments', *Journal of Neurology, Neurosurgery, and Psychiatry* 80 (9), September 2009.

Taylor, Shelley E., *Positive Illusions: Creative Self-Deception and the Healthy Mind*, Basic Books, 1991.

Twain, Mark, *On the Decay of the Art Of Lying*, FQ Books, 2010.

Vasek, Marie E., 'Lying as a skill: The development of deception in children', in Mitchell and Thompson 1986.

Vrij, Aldert, *Detecting Lies and Deceit: The Psychology of Lying and the Implications for Professional Practice*, John Wiley & Sons, 2002.

Vrij, A., Leal, S., Mann, S., Warmelink, L., Granhag, P., and Fisher, R. (2010), 'Drawings as an innovative and successful lie detection tool', *Applied Cognitive Psychology* 24, 587–94.

Vrij, Aldert ,and Semin, G.R. (1996), 'Lie experts' beliefs about nonverbal indicators of deception', *Journal of Nonverbal Behavior* 20, 65–80.

Watters, Ethan, 'The Devil in Mr Ingram', *Mother Jones*, July–August 1991.

Weiner, Tim, Johnston, David, and Lewis, Neil, *Betrayal: The Story of Aldrich Ames, an American Spy*, Richard Cohen Books, 1996.

Wenger, Andrew, and Flowers, Blaine (2008), 'Positive illusions in parenting: Every child is above average', *Journal of Applied Social Psychology* 38 (3), 611–34.

Wegner, D.M., and Wheatley, T.P. (1999), 'Apparent mental

causation: Sources of the experience of will', *American Psychologist* 54, 480–92.

Weiss, B., and Feldman, R.S. (2006), 'Looking good and lying to do it: Deception as an impression management strategy in job interviews', *Journal of Applied Social Psychology* 36, 1070–86.

Wilde, Oscar, *The Decay of Lying*, Penguin, 1995.

Wilson, Timothy, *Strangers to Ourselves*, The Belknap Press of Harvard University Press, 2002.

Woods, Kevin M., and Stout, Mark E., 'Saddam's perceptions and misperceptions: The case of "Desert Storm"', *The Journal of Strategic Studies* 33 (1), February 2010, 5–41.

Wrangham, Richard (1999), 'Is military incompetence adaptive?' *Evolution and Human Behavior* 20, 3–17.

Wright, Lawrence, *Remembering Satan: Recovered Memory and the Shattering of a Family*, Serpent's Tail, 1994.

Wright, Robert, *The Moral Animal*, Abacus, 1996.

Yamagishi, Toshio, et al. (1999), 'Trust, gullibility and social intelligence', *Asian Journal of Social Psychology* 2, 145–61.

Zagorin, Perez, *Ways of Lying: Dissimulation, Persecution and Conformity in Early Modern Europe*, Harvard University Press, 1990.

Zannino, Gian Daniele et al., 'Do Confabulators really try to remember when they confabulate? A case report', *Cognitive Neuropsychology* 25 (6), September 2008, 831–52.

Zborowski, Mark, 'Cultural components in responses to pain', in Michael H. Logan and Edward E. Hunt (eds), *Health and The Human Condition*, Wadsworth Publishing Co., 1978.

Bibliography

Zipperstein, Steven J., 'Underground Man: The curious case of
Mark Zborowski and the writing of a modern Jewish classic',
Jewish Review of Books 2, Summer 2010.

Acknowledgements

I am indebted to many people for sharing their time and expertise with me in various ways during the writing of this book. Any remaining errors are entirely my responsibility.

The following people were generous enough to take time to talk to me about their work: Dick Byrne, Jane Campbell Moriarty, Nancy Darling, Avinash Dixit, Petter Johansson, Aikaterini Fotopoulou, Robin Fox, Chris Frith, Ruben Gur, Stephen Holmes, Robert Hunter, Daniel Langleben, Charles Limb, Kang Lee, Will Self, Hunter Somerville, Victoria Talwar and Kevin Woods. My thanks to all. Thanks also to the many experts to whom I didn't get to talk, but whose ideas and research inform this book.

The enthusiasm and energy of my agent Nicola Barr saw this book get off, and stay off, the ground. Richard Milner, Joshua Ireland and the rest of the team at Quercus provided excellent support and advice throughout. Antonia Senior and Michael Henderson of the *Times* commissioned me to write a piece about lying for *Eureka* magazine at a time when I was wondering if it would make a good topic for a book, as did James Crabtree at *Prospect*. My thanks to all.

A special thanks to Professor Martha Farah and her team at the Centre for Neuroscience and Society, at the University of Pennsylvania. In 2010 I was lucky enough to attend Neuroscience Boot Camp, a course that Martha runs for non-neuroscientists looking for an introduction to the field. I enjoyed it immensely and gained a store of intellectual stimulation that will last for years. I'm grateful to the brilliant scientists there who made the effort to explain the topic in terms even I could understand, and to my fellow Boot Campers for many fascinating conversations and much laughter over muffins, coffee and beer.

I fondly recall a lovely afternoon in Oxford talking to Kate Fox and Henry Marsh, who shared with me their unique perspectives on this topic and sent me down many fruitful paths of enquiry; I thank them for their generosity, hospitality and good will. I'm very grateful to Joanne Bain for reading the entire manuscript in draft and passing on her astute and perceptive comments. Ed Docx was, as always, an indispensable voice of encouragement and support throughout, and a wise counsel. I'm particularly indebted to Stephen Brown, who was kind enough to spend a lot of time with the manuscript. He held it to a high standard, and raised its levels of narrative discipline and intellectual rigour. My thanks go to the staff at the British Library and the Wellcome Library, and to Jeremy and his team at Brill, on Exmouth Market, for the good cheer and excellent coffee. Others who contributed ideas, talked things

Acknowledgements

over with me or bucked me up when I needed it include David Bain, Laura Barton, Emma Docx, Stewart Wood, and my parents, Bryan and Margaret Leslie. Finally, a special thanks to Alice Wignall, my closest editor in every sense, who wielded her red and pink pens with enormous skill and sensitivity, helped me to keep faith in this book whenever my confidence in it flagged, and agreed, at the end of it all, to be my wife.

Index

Index

Index

Index

Index